Burmese Silver Art

BURMESE SILVER ART

Masterpieces Illuminating Buddhist, Hindu and

Mythological Stories of Purpose and Wisdom

David C. Owens

 **Marshall Cavendish** Editions

Published in 2020 on behalf of David C. Owens by Marshall Cavendish Editions
An imprint of Marshall Cavendish International

Marshall Cavendish International (Asia)
1 New Industrial Road
Singapore 536196
Tel: (65) 6213 9300
genref@sg.marshallcavendish.com
www.marshallcavendish.com/genref

A member of the
Times Publishing Group

Other Marshall Cavendish Offices:
Marshall Cavendish Corporation, 800 Westchester Ave, Suite N-641, Rye Brook,
NY 10573, USA • Marshall Cavendish International (Thailand) Co Ltd, 253
Asoke, 16th Floor, Sukhumvit 21 Road, Klongtoey Nua, Wattana, Bangkok 10110,
Thailand • Marshall Cavendish (Malaysia) Sdn Bhd, Times Subang, Lot 46,
Subang Hi-Tech Industrial Park, Batu Tiga, 40000 Shah Alam, Selangor Darul
Ehsan, Malaysia

Marshall Cavendish is a trademark of Times Publishing Limited

National Library Board, Singapore Cataloguing-in-Publication Data
Name: Owens, David C.
Title: Burmese Silver Art: Masterpieces Illuminating Buddhist, Hindu
and Mythological Stories of Purpose and Wisdom / David C. Owens.
Description: Singapore : Marshall Cavendish Editions, 2020. |
Includes bibliographic references and index. | "Published on behalf
of David C. Owens" – Title page verso.
Identifier(s): OCN 1141422908 | ISBN 978-981-4868-88-4 (hardcover)
Subject(s): LCSH: Silverwork–Burma–19th century. | Symbolism in art. |
Buddhist art and symbolism–Burma. | Hindu art–Burma.
Classification: DDC 739.23809591–dc23

Printed in Singapore

Contents

Preface

The silver art illustrated and described in this book was crafted in the years between approximately 1850 and 1930 in a land known to the English-speaking world as Burma. Therefore, the author uses the contemporary English names of this period for the country, political divisions, major towns and geographical features. The military government of the Union of Burma changed the official English name of the country to the Union of Myanmar in 1989. At the same time, place names chosen by the colonial British in the 19th century were discarded, and other English names were changed to better reflect Burmese pronunciation. For example, Rangoon became Yangon. Burma is officially known today as the Republic of the Union of Myanmar.

Three actualities sowed the seeds that grew into this book. The first is a wanderlust coded into my genetic condition, which led me to first visit Burma in 1993 and return many times thereafter. The second is a long and valued friendship with Sao Ratana Hseng Leun of Vancouver, Canada. She is the youngest daughter of Sao Shwe Thaike and Sao Hearn Hkam. Sao Shwe Thaike was the last Shan Saohpa, or prince, of Yawnghwe State and the first President of independent Burma from 1948 to 1952 following the end of British colonial rule. Leun's remarkable early life and experience in Burma kindled a profound historical and cultural interest in the country and in the Shan States. Leun also connected me to her network of family and friends in modern Myanmar, who have enlightened me on so many facets of life in the country, both past and present. The third actuality was incidental and serendipitous. I accompanied my wife to the Isan Gallery in Singapore, ostensibly to view exquisite hand-woven silk textiles from Thailand, but to my surprise, also discovered a display of mesmerizing Burmese silverwork. A ceremonial offering bowl purchased that day in 2013 was the beginning of the collection exhibited in this book (the Noble Silver Collection).

Building the collection has always been a joint labour of love with my wife Kathleen. She shares my curiosity in deciphering the visual narratives that adorn the silverwork and has a sharp eye for silverwork quality and value. Kathleen has also provided sterling support, both material and emotional, to the nurturing and compilation of this book. My thanks to Kathleen – without her constant encouragement and fortuitous interest in Thai textiles, neither the silverwork collection nor a book to share the delight of Burmese silver art would have materialized. My thanks are also due to Charlie Lim, a Singaporean artist and photographer who created the superb photographic images of the silverwork. Charlie is a wonderfully creative photographer, adept at controlling light and always vigilant to the detail of every shot.

A warm expression of gratitude is also due to the many friends who have contributed their knowledge, experience, guidance, enthusiasm and personal support to all aspects of building the silverwork collection, conducting research and writing the book. Those in Myanmar deserving of special acknowledgement and kind appreciation include David Fu, Than Htun, Kin Maung Toon, Saw Sanda Soe, Princess Hteik Su Phaya Gyi (granddaughter of King Thibaw and his wife Queen Supayalat), Sao Shwe Ohn and Sao Hseng Zanda Siri. In Singapore, Percy Vatsaloo was an indispensable mentor in the field of Burmese silverwork and unstinting in his support for this book and the development of the collection. Michael Backman, Joseph Cohen and Wynyard Wilkinson in London and Neil and Digna Ryan in Penang also generously shared their knowledge and provided invaluable encouragement to write this book. My thanks also to the many authors listed in the bibliography whose publications have provided the knowledge upon which I have drawn so extensively in the process of researching Burmese silverwork and writing *Burmese Silver Art*. Finally, I must express my appreciation and gratitude to Marshall Cavendish International (Asia) Pte Ltd for undertaking to publish this specialist art book. Glenn Wray and Justin Lau at Marshall Cavendish have guided the book, and the author, through the publication process with consummate skill, efficiency and equanimity. I thank Glenn and Justin for nurturing *Burmese Silver Art* and delivering a book worthy of the exceptional quality and value of Burmese silverwork.

Any errors, omissions or inadvertent misrepresentations in the content of the book are entirely the responsibility of the author. I welcome all and any corrections, additions and feedback.

CHAPTER ONE

Prologue

Burmese Silver Art is the first publication since 1904 dedicated exclusively to the exhibition of silverwork handcrafted in Burma during the mid-19th to early 20th centuries – a period coined the 'Burmese Silver Age'.

1.1 Salted fish storage jar, c. 1890

1.2 Decorative narrative – Vidhura-Pandita Jataka

The body of work created by master silversmiths during this time is characterized by superb technical workmanship and a unique decorative style featuring detailed illustrations of narratives from Buddhist and Hindu religious traditions, Burmese folk tales and mythology. These ancient narratives also embody profound ethical wisdom on transcendent notions of virtue, morality and nobility. This distinctly Burmese genre of silverwork has wonderful aesthetic value, eloquent decoration and is little known or understood.

Objectives and Motivation

The primary objective of this publication is to showcase in a photographic gallery 100 alluring Burmese silver artefacts that represent some of the finest-quality work from the Silver Age (Fig. 1.1). A second objective is to elucidate the captivating visual narratives that adorn much of the silverwork (Fig. 1.2). An understanding of the historical sources and meanings of these narratives provides a more complete insight into the cultural and artistic importance of the silverwork. Many of the narratives described in this work are little known outside of Burma or the predominantly Buddhist countries of Asia.

All authors have a motivation for their work. The motivation for *Burmese Silver Art* was the contention that a book exclusively on the subject was fully deserving and long overdue. Fully deserving, because the silverwork is of exceptional artistic merit and cultural value, and long overdue because the last dedicated work – *Modern Burmese Silverwork* by Harry L. Tilly – was published in 1904. Tilly was motivated to write because of his deep personal interest in many Burmese art forms and his passion to preserve their traditions. This author's passion is more simply to collect and study the silverwork that Tilly fostered and so much admired. The outcome of this passion is now the 'Noble Silver Collection' of Burmese silverwork. This collection has been assembled over an energetic eight-year period, largely from art galleries and private collectors in Singapore, Yangon, Mandalay, London and Hong Kong. Chapter 3 of this book illustrates 100 of the most important silver artefacts in the collection. This is the first catalogued exhibition of these pieces.

This book does not profess to be a scholarly work. It is a general interest publication by a private collector to showcase Burmese silver art to the widest possible audience. To achieve this purpose, the book comprises two essential chapters: one, a 'virtual' gallery of compelling photographs of individual pieces of silverwork accompanied by catalogue-style descriptions; and, two, the detailed illustration and deciphering of the many religious and mythological stories that adorn the silverwork. The book also features an introductory chapter containing historical and technical information on Burmese silver art. An Appendix to the book includes pertinent information on silver metal, including its genesis, properties, mineral occurrence, applications and tarnish prevention. A comprehensive bibliography at the end of the book acknowledges the indispensable source literature for historical, scientific and technical information.

There are also subjective opinions and conjecture in the book regarding many aspects of Burmese silver art. These are based on the author's research in Burma and the hands-on study of many silver artefacts of variable form, decorative style and quality. The cogency of the author's opinions and conjecture is for the reader to decide.

1.3 Betel box, c. 1910

1.4 Treasure or cheroot box, c. 1910

1.5 Ceremonial offering bowl, 1853

Burmese Silverwork

'Burmese silverwork' as a descriptive term encompasses a wide range of artefact designs, functionality and decorative styles. The archetypal silverwork is the ceremonial offering bowl that resembles the form and function of the traditional alms bowl (*thabeik*) carried by Buddhist monks (Fig. 1.5). This form of silverwork is the focus of the Noble Silver Collection. The silver bowls were typically commissioned by wealthy Burmese and used for ceremonial offerings, religious and secular rituals, votive objects and status display in the home. Other traditional forms of Burmese silverwork featured in the book's virtual gallery include cylindrical betel boxes (Fig. 1.3), rectangular cheroot and treasure boxes (Fig. 1.4), rice and dried fish storage jars, lime boxes, water bowls and vases. In form, decorative style and ownership, these works constitute a 'domestic' class of silver.

Silversmiths also created cross-cultural artefacts that incorporate elements of both Burmese and European style and utility. This type of work was typically commissioned by foreign residents of Burma as gifts, trophies and keepsakes. It is an 'export' class of silverwork. There is no evidence of commercial-scale manufacturing of silverwork for export during the Silver Age.

Master silversmiths also crafted a special and limited class of silverwork for international and domestic art competitions sponsored by the British colonial administration in India in the late 19th and early 20th centuries. This work was often highly ornate and served as ceremonial centrepieces and display objects. An example of this class by a master silversmith is currently exhibited in the silver gallery of the Victoria and Albert Museum in London.

Historical and Cultural Background

Silverwork (*pan htyan*) is recognized as one of Burma's traditional art forms. It has an ancestry dating back to the city-state Pyu civilization that occupied the central Irrawaddy river valley in modern Burma (Myanmar) from about 100 BCE to 900 CE. The oldest extant Pyu silverwork was discovered in 1926 during the archaeological excavation of the Khin Ba burial mound adjacent to the Pyu city of Sri Ksetra (Figs. 1.6–8). The mound contained a treasure trove of over 50 artefacts, including a rich and varied selection of silver objects. Among these objects were decorated silver bowls and plates that are reminiscent of Silver Age work crafted almost 2,000 years later. Some art historians ascribe Pyu artistic style to Indian influence from Andhra Pradesh and the contemporary Gupta Empire.

The source of the two most popular decorative narratives found on Silver Age work – the Buddhist Pali Canon and the Ramayana – reflect a much older Indian influence on Burmese silver art. The Theravada branch of Buddhism believes that the scriptures in the Pali Canon represent the original words and teaching of the Buddha who lived in northern India in the 6th to 5th centuries BCE. The Ramayana is an epic poem containing the teachings of ancient Hindu sages. It was written by the Indian poet Valmiki. The verses recount the life of Prince Rama during the Vedic period (c. 1500–500 BCE) of Indian history.

The recurrent use of Buddhist and Hindu decorative iconography is a singular characteristic of Burmese silverwork.

1.6 Information board, Khin Ba mound, Department of Archaeology and National Museum, Myanmar

1.7 Discovery of the silver reliquary in the mound chamber, Charles Duroiselle, 1926

1.8 Khin Ba burial mound, Sri Ksetra, Myanmar, 2017

1.9 Traditional silversmith, Ywataung village, Sagaing, 2015

This characteristic imbues the work with a religious and spiritual value that is only revealed by interpreting and understanding the detail of the iconography. The original owners of the silverwork would have utilized the visual narratives on the artefacts to teach and reinforce Buddhist and Hindu precepts and wisdom. This fervent emphasis on religious silver art is not found in the silverwork traditions of other Asian countries.

Prior Publications

The claim was made earlier in the Prologue that a publication dedicated to revealing the achievements of Burmese silversmiths in the mid-19th to early 20th century was long overdue. A brief account of the English-language literature on Burmese silverwork is required to support this claim. Two short monographs by the Englishman Harry L. Tilly, dated 1902 and 1904, constitute the metaphorical 'canon' of writing on Burmese silverwork (Fig. 1.10). These works comprise only 61 pages in total, although the information, commentary and photographic plates in both works are a rich and invaluable source of knowledge on many aspects of Burmese silverwork from a contemporary expert. No other books exclusively on Burmese silverwork have been published since Tilly's 1904 monograph.

More recently, other eminent authors have provided important accounts and illustrations of Burmese silverwork in chapters from books that otherwise focus on silversmithing traditions in India or Southeast Asia. The four most important of these chapters are found in the books *Silverware of South-East Asia* by Sylvia Fraser-Lu (1989); *Burmese Crafts: Past and Present* by Sylvia Fraser-Lu (1994); *Indian Silver 1858–1947* by

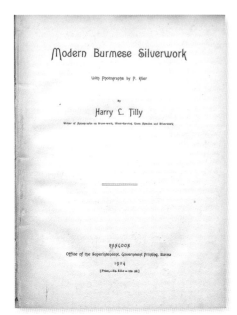

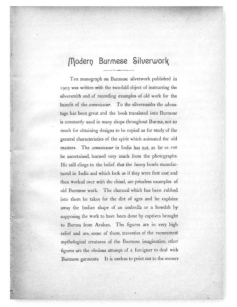

1.10 Pages from Harry L. Tilly's 1904 monograph

1.11 Silversmith's trademark –
Maung Shwe Yon, c. 1880

Wynyard R.T. Wilkinson (1999); and *Delight in Design: Indian Silver for the Raj* by Vidya Dehejia (2008). All four of these titles inspired the author to collect, study and write this book. Other traditional forms of Burmese art and craft, including lacquerware, textiles, wood and stone carving and bronze sculptures, have already been illustrated and described in a wide variety of publications ranging from specialist and general interest books to academic papers. Many of these other traditional art forms were also produced in high quality during the 19th and early 20th centuries.

The author's efforts to uncover Burmese-language information on silversmithing proved unsuccessful. The difficult task of conducting Burmese archival research requires language skills and fortitude unavailable to the author. A more productive and enjoyable means of gathering information was to spend time discussing silverwork with collectors, silversmiths, gallery owners and friends in many parts of Burma over the last eight years.

Provenance

An official system of silver hallmarking to certify provenance has never existed in Burma. It was also rare for silversmiths to inscribe their name or initials on domestic class artefacts and no workshop records are known to survive that would help to establish provenance. It is also difficult to establish clear provenance for a substantial proportion of silverwork made in China, India, Thailand and other Asian countries in the 19th and early 20th centuries. In Burma, the silversmith's anonymity reflects religious and cultural values. Buddhist strictures on vanity, pride and material possession are strong rationales for the silversmith to remain anonymous.

An uncommon exception to this practice is found on some silverwork produced by master silversmiths for either foreign patrons or specifically for national and international art competitions sponsored by the British India colonial government. W.R.T. Wilkinson (1999) lists the names of 37 silversmiths who were officially recorded as contestants in these competitions and any surviving work by these silversmiths is particularly coveted and valued by collectors. H.L. Tilly (1902 and 1904) also describes and illustrates prize-winning pieces by documented master silversmiths. There is also design and decorative style evidence to suggest that master silversmiths produced both signed and unsigned versions of successful or popular silverwork. The traditional domestic offering bowl typically bears no inscription of the silversmith's name or his workshop.

That is not to say that domestic silverwork is devoid of all provenance information. One third of the pieces in the Noble Silver Collection are inscribed with context information, including one or more of the following: the owner's name and title, the completion date of the piece, the owner's township residence and a short inscribed message. The completion date is the most valuable information. It establishes an outline technical and artistic chronology of the Silver Age and a reference base for estimating the age of non-dated silverwork.

Silversmiths also commonly inscribed a whimsical mark on the underside of the object, typically an animal, mythological creature or floral motif. In most instances these marks have little provenance value, because there are no known records that correlate specific marks to a silversmith's name or period of work. One exception is the 'seated deer' trademark (Fig. 1.11) used by the master silversmith Maung Shwe Yon and his son's silversmithing company, Mg Shwe Yon Bros. A tiger trademark used by an unknown silversmith is one of the more common trademarks on surviving silverwork.

The final determination of authenticity and age of the silverwork in the Noble Silver Collection rests on the inscribed provenance data and the intangible property of practical experience gained by handling a wide variety of silverwork and studying its form, design, technical workmanship and decorative quality. This experience is also acquired by the exchange of knowledge, information and opinion with other silver collectors and gallery owners specializing in Burmese

1.12 Artistic rendition of human form using repoussé and chasing techniques, c. 1880

1.13 Sita's face magnified to illustrate the litmus test of quality workmanship, c. 1915

silverwork. In the author's experience, the paramount criteria for assessing provenance and value in the absence of hallmark-like inscriptions are the artistic and technical qualities of the ornamentation. Critical to this assessment is an evaluation of the silversmith's ability to accurately and aesthetically render human and animal anatomy. Only the finest silver artists were able to portray a sense of emotion on a human face or imbue a human form with body language to suggest some conscious thought or intent (Figs. 1.12 and 1.13). A pragmatic aphorism for a provenance and value assessment might read: 'Look first at the face and body details!'

Silverwork that reproduces the traditional designs and decorative themes of the Silver Age is still handcrafted today in a few silversmithing centres in Burma (Fig. 1.9) and perhaps in Chiang Mai, Thailand. This work is easily distinguished from old silverwork by its lower technical and aesthetic quality.

There are no known living silversmiths with the artistic and technical skill to reproduce the master work of the late 19th and early 20th centuries.

Visual Narratives

The visual narratives, or storyboards (Fig. 1.14), that decorate silver offering bowls, betel boxes, treasure and cheroot boxes, storage jars, drinking vessels and other medium- to large-size artefacts are a defining characteristic of Burmese silver art. It was the curiosity to understand the history, content and wisdom of these narratives that, above all, inspired the passion to collect and research the art form. A publication to showcase the allure of Burmese silverwork would be incomplete without revealing the meaning and significance of the visual narratives.

1.14 A 360-degree storyboard of the Mahajanaka Jataka tale on a ceremonial offering bowl, c. 1925

1.15 Punnaka and his supernatural horse (from the Vidhura-Pandita Jataka), 1925

The two most common literary sources for the visual narratives are sacred Buddhist texts and the Ramayana poem from the Hindu religious tradition. Buddhist narratives illustrated in this book originate in the biography of the early life of the Buddha, the Jataka tales (Fig. 1.15) and poetry composed by the first Buddhist nuns. Jataka storyboards represent the classical decorative expression of Burmese master silversmiths. The Jataka tales are ancient stories of the many previous incarnations of the last Buddha, known as Gautama Buddha in his final life on earth.

Jataka are important historical texts because they convey and serve to teach the fundamental ethical values of Buddhism. They typically illuminate specific virtues required to achieve nirvana. These include generosity, good conduct, wisdom, energy, truth, determination, loving-kindness and equanimity. The wisdom of these values is surely universal and timeless. A silver artefact decorated with a Buddhist narrative also served another purpose. It was a source of karmic merit for both the silversmith and his patron. Karmic merit is a Buddhist metaphysical abstraction that determines in part the condition of one's current existence and future reincarnation in the endless cycle of life, death and rebirth. Moral precepts and values are also integral to the Jataka tales and the epic Ramayana poem (Figs. 1.16–21). The deeper wisdom found in these narratives speaks to the importance of character and righteous conduct in the eternal conflict between good and evil.

Many of the stories illustrated and described in this book are allegorical and complex narratives. Exceptional skill was required by the silversmith to condense the story events into a small number of representative scenes without losing the essence or wisdom of the narrative. Also, since this book by necessity can only illustrate select scenes from each artefact and provide a short abstract of the complete narrative, the author would encourage readers to seek out and read the complete original versions of these ancient tales to fully appreciate their drama and spiritual meaning.

Regional Silverwork

Decorative and applied silver art has a long tradition in Southeast Asia, India and China. This work is generally well known by virtue of research, publication and exhibition. Burmese silver art by comparison is less familiar to silver

1.16 The Ramayana poem depicted on Offering Bowl S106

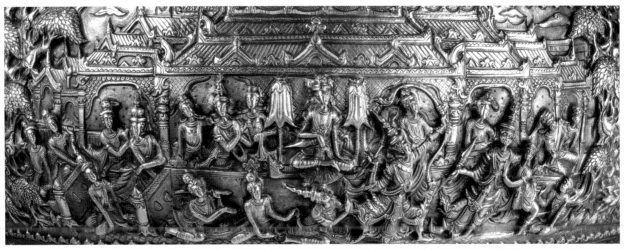

1.17 Rama defeats Ravana in an archery competition and wins the honour of marrying Sita

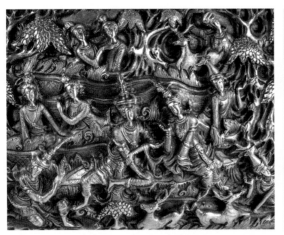

1.18 Sita begs Rama to capture a golden deer

1.19 Rama slays the demon deer

1.20 Ravana captures Sita

1.21 Ravana abducts Sita to Lanka Island on his flying chariot

1.22 Silver pedestal stand, tray and cover, 1891. A presentation to J. Pitt Kennedy, Recorder of Rangoon and Moulmein. Height 60 cm.
Victoria & Albert Museum, London

collectors, art historians and the broader world of Asian art and culture. One important reason for this limited recognition is the relative political, economic and social isolation of Burma (Myanmar) from the rest of the world since about 1962. This isolation also resulted in the hoarding of high-quality old silverwork by Burmese families until the late 20th century. Until this time, Burmese silverwork owned or exhibited outside of the country (Fig. 1.22) was generally limited to artefacts 'exported' in relatively small numbers by the resident foreign population in Burma prior to independence in 1948.

Burmese silver art was arguably more widely recognized and admired in the international art world in the late 19th and early 20th centuries than it is today. J.H. Rivett-Carnac, writing in the *Journal of Indian Art and Industry* in 1902, states that 'Burmese silver is deservedly the most celebrated and is the boldest and most meritorious in execution'. This view was confirmed when the master silversmith Maung Yin Maung from Rangoon won the First Prize with Gold Medal for his table centrepiece at the important Indian Art Exhibition at Delhi in 1903

(Fig. 2.24) and Maung Po Kin won the First Prize and Silver Medal for the best silver bowl in the same competition. This exhibition coincided with the grand imperial Delhi Durbar held in 1903 by the British to celebrate the succession of Edward VII as Emperor of India. The official catalogue of the exhibition by George Watt (1903) records that the best samples of Burmese silverwork loaned to the exhibition 'could have been disposed of several times over' had they been for sale. Tilly (1904) derides Indian attempts to copy old Burmese silver and states emphatically that 'Burmese handicraftsmen do not reproduce, they create'.

There is also a strong silversmithing tradition in China, Thailand, Malaysia and Indonesia. Chinese 'export' silver from the late 18th to mid-20th centuries was not well studied or widely collected until the 1970s, when it was 'rediscovered' by scholars and silver collectors in Europe and the United States. Silverwork from Thailand and Malaysia is rarely decorated with the exuberance and penchant for high-relief storytelling that characterizes Burmese silverwork, although some designs and decorative styles are common to all three bodies of work. Indonesia has a silversmithing tradition centred on the town of Gede near Yogyakarta, which dates to the 16th century. This tradition was revitalized by the Dutch in the 1930s and today silversmiths make bracelets, pendants, bowls, rings and other small pieces using filigree, inlay and casting techniques. Cambodia and Laos also produce small silver artefacts with distinctive designs and decoration.

The Allure

Burmese silverwork holds great allure – it is deeply and mysteriously fascinating. The medium of silver metal, the pleasing balance of the physical forms, the tactile nature of an offering bowl, the sublime artistry of the decoration, the extraordinary skill of the silversmith and the wisdom of the visual narratives all contribute to this wonderful allure. *Burmese Silver Art* attempts to capture, or at least represent, some of these qualities in the galleries, photographic images and text that follow. The author hopes the reader is surprised, delighted and informed by this work.

CHAPTER TWO

A Frame of Reference

There is a 2,000-year old cultural tradition of silversmithing in Burma dating back to the Pyu Period (100 BCE–900 CE). The surviving Pyu silverwork includes a magnificent Buddhist reliquary (Fig. 2.2), gilded plates (Figs. 2.1 and 2.4), decorated bowls (Fig. 2.6), Buddha images, miniature stupas, jewellery and coins. This important work is arguably the oldest and finest-quality Buddhist silver art discovered in South and Southeast Asia.

2.1 Gilded silver Pyu peacock plate, c. 5th century
National Museum of Myanmar, Naypyitaw

2.2 Pyu silver reliquary, c. 5th century. National Museum of Myanmar, Yangon
Photo: Metropolitan Museum, New York and National Museum of Myanmar, Yangon

Pyu Period

Most of the surviving Pyu silverwork is displayed in the National Museum of Myanmar in Yangon, the National Museum in Naypyitaw and the Sri Ksetra Archaeological Museum in Pyay.

The Pyu people first appear in the archaeological records in the late first millennium BCE in the central dry zone of Burma. They spoke a Tibeto-Burman language and archaeologists debate whether the Pyu evolved from a much older Bronze Age society in the Samon River area of central Burma or migrated directly from southwest China. The pre-historical roots of the Pyu may have been the high plateaus of Qinghai and Gansu in northwest China. There are references to a Piao people in Chinese chronicles from the Jin dynasty in the 3rd century CE to the Tang dynasty in the 9th century CE. Other ancient texts suggest that the Pyu called themselves 'Tircul'.

The Pyu were the first hierarchical urban civilization in Southeast Asia and the first to build city-states enclosed by fortified brick walls. These cities and other smaller settlements were all located within the basins of the Irrawaddy and Chindwin rivers in central Burma (Fig. 2.3). Pyu settlements ranged in size from less than 10 hectares (ha) up to 1,452 ha. Sri Ksetra (1,452 ha), Beikthano (859 ha) and Halin (629 ha) were the largest royal cities and the centres of Pyu religious, economic and cultural life.

Pyu engineers also constructed sophisticated water irrigation systems and mastered skills in ferrous and non-ferrous metalworking. Silver-copper alloy coins imprinted with Buddhist and Sanskrit motifs have been found in quantity at many Pyu sites. The silver content ranges from about 30 per cent to over 80 per cent, which suggests the coins were minted in several locations. It is uncertain if the Pyu silver coins were used for monetary exchange or some form of symbolic or token value.

A sophisticated and literate culture developed during the 1,000-year Pyu period. Dynastic and religious inscriptions on stone, silver and leaf artefacts, written in the Pyu, Sanskrit and Pali languages, reveal the influence of Brahman, Theravada Buddhist and Jain religious traditions from India as early as the first millennium CE. Indic influence also permeates many other aspects of Pyu culture and society, including Buddhist architecture, religious art, funerary customs, kingship rituals, dynastic names, artistic symbols of power, pottery design and decoration, coin symbols and even brick dimensions. Cultural influence also flowed along early trade routes that linked Pyu city-states to contemporary China and the Roman Empire.

Pyu silversmiths created a wide range of sophisticated Buddhist and secular artefacts. A treasure trove of these artefacts was discovered in 1926 in an undisturbed 5th-century royal relic chamber which lay underneath the Khin Ba mound in Sri Ksetra. This one-metre-square, brick-lined chamber contained over 50 silver and gold artefacts, including the magnificent 'Great Silver Reliquary' (Fig. 2.2), 20 leaves

2.3 Major cities during the Pyu period

2.4 Gilded and decorated silver Pyu plate, c. 5th century
Sri Ksetra Museum, Pyay, Myanmar

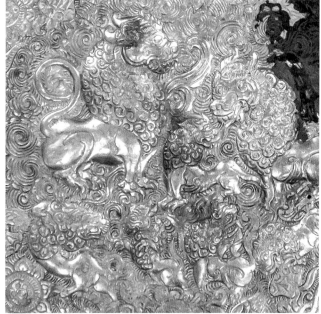

2.5 Detail from Fig. 2.4 – repoussé lions and cubs

of golden Pali text, silver votive stupas, silver Buddhas, silver Bodhisattvas, and silver bowls, betel boxes, cups, bells, rings, butterflies, petalled lotuses, sheets and coins. Farmers and archaeologists have also discovered silver artefacts at many other Pyu settlements. The regal silver plate from Sri Ksetra (Figs. 2.4 and 2.5) confirms that Pyu silversmiths had already mastered the decorative skills of repoussé and gilding by the middle of the first millennium CE. The classic shape and decorative style of the Pyu bowl illustrated in Fig. 2.6 is reminiscent of the archetypal ceremonial offering bowls of the 19th and early 20th centuries.

The Pyu civilization effectively vanishes by the end of the 9th century after a period of gradual decline that began in the previous century. This decline was probably due to repeated invasions by a Tibeto-Burman tribe from Nanzhao in southwest China and a related contraction of the economy. Historical chronicles record that in 832 CE the Bamar tribe from Nanzhao sacked a Pyu city, either Halin or Maingmaw. This event may have initiated a gradual political, economic and cultural assimilation of the Pyu people with the more powerful Bamar tribe.

The final eclipse of the Pyu occurred in the mid-10th century, when King Anawrahta founded the Bamar kingdom at Bagan. The archaeological record of the Bagan period from the 10th to the 13th centuries does not include any important silver artefacts, although burial tomb inscriptions describe interred silver objects, and it is likely that silver regalia and ornamentation were present at the royal court of the Bagan kings. There is no evidence that silver coins were used extensively during the Bagan period.

Burmese silverwork of artistic or cultural significance is also missing from the archaeological record for the long period of history between the Bagan era and the early 19th century. However, written accounts of a Portuguese priest to the Kingdom of Arakan in 1634, and the first official British mission to the Konbaung dynasty court at Ava by Michael Symes in 1795, describe silver thrones, silver regalia, silver ornamentation and silver money. It is also recorded that Siamese silversmiths captured during the Burmese-Siamese wars of the 16th to 18th centuries were permanently relocated to work in Burma.

Silverwork and silver coins have been constantly recycled in the silversmith's furnace throughout human history. This destiny no doubt befell much of the 'missing' silverwork from long periods of Burmese history. There are many reasons and causes to account for the recycling, including war, revolution, political and social change, wealth preservation, protection against fiat money and – most tragically – the theft and looting of artefacts from ancient and sacred burial tombs and royal palaces. Conflict in all its forms is perhaps the major catalyst for silver recycling, and Burma has a long and bloody history of war. The Mongol Empire launched three invasions in the 13th century; Burma fought 18 wars with neighbouring Siam (Thailand) between 1547 and 1855; the Chinese Qing dynasty armies invaded Burma four times in the 18th century; there were three Anglo-Burmese wars in the 19th century; and Japanese forces overran the country in the 1940s. The nation's history has not been conducive to the preservation of its cultural and artistic heritage.

2.6 Pyu silver bowl, c. 5th century
Sri Ksetra Museum, Pyay, Myanmar

The Burmese Silver Age

The 'Burmese Silver Age' is a descriptive title coined by the author for the period between about 1850 and 1930, when Burmese silversmiths handcrafted an exceptional and important body of artistically and technically high-quality silverwork.

This achievement is particularly noteworthy because Burma at the time was not an economically and artistically sophisticated country compared to Europe, China and the United States. It was in fact a largely undeveloped rural country with little infrastructure to nurture and support silversmithing. Private collections of the surviving work from the Burmese Silver Age are known to exist in Burma, Singapore, Thailand, France, England, Austria and the Middle East. The permanent collections of several museums in Asia, Europe and North America include representative examples of Burmese silverwork. Chinese, Indian, Thai and Cambodian silverwork is by comparison better known, published and publicly exhibited.

The extraordinary and rapid growth of silversmithing in mid- to late-19th century Burma was a result of many factors. Two key factors stand out from the wide perspective: first, the serendipitous advent of a new generation of gifted silversmiths; second, the momentous impact of incremental British colonization following the three Anglo-Burmese Wars

of 1825–26, 1852–53 and 1885 (Fig. 2.8). Colonialism fundamentally changed the political and economic structure of Burma: the king was exiled (Fig. 2.7), royal prerogatives and laws were abolished, mercantile capitalism replaced a semi-feudal

2.7 King Thibaw and Queen Supayalat escorted aboard the PS *Thooreah*, Mandalay, 29 November 1885

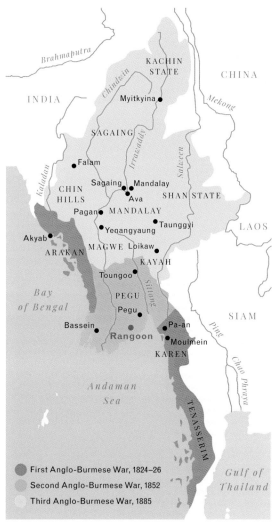

2.8 British colonial expansion in Burma, 1824–85

residents in Burma were a secondary, but important, market for silverwork during this same period. The acme of the Silver Age occurred in the early 20th century, and a rapid decline in silverwork output and quality appears to have begun in the late 1920s. This decline coincides with the international Great Depression and the widespread civil unrest and rebellion against British colonial rule in Burma in the early 1930s.

Very little information in the English language is available on the identities and biographies of the two generations of silversmiths who defined the Burmese Silver Age. Journeyman silversmiths were well established in small town workshops all over Burma at the turn of the 19th century and their anonymous images appear in several contemporary travel books written by Europeans. Some master silversmiths working in the larger towns and cities are identified by name only, with no surviving record of their individual work. Harry L. Tilly's 1902 and 1904 monographs illustrate and identify the work of a small number of preeminent silversmiths who submitted work to important national and international art competitions. These events were sponsored by the British India colonial government as part of

economy and the unified country was systematically opened to foreign investment and international trade for the first time in its history. This formidable and rapid change transformed the world of Burmese silversmithing.

The change was legal, economic and human in character. Legal because royal sumptuary laws proscribing silver ownership to all except royalty, high court officials and a few elite private families were abolished after 1885. Economic because a fast-expanding economy after 1885 created a burgeoning class of affluent Burmese. And human because master silversmiths previously cloistered in the royal palace at Mandalay under the patronage of the king were now released to either train a new generation of silversmiths or take commissions from an increasing number of nouveau-riche Burmese.

Typically, the new wealth and disposable income belonged to entrepreneurs and traders, timber and agricultural developers, and middle- to high-ranking colonial government officials. These groups constituted the primary market for silver art in Burma from about 1850 to 1930. British and other foreign

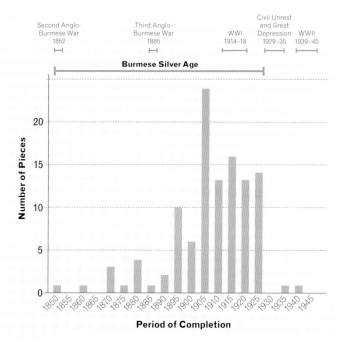

2.9 Burmese Silver Age: Dated artefacts in the collection and a historical timeline

their policy to encourage and develop traditional Burmese art. Another element of the policy was the opening of a 'commercial' art workshop in Rangoon in 1883. Tilly also informs on the prizes awarded at some of the important art competitions and provides brief biographical information on two of the most esteemed prize-winning Burmese master silversmiths – Maung Shwe Yon and his son Maung Yin Maung from Rangoon.

Figure 2.9 is a frequency bar chart of the inscribed ages of 111 pieces of silverwork made during the period 1850 to 1945. Historical events that had a significant impact on life in Burma during this period are identified in a timeline above the bar chart. The frequency distribution of the age data approximately defines an asymmetric curve with a gently rising gradient from 1850 to about 1885, a crest around the interval 1905–10 and a precipitous decline after 1925–30. It is the author's hypothesis that this age frequency curve is a broad proxy for the overall rise and fall of the Burmese Silver Age.

The sample population of dated silverwork comprises 50 objects from the Noble Silver Collection and 61 from another private collection. It is noted, however, that this sample population is statistically small, and the age frequency curve may not be representative of all surviving silverwork from the period.

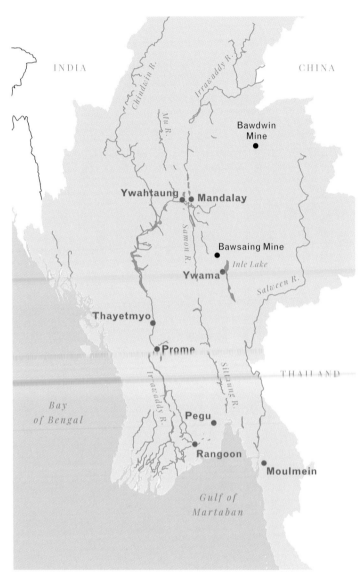

2.10 Major silversmithing centres and silver mines, 1850–1930

Silversmithing Centres

There were eight principal silversmithing centres in Burma during the period 1850 to 1930 (Fig. 2.10): Rangoon, Pegu and Moulmein in Lower Burma; Prome, Thayetmyo, Mandalay and Ywahtaung in Middle Burma; and Ywama floating village on Inle Lake in the Shan States. Other small towns in the country also supported small-scale workshops. The village of Ywahtaung in Sagaing district claims to be an 800-year old silversmithing centre with ancestral links to the Pyu people of the first millennium. Other Ywahtaung ancestors include highly skilled Siamese silversmiths from Ayutthaya and Chiang Mai who were captured during the 18th-century Siam-Burmese Wars and permanently resettled in Sagaing district. Ywama village in the Shan States also has a long pre-colonial history of silversmithing.

'Lower Burma', 'Middle Burma' and the 'Shan States' are regional classifications based on an amalgam of criteria including geography, political history and the predominant decorative style of the silverwork. Lower Burma silverwork is characterized by ornate, high-relief repoussé style decoration (Fig. 2.11); the distinctive Middle Burma style features a flat surface decorated using the piercing, or perforation, technique to create open spaces (Fig. 2.12); and Shan silverwork is readily distinguished by its typical floral, faunal and astrological decorative motifs, executed using both repoussé and piercing techniques (Fig. 2.13). It should also be noted that regional style attribution is not definitive in the absence of any supporting information on the artefact.

Transitional styles of form and decoration also complicate the assignment of regional provenance. Writing in 1904, Tilly

2.11 Lower Burma decorative style

2.12 Middle Burma decorative style

2.13 Shan States decorative style

2.14 'Domestic' silverwork: Offering bowl illustrating a Buddhist Jātaka tale

2.15 'Export' silverwork: Milk pitcher displaying cross-cultural form and decoration

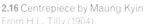

2.16 Centrepiece by Maung Kyin
From H.L. Tilly (1904)

2.17 Silverwork varieties, 1900
From *Burma* by M. and B. Ferrars

had the benefit of first-hand contemporary knowledge and describes 'two main schools of Burmese silverwork, viz., those of Rangoon and of Thayetmyo. Rangoon – precise, formal and accurate but tame; Thayetmyo – bold imaginative, but inexact and vague'. It is difficult today to recognize these schools with certainty, especially within the large body of silverwork crafted after 1904.

The Body of Work

Burmese silverwork can also be broadly classified into 'domestic' and 'export' categories based upon the principal sales market for the work. Most of the silverwork in the Noble Silver Collection is categorized as 'domestic'. It was made primarily for Burmese patrons to serve religious and secular purposes in the home and in the community. 'Export' silverwork was typically made for foreigners resident in or visiting Burma and taken out of the country to homes in Britain and Europe. The form of this work can embody a European function – a teapot, for example – and the decoration often includes cross-cultural designs and motifs. 'Competition' silverwork is a third and minor category of work in terms of the number of pieces made, but highly important in respect to the artistry and magnificence of the workmanship.

The ceremonial offering bowl illustrated in Fig. 2.14 is a good example of 'domestic' silverwork. It is entirely Burmese in form, decorative style and utility. The high-relief narrative comprising the central decorative band illustrates the Sama

Jataka from Buddhist scripture. Figure 2.15 is an 'export' category silver milk pitcher decorated with cross-cultural motifs. The cast handle is in the form of a *naga*, or dragon, while the cartouches on the bulb of the pitcher are filled with dancing women and posturing males – images not obviously associated with traditional Burmese culture or Buddhism. Figure 2.16 is a splendid example of 'competition' category silverwork. It is a large, grandiloquent centrepiece made by Maung Kyin from Mandalay that placed second in a national art competition in 1904. This artefact is not in the Noble Silver Collection.

A photo dated 1900 from the book *Burma* by Max and Bertha Ferrars (Fig. 2.17) portrays many forms of contemporary 'domestic' silverwork, including offering bowls, a betel box and a food container on a pedestal, storage jars, water cups, a sword and dagger handle in silver, a silver scabbard and a lime box. Other artefacts in the silversmith's 'domestic' repertoire comprised treasure and cheroot boxes, manuscript cylinders, fruit bowls, spittoons, temple vases, belt buckles and scale models of Buddhist stupas. Silver jewellery rarely features in either contemporary photographs or the surviving body of work from the Silver Age. Minority ethnic groups who live in the mountainous border regions of east and northeastern Burma have traditionally fashioned silver jewellery. This is considered a separate genre of silverwork.

The popular designs of 'export' silver reflect foreign taste and utility. Some examples include tea and coffee services, serving salvers, wine goblets, claret jugs and candlestick holders. Silversmiths also decorated traditional-style offering bowls

2.18 Buddhist shrine in a private home, Ywama Village

with motifs designed to appeal to foreigners, including idyllic village-life scenes, Burmese landmarks and human figures with statuesque Greco-Roman anatomy. Foreigners also purchased silverwork that was originally made for the domestic market or for art competitions. These artefacts were typically used as competition trophies, administrative awards, gifts for services rendered, ceremonial awards for military service, and everyday souvenirs. It was not uncommon for these artefacts to be engraved in English with information relevant to the gift, award or prize. Europeans also purchased some of the finest 'domestic' and 'competition' silverwork to furnish private art collections.

The Burmese purchased silverwork for a variety of reasons and functions. Archetype ceremonial bowls decorated with religious iconography were commonly used to display and distribute rice, food and other gifts to the monastic community during many religious and secular festivals. Inside the home, the bowls functioned as devotional objects to help teach and reinforce Buddhist scripture and Hindu values. A variety of silver artefacts (Fig. 2.18) containing water, food and flower offerings were typically placed in front of Buddha statues in private family shrines. Filling offering bowls in the home with seasonal flowers and fruit was an attractive secular use of

silverwork. The display of rich silver artefacts in the home also served to project the owner's wealth and social status.

The Silver Age ended soon after 1930. The specific reasons are not documented, although the turbulent history of Burma in the two decades after 1930 is more than enough to account for the demise of high-quality silversmithing and the collapse in demand for traditional silver art.

Today, the Burmese silversmithing tradition is only practised on a small scale in Ywahtaung village in Sagaing and Ywama floating village in Shan State. Reports of silversmithing in modern-day Yangon (Rangoon) have not been verified. Silverwork made in Ywahtaung and Ywama is sold to both the local and tourist markets. Much of the traditional religious demand for offering bowls is now satisfied by low-value, mechanically pressed aluminum bowls from China (Fig. 2.19). Regrettably, handcrafted silversmithing is an anachronism in modern Burma. There are few, if any, silversmiths with the mindset, the narrative knowledge and the skills to continue the time-honoured traditions of the old master silversmiths.

Contemporary Documentation

A few English-language articles published in the late 19th and early 20th centuries describe and celebrate the aesthetic value and the technical quality of Burmese silverwork. The authors of these indispensable articles were often British colonial officers with official responsibilities to document and promote traditional Indian and Burmese arts and crafts. The earliest known of these articles, 'Burmese Silverwork' by John Lockwood Kipling, appeared in *The Journal of Indian Art* in 1886 (Fig. 2.20) and described silverwork exhibited at the Calcutta International Exhibition of 1883–84. The journal piece contains two parts: the first is a critical survey of Indian and Burmese silverwork written in an imperious colonial style; the second part is a discussion on all aspects of Burmese silverwork

2.19 Rice offerings in Chinese aluminium bowls

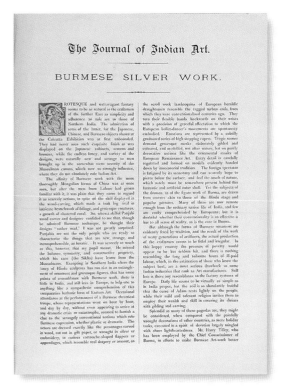

2.20 First comprehensive report on Burmese silverwork
J.L. Kipling, October 1886

written by the renowned Harry L. Tilly. According to Kipling, Tilly was first employed by the Chief Commissioner of Burma 'to make Burmese art-work better known' – a task that remains unfulfilled to this day!

Tilly's early opinion of Burmese silverwork in 1886 was unequivocal: 'The silver-work of Burma is much thought of by connoisseurs all over the world, and under the guidance of Europeans it is being improved, whilst the national characteristics are jealously guarded.' Figure 2.21 is a line-drawing of high-quality Burmese silverwork exhibited at the Calcutta exhibition. In a side-note to the literary history of Burmese silverwork, it is interesting to note that John Lockwood Kipling was the father of Rudyard Kipling, a popular Indian-born English writer, journalist and poet who won the Nobel Prize for Literature in 1907. Rudyard Kipling is best known in Burma for his classic poem 'Mandalay', which was inspired by a chance encounter with a beautiful Burmese girl at the Kyaik-Than-Lun Buddhist temple in Moulmein in 1899.

Harry L. Tilly is indisputably the most important contemporary source of information, illustration and opinion regarding late 19th and early 20th-century Burmese silverwork. He wrote two short monographs, *The Silverwork of Burma* in 1902 and *Modern Burmese Silverwork* in 1904. Both monographs were published by the Government Printing House in Rangoon. Interestingly, the 22-page 1902 monograph is a near verbatim copy of his contribution to the article by J.L. Kipling published

16 years earlier in the *Journal of Indian Art*. This monograph was also translated into the Burmese language for the 'benefit' of Burmese silversmiths and, according to Tilly, 'is constantly used in many shops in Burma, not so much for obtaining designs to be copied as for the study of the general characteristics of the spirit which animated the old masters'. The 1904 monograph comprises eight pages of text and 14 illustrations of exceptionally high-quality and prize-winning Burmese silverwork.

Tilly is the only source of information in English on the identity of the late 19th-century master silversmiths. In 1902 Tilly also organized the collection of Burmese silver artefacts that were exhibited with much acclaim at the prestigious Indian Art Exhibition at Delhi in 1903. Tilly's last known work, titled *The Art Industries of Burma*, was published in 1913 in the *Journal of Indian Art*. This short piece emphasized the value of domestic art competitions in the furtherance of traditional Burmese silversmithing. Tilly also wrote informed monographs on Burmese glass mosaics and woodcarving. His last known colonial position was Chief Collector of Customs in Rangoon in 1913.

Other illustrations and short descriptions of Burmese silverwork are found in 19th- and early 20th-century books by British and European authors who travelled extensively throughout Burma and documented many characteristics of the people and their culture. The best example of this genre of work is arguably *Burma* by Max and Bertha Ferrars (1900).

2.21 Silver offering bowls. Kipling, 1886

Silversmiths and Patrons

The Burmese Silver Age is defined by the work of an unknown number of remarkably gifted silversmiths who rose to prominence as artists in the late 19th century and left behind a legacy of unique and exceptional quality silver art. This legacy is the work of at least two generations of Burmese and Shan silversmiths over a period of about 80 years. The apogee of this long artistic period were the years spanning the end of the 19th century and the beginning of the 20th century. Little is known about the identity and lives of most of the silversmiths. They rarely signed their work in deference to Buddhist strictures on any display of personal vanity, pride or attachment to impermanent objects.

Less than one-tenth of all the silver artefacts in the Noble Silver Collection are inscribed with the silversmith's name. Most of these names are inscribed in the English language form of the Burmese name, suggesting the work was made for either foreign patrons or international art competitions.

Conversely, almost one-third of the collection is inscribed with the owner's name, written in Burmese script. This custom had practical value since ceremonial silverwork was commonly lent to family members and community friends for important Buddhist and secular festivals and ceremonies. Figure 2.22 portrays silverwork displayed at a novitiation ceremony featuring boys dressed as 'princes' to symbolize the life of Prince

Siddhartha Gautama before he renounced his royal destiny and began his journey towards Buddhahood. Later in the novitiation ceremony, the heads of the boy 'princes' will be shaved and they will change into the simple robes of a monk.

The only substantive information on the identity and work of any individual Burmese silversmith is, not unsurprisingly, found in Harry L. Tilly's monographs of 1902 and 1904. These wonderfully illustrated publications are in large part dedicated to the work of an elite group of contemporary, prize-winning Burmese master silversmiths. They contain a treasure trove of information on the names of the silversmiths, residency, quality and style of work, prize record and, in one case, biographical information on a two-generation family of esteemed silversmiths. The 1904 monograph also includes a full-page, formal studio photograph of perhaps the most gifted and acclaimed eight master silversmiths of the Burmese Silver Age (Fig. 2.23). Each silversmith is superbly attired in traditional Burmese dress, and competition winners proudly wear their prize medals. The only other known source that identifies the names and residence of prestigious silversmiths is a list published in 1999 in a book titled *Indian Silver 1858–1947* by Wynyard R.T. Wilkinson. This source lists 37 silversmiths who exhibited work at international art competitions between 1875 and 1910.

The two master silversmiths most frequently illustrated and admired by Tilly are Maung Shwe Yon and his son Maung Yin Maung from Rangoon. Maung Shwe Yon died in 1889 and his son became the preeminent and most celebrated master silversmith of his generation in the first decade of the 20th century. The pinnacle of his career came in 1903 when he was awarded the only First Prize with Gold Medal for 'silver plate' in India at the prestigious Indian Art Exhibition in Delhi. The prize-winning piece was an ornate centrepiece (Fig. 2.24), described by Tilly as a *kelat* which was 'used to carry before royalties on occasions of State and containing condiments or scent or a handkerchief'.

The Delhi art competition was held in conjunction with the magnificent Delhi Durbar organized by Lord Curzon, Viceroy of India, to celebrate the coronation of Edward VII as King of England and Emperor of India. Maung Po Kin, also from Rangoon, won the First Prize with Silver Medal in the category

2.22 Silver offering bowls displayed at a Buddhist novitiation ceremony, c. 1920

2.23 Studio portrait: Eight master silversmiths
From H.L. Tilly, 1904

2.24 Centrepiece by Maung Yin Maung
From H.L. Tilly, 1904

of 'bowls' at the same competition in Delhi for his *swun ok,* a 'receptacle for carrying rice or any other food offered to monks or a pagoda'. Both prize-winning pieces are based on the design of silverwork deployed during Konbaung court ceremonies and rituals. Maung Yin Maung and Maung Po Kin are wearing their Delhi prize medals in the studio photograph of master silversmiths in Tilly's monograph (Fig. 2.23).

The large body of silverwork made during the Silver Age ranged in size and value from the plain, functional lime box made by village and small-town silversmiths (Fig. 2.25) to the grand, ostentatious competition centrepieces made by the master silversmiths. There was also a wide variation in the dimensions, silver thickness and decorative quality of the

classic offering bowls. The original cost of any piece of silverwork would have been determined by the value of the silver content, the quality and complexity of the decoration, and the status of the silversmith. Small lime boxes were widely owned by virtue of their relative affordability, whereas the cost of the finest-quality offering bowls and betel boxes limited their sales to a small class of affluent Burmese (Fig. 2.30). Inscriptions on the base of many offering bowls identify the name, honorific title and gender of these affluent patrons. In the Noble Silver Collection, the bowl inscriptions record a near equal number of male and female owners. This probably reflects the traditional and prime role played by women in managing budgets and wealth in many Burmese households.

2.25 Burmese silversmiths. From H.L. Tilly (1902)

2.26 F. Beato Ltd art emporium, Mandalay, 1894
Photo: Canadian Centre for Architecture

P. KLIER & Co., PHAYRE STREET, RANGOON.

(Next door to Messrs. Thos. Cook & Son.)

Dealers and Manufacturers in BURMESE MASTERPIECES of WOOD and IVORY CARVINGS, BURMESE ART SILVERWARE, and CURIOS. Awarded Medals.	Largest selection of Views of BURMA and PICTORIAL POST-CARDS. Amateurs' work undertaken. Developing and Printing carefully executed.

Studio and Head Office :
3. SIGNAL PAGODA ROAD.

2.27 P. Klier advertisement
'Burmese Art Silverware', c. 1900

F. BEATO, LTD.,
COLOMBO,
DEALERS IN CURIOS.

BURMESE	BURMESE
Carvings,	Washing Silks,
Furniture,	Hand-Painted
Silverware	D'oylies,
Of all descriptions.	Fans, &c.

SILVER, BRONZE, AND ALABASTER BUDDHAS.
All Goods marked in Plain Figures.
All Burmese Silver Goods Guaranteed of Sterling Quality.
Head Office: **Mandalay, Upper Burma.**

2.28 F. Beato advertisement
'Burmese Silverware', c. 1900

P. ORR & SONS,
JEWELLERS
TO HIS MAJESTY THE KING.
RANGOON.

VISITORS TO BURMA
SHOULD INSPECT OUR STOCK OF

Burma Rubies - -
Peridots & Sapphires.

Burmese Silverware, Coins and Curios.

2.29 P. Orr & Sons advertisement
'Burmese Silverware', c. 1910

Foreign patrons of Burmese silverwork included colonial government officials and civil servants, military personnel, business corporations, non-government organizations and the first influx of international tourists. One of the preferred vendors of high-quality silverwork was Mg Shwe Yon Bros, goldsmiths and silversmiths of Rangoon. The company's name and address were often inscribed in English on the base of their work. Silverwork presented as an achievement award, sporting trophy, retirement gift or as a keepsake often bears an inscription around the rim of the piece recording the recipient's name and the occasion of the award or gift. One intriguing rim inscription on a small offering bowl in the Noble Silver Collection honours the village headman U Po Myit for 'assistance rendered by him in arresting (an) absconder wanted in F.I.R. No.99/26 Lugaungyun P.S.'. The fate of the absconder is not recorded, although his capture was evidently of some importance to merit the award of a valuable silver bowl.

The business of commissioning and purchasing high-quality silverwork could be conducted in several renowned foreign emporiums in Rangoon and Mandalay. These 'western'-style retailers specialized in a comprehensive range of Burmese artwork, crafts, jewellery and local curios. The most recognized of these businesses were Coombes & Co. of London and Rangoon; P. Orr & Sons of Rangoon (Fig. 2.29); Philip Klier & Co., a renowned German photographer and entrepreneur with a head office at 3 Signal Pagoda Road, Rangoon (Fig. 2.27); and F. Beato Ltd. of London and Colombo (Fig. 2.28), who opened an art and antique store on C Road in Mandalay in 1894 (Fig. 2.26), and a branch in Rangoon a few years later. Felice Beato (1832–1909) was a prolific and ground-breaking British-Italian photographer who is famous for his albumen silver portraits and images of war, architecture and everyday life in India, China, Japan and Burma in the mid-19th century. He also produced an early mail-order catalogue for the export of goods and guaranteed that all silverwork was 'sterling quality'.

2.30 Studio portrait: An affluent Burmese lady and her silver offering bowls, c. 1920

2.31 How a silver bowl is made, from silver ore (right) to decorated artefact (left), Ywama village, 2015

Silversmithing

An echo of the Burmese Silver Age can still be found today in Myanmar. A visit to the surviving silversmiths located in Ywahtaung, near Mandalay, and in the floating village of Ywama (Fig. 2.34) on Inle Lake in the Shan States is a journey back in time to the late 19th and early 20th centuries. Metallurgical procedures, forging methods, decorative techniques and the silversmith's simple toolbox (Fig. 2.37) have all changed little over 150 years. In fact, the simple technology, workflow and hand tools used today were first developed by the Sumerians, who crafted silver art in ancient Mesopotamia in 3,000 BCE.

How silver art is made by hand is not always self-evident when viewing the artefact. As a result, it is difficult for the observer to fully appreciate and value the silversmith's technical and artistic expertise. Therefore, an illustrated summary of the silversmithing process is described below to help resolve this difficulty and further the understanding of Burmese silverwork. The information is sourced from the generic literature on silversmithing and the author's observations of silversmiths working in Ywahtaung and Ywama villages.

Figure 2.31 is a 'tourist schematic' from Ywama village to illustrate the principal steps in transforming natural silver ore into a small decorated silver bowl. Intermediate stages, from right to left, include a silver bullion bar, a precursor silver alloy disc, the first stage of raising the bowl from the disc, the final form of the bowl, the filling of the bowl with natural pitch for internal support during the decoration phase, and the polished final product. The detailed technical process for crafting a classic Burmese silver offering bowl can be divided into four summary stages:

1. Metallurgical: A molten silver-copper alloy is poured into a ceramic mould to create a saucer-shaped precursor disc with a flat surface and a convex profile. The diameter of the disc is approximately equal to the width plus the height of the desired bowl.

2.32 Precursor components of a silver-copper alloy: Ingot silver and scrap silver and copper

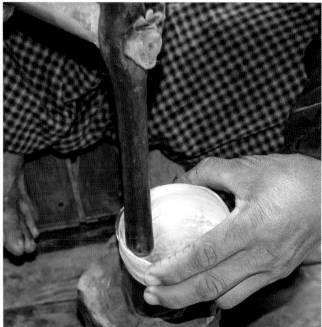

2.33 Raising a bowl from a silver alloy disc

2. Forging and Forming: The controlled cold-working of the disc using a hammer to raise the desired shape and dimensions of the bowl. This work hardens the silver and the nascent bowl needs to be regularly annealed to restore metal ductility and malleability.

3. Decoration and Shaping: The sketching of the design and narrative on the bowl prior to executing the detailed decoration using a combination of repoussé, chasing, piercing and other silversmithing techniques. Annealing is also required during this stage.

4. Finishing: The washing, burnishing and final polishing of the bowl.

Metallurgical

Pure silver is too soft for silver art. It is prone to cracking when overworked and is easily damaged by physical abrasion and impact. To overcome these disadvantages, silver is typically combined with between 5 per cent and 10 per cent copper to produce a silver alloy with optimum metalworking properties. The most common alloy is 'sterling' silver, containing 92.5 per cent silver and 7.5 per cent copper. Burmese silversmiths often produced the required silver-copper alloy by the direct melting of Burmese and Indian rupee coins with a pre-existing content of about 91 per cent silver and 9 per cent copper.

2.34 Ywama floating village – Silversmith and showroom, 2015

2.35 Annealing the silver bowl in a charcoal furnace

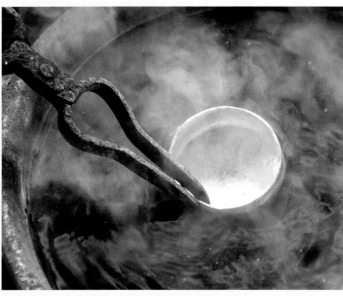

2.36 Quenching the bowl in water after annealing

Customized silver alloys were also made by melting silver bullion bars and copper metal in a high-temperature charcoal furnace (Fig. 2.32).

Forging and Forming

The raising of the silver alloy disc into the form of a bowl is achieved in controlled stages. The disc is first beaten with a straight-edged hammer at an angle of 45 degrees to create a lip around the disc. The lip is then raised to the full height of the bowl by using a raising hammer to beat the flat part of the disc in a spiral direction from its outer edge to the centre and back again in a series of courses (Fig. 2.33). This raising process requires skill and experience, since the silversmith must maintain both the thickness and symmetry of the bowl during the forming process.

Finally, when the bowl is raised to the desired height, it is beaten with a heavy hammer on a curved anvil to produce the final profile of the design. This work stage requires weeks of patient and consistent hammering to craft a large offering bowl. Modern power lathes, drop-and-pull hammers and mechanical presses are now used to fabricate metal bowls on a commercial scale. Generally, the aesthetic quality of a hand-raised silver bowl is superior to a mechanically made bowl.

It is essential to repeatedly anneal the silver during the raising of the bowl to preserve the metal's workability. This requires the heating of the bowl in a charcoal furnace to a

2.37 Silversmith's simple tool box

dull red colour (Fig. 2.35) and a temperature of about 650°C, followed by immediate quenching in cold water (Fig. 2.36). Burmese silversmiths estimated the annealing temperature from experience and used only human-powered bellows to supply compressed air to the furnace.

2.38 Chasing work on a resin-filled bowl

2.39 Scrubbing the finished bowl with soap nuts and water

Decoration and Shaping

The embellishment of the silverwork is a multi-staged technical and artistic process. The skills employed determine the quality and value of the finished artefact. A simplified description of the workflow is as follows:

1. A compound of natural resins and binders is poured into the bowl and a short wooden pole is placed in the mix before it hardens to create a working handle. The hard resin compound acts as a brace for the metal when the silversmith uses a compressive hammer and tools to decorate the bowl (Fig. 2.38).

2. The master silversmith traces the primary decorative elements on the exterior of the bowl in pencil. These elements include the outline of the visual narrative, the floral ornamentation and the banded geometric designs. The pencil outlines are next inscribed on the metal surface using a steel graver.

3. The rough outline of the low-relief areas of the design is punched into the metal using a simple hammer and a range of steel punches. This action simultaneously forces the adjacent metal upwards and creates the initial boundaries of the high-relief decoration.

4. The resin compound is melted and removed.

5. The silversmith uses the ancient repoussé technique to push out the detailed outlines of the high-relief decoration from the inside of the bowl.

6. The bowl is again filled with resin and the decorative detail is completed using a hammer and a variety of chasing tools, liners, punches, matting tools, stamps and engravers. At this stage, annealing is also required to restore the softness and ductility of the metal, which is essential for small-scale precision work. This final stage provides the silversmith with the opportunity to use the simple tools of the trade to expresses his full artistic imagination and technical skills.

Finishing

There are three common finishing tasks: first, the bowl is placed in a boiling solution of aluminum sulphate (alum) to dissolve surface residues; second, it is scrubbed clean with soap nuts and water (Fig. 2.39); and finally, the unadorned areas of plain silver are burnished to a high polish. The best-quality ceremonial offering bowls measuring about 25 centimetres in diameter took about a year to complete. Work time was also dependent on the size of the workshop, since a large shop employed apprentices and junior silversmiths to perform the less-skilled work.

Other Techniques and Skills

The full repertoire of techniques and skills used by Burmese silversmiths included piercing, niello work, casting, die forming, filigree work and gilding.

Piercing, or perforation, is a decorative technique used to create open spaces in the silver using a punch, saw or file. The result is a latticework design. In high-quality pierce work, the metal to be removed is first punched inwards and then completely excised after heating. This method creates a clean edge to the open spaces. A rough edge remains if the pierced metal is not fully removed. A skilled silversmith may remove up to 50 per cent of the object's silver mass in creating a detailed latticework design. The detailed decoration and narratives are chased onto the silverwork after the pierce work is completed. Pierce work is a characteristic regional style of Middle Burma.

Niello is an inlay technique used to create a contrasting black-and-silver finish on silver artefacts. The name derives from the Latin *nigellum*, meaning 'blackish'. The niello finish is achieved by filling a lattice pattern on the silver object with a black powder mix comprising copper, lead, silver and sulphur, and heating the object in an oven to about 370°C. This was a skilled but dangerous occupation. The mixing of the niello powder and the high-temperature fusing of the powder created highly poisonous sulphur dust and fumes. Burmese niello artefacts are uncommon except in the form of small lime boxes.

Casting is a technique to create three-dimensional silver objects by pouring molten silver into a design mould (Figs. 2.40 and 2.41). Cast silver pieces were made as stand-alone artefacts, finials and small decorative attachments that were soldered onto larger artefacts. Die forming was a time- and cost-efficient technique for reproducing multiple copies of silverwork pieces with the same rough imprint of a popular decorative design. A common die design was the iconic 'Konbaung royal family' image (Fig. 2.42) that was often featured on the lid of rectangular lime boxes. The silverwork copies are made by pressing, or forcing, annealed silver against a pre-formed brass or steel die.

Silver filigree decoration is most often seen as a minor design element on silverwork made for international art competitions and exhibitions. It is created by soldering together fine silver wire. Gold leaf gilding was rarely used in Burma.

2.40 Casting molten silver alloy into an elephant head mould

2.41 Cast elephant head

2.42 Konbaung royal family brass die for a lime box lid, c. 1920

2.43 Bawdwin silver mine – the open-pit development, 2015

Silver Sources

Silver has played a role in the cultural and economic history of Burma since the beginning of the Pyu period in the first millennium CE. The most important general sources of the metal were trade – particularly with India, China and Britain – and natural silver deposits in the Shan States. Much of the mid-19th to early 20th-century silverwork was made from recycled Burmese and British India coins.

Trade Routes

The historical land and sea routes that link Burma to neighbouring India and China have existed since at least the beginning of the first millennium when the Pyu civilization first traded with the wealthy kingdoms of northern and southeast India. Silver coins with Indo-Brahmic designs have been uncovered at many Pyu sites in central Burma, and many Pyu silver artefacts reflect the influence of Indian culture and design. The source of the silver for the coins and artefacts is not recorded – although, in the absence of any confirmed Pyu Period silver mines or smelters, it is logical to deduce that Pyu silver was sourced in India, where silver mining and processing were already established.

The mountainous route connecting Burma and the Shan States with southwest China has been used since at least the Tang dynasty in the 7th century CE. This route brought Chinese court officials, armies and trade to Burma. The Nanzhao kingdom from Yunnan invaded the Pyu states in the 9th century and Chinese Qing dynasty armies followed in the 18th century. It is also probable that Yunnan exported silver bullion to Burma for a wide range of uses. This region of southwest China is rich in silver and other metallic mineral deposits and the history of mining and smelting is older than the Tang dynasty.

International seaborne trade in the 18th to 20th centuries was another source of silver bullion. The British East India Company imported silver bars to the port of Syriam after the Second Anglo-Burmese War of 1852. The silver paid for ship construction, repair and general trade.

BAWDWIN MINE PICTORIAL VIEW

2.44 Schematic cutaway view of the surface and underground development of Bawdwin silver mine, c. 1980

Silver Mines

The complex geological history of Burma has endowed the country with rich mineral deposits of copper, lead, zinc, silver and other minor metals. The Bawdwin silver-lead mine near Lashio in northern Shan State was one of the most prolific sources of silver in the world (Figs 2.43 and 2.44). The mine's name derives from the Burmese words *baw*, meaning silver, and *dwin*, indicating a hollow or hole in the ground. A rock inscription near the mine records that 'mining was begun by the Chinese in the ninth year of the rule of Emperor Yongle of the Ming dynasty' – equivalent to the year 1412 in the Gregorian calendar. Older Chinese chronicles also refer to unidentified Burmese silver mining in the 12th century.

Between 1412 and 2009, Bawdwin produced approximately 175 million ounces, or 5,000 tons, of silver metal. The bulk of silver production was from a 'modern' British-financed and -built mine that operated between 1909 and 1939. Some 120 million ounces, or about 70 per cent of the total historical mine output, was produced during this 30-year period. The Bawdwin mine is now closed, although silver ore reserves remain, and the open-pit and original underground mine facilities exist on a care and maintenance basis.

There is an interesting historical footnote to the history of the Bawdwin mine regarding the naming of the 'Tiger Tunnel' – the primary access tunnel to the underground mine workings. In April 1914, the general mine manager discovered a tiger deep inside the tunnel and was forced to beat a hasty retreat to the surface in fear for his life. Henceforth, the tunnel was named 'Tiger Tunnel' to memorialize the event. The manager

was a geologist and mining engineer by the name of Herbert C. Hoover, who later became the 31st President of the United States in 1929. Figures 2.45 and 2.46 illustrate the tunnel entrance in c. 1925 and during the author's visit in 2015. The 1925 photo was taken by a mine engineer who was a contemporary of Herbert C. Hoover and the father-in-law of the author's maternal uncle.

Geologically, Bawdwin is defined as a structurally deformed volcanogenic lead-zinc-silver deposit. The silver occurs primarily within the molecular structure of galena (Fig. 2.47), a common lead sulphide mineral. Lesser amounts of silver are found in acanthite (Fig. 2.48) and argentite, two chemically related silver sulphide minerals. When the Bawdwin deposit

2.45 Tiger Tunnel at Bawdwin mine, c. 1925 Photo: Derek and Helen Langslow, England

2.46 Tiger Tunnel nameplate, 2015

2.47 Galena, the principal source of lead and silver

2.48 Acanthite, a common silver mineral, Bawdwin mine, 2015

2.49 Burmese 999 silver ingot (3.5 kilograms), Ywahtaung village, 2014

was discovered at least 600 years ago, the surface mineralization was oxidized. It is probable that the oxidized mineralization contained visible native silver, which would have attracted the attention of the first miners. After the native silver had been mined out, the ancient metallurgical process of cupellation would have been used to separate silver metal from the oxide and sulphide lead ore. Silver was also produced from smaller mines in the Bawsaing district near Heho in southern Shan State from about the 14th century. A Chinese-Burmese joint venture company currently operates a modern silver-lead-zinc mining business in the same district.

The end products of the Bawdwin and Bawsaing mining and smelting operations were predominantly silver ingots and bars with a presumed fineness of about 99.9 per cent silver (Fig. 2.49). The historical downstream uses of this silver would have included Burmese 'lump' silver currency, silver coinage, trade and government financing, royal court consumption and silver artefacts. The early 20th century was the apogee of the Burmese Silver Age and the peak period of silver production from the Bawdwin mine. This coincidence may be causally related.

Lump Silver Currency and Silver Coins

Silver coins and other physical forms of silver metal with monetary value were in wide circulation in Burma during the 19th and early 20th centuries. Trade and commerce relied on this silver currency and it was increasingly used as a store of new wealth. A proportion of the metal was also recycled in the silversmith's furnace to be reincarnated as silver art.

'Lump' silver was a common currency in Burma prior to the introduction of regulated silver coins in 1865. There were many shapes and weights of lump silver, including 'flower' silver, 'oyster shell' silver and 'sycee' silver (Fig. 2.50), used more commonly in northern Burma and close to the Chinese border.

In practice, lump silver was simply cut, clipped and weighed to satisfy the value of the payment. Henry Yule, who led a British mission to the Burmese court of Ava in 1855, described the varieties of lump silver in circulation: 'the finest silver current in Burma is called *Baw*. It contains three or four per cent of alloy (copper), but not more'. He also recorded that *dain*, containing 95 per cent silver, was commonly used for foreign trade and exclusively for Chinese trade. Flower silver, known as *Yowet-ni*, contained 85 per cent silver and was used for domestic business. Yule added that the 'currency' system was further diversified by the circulation of low-quality lump silver containing anywhere between 50 per cent and 80 per cent silver. It is not recorded which, if any, variety of lump silver was used by contemporary silversmiths. The colour, density, softness and value of all silverwork made from lump silver would be directly dependent on the fineness of the source silver.

Government-minted silver coins were probably the preferred source of a silver alloy for crafting all forms of Burmese silverwork from about the late 19th century. The alloy composition of these coins was 'guaranteed' at about 91 per cent silver and nine per cent copper and other minor metals. It was an ideal alloy for crafting high-quality silverwork and contained close to the 92.5 per cent 'official' silver content of sterling silver. The coins were also used as a store of financial wealth by the newly rich Burmese in the early 20th century, with some families choosing to diversify their financial assets and convert surplus coins into silverwork. This conversion was probably an important driver of the Silver Age. The final size, weight and fineness of the silverwork was a function of the number and tenor of the coins used to make each artefact. A few pieces in the Noble Silver Collection are inscribed with the number or weight of the silver coins used by the silversmith.

Burmese 'Peacock' one-kyat coins and British India one-rupee coins (Fig. 2.52) were the most common coins melted down to make silverwork. Peacock coins were so named because they were struck with the design of a peacock in full

2.50 Lump silver currency in various shapes: Flower, oyster shell and sycee, c. 19th century

display on the obverse face of the coin. This coin was first minted by King Mindon in Mandalay in 1865 using an imported mint from Birmingham, England. The chimney and walls of the mint are still standing today within the reconstructed Konbaung royal palace in Mandalay (Fig. 2.51). Over 26 million one-kyat coins and 10 million one-half, one-quarter and one-eighth kyat coins were minted between 1865 and 1885. The mint was closed following the British annexation of Burma in 1885, and all Peacock coins were subsequently withdrawn from circulation and gradually replaced with British India rupees.

British colonial records suggest that many of the Peacock silver coins were not exchanged by the Burmese for equivalent British India rupees, but either hoarded or used for other

purposes. It is probable that many of the coins that were no longer legal tender were recycled by silversmiths during the Silver Age. The official British report on the currency exchange indicates that Peacock coins were surrendered in extraordinarily low numbers. A total of 36 million Peacocks in four denominations were minted in Mandalay. When the exchange period ended in 1889, only 7.5 million of these coins had been returned. On face value, the 28.5 million 'missing' coins of all denominations represent a very large inventory of silver – about 200,000 kilograms, or seven million ounces. These figures arbitrarily assume that 75 per cent of the 'missing' coins were the common one-kyat denomination, with an average weight of 11 grams and a silver content of 91.2 per cent. The precise number of hoarded Peacock coins is unknown, although it is evident that a significant value of silver metal remained in private ownership after 1889 in the form of silver coins.

Other coins recycled by Burmese silversmiths may have included the Spanish *real*, otherwise known as a Spanish dollar or 'pieces of eight', and the French Indochinese *piastre* (Fig. 2.52). The *real* was a common trade currency in Southeast Asia from the 17th to the 19th centuries and the *piastre* was in circulation during the 19th and 20th centuries.

2.51 Mandalay mint (Konbaung era), photographed in 2016

2.52 Silver coins: (From top) British India rupee, Konbaung Peacock and French Indochinese *piastre*

CHAPTER THREE

One Hundred Silver Artefacts from the Noble Silver Collection

This chapter is a photographic exhibition of 100 fine-quality Burmese silver artefacts from the period 1850–1930. The elegant images are the work of the acclaimed Singaporean artist-photographer Charlie Lim. A caption to each photo tabulates catalogue data for the artefact. Selected artefacts are described and appraised. All the 100 artefacts are from the Noble Silver Collection. They are arranged in the following eight 'galleries', according to the physical form and function of the artefact.

1. Betel Boxes and Food Platters
2. Cheroot, Treasure and Dried Food Boxes
3. Master Silversmiths
4. Ceremonial Offering Bowls
5. Food Storage Jars
6. Lime Boxes
7. Drinking Vessels and Vases
8. Variety Silverwork

How to Read the Captions: An Example

Offering Bowl (S115), c. 1880 ⟶ *Form or function | Inventory number | Year of completion (inscribed or estimated)*

Maung Shwe Yon ⟶ *Silversmith*

Lower Burma ⟶ *Regional style*

Patacara Therigatha ⟶ *Decorative design or visual narrative*

'M.S.Y.' ⟶ *Base inscription (English translation)*

Wt 1,754 g ▪ D 26 cm ▪ H 17.5 cm ⟶ *Weight, Diameter, Height*

3.1 Betel Box (S9), c. 1910
Lower Burma
Sama Jataka
Wt 1,773 g ▪ D 25 cm ▪ H 40 cm

3.2 The Noble Silver Collection

The largest number of artefacts are displayed in the 'Offering Bowls' gallery. This silverwork is the focus of the Noble Silver Collection and the classical artefact of the Burmese Silver Age. A simple statistical analysis of the complete collection is provided in bar-chart form in Appendix 2. A small 'side-gallery' at the end of Chapter 3 contains a pictorial catalogue of the whimsical inscriptions commonly inscribed by the silversmith on the underside of the artefact. The intriguing and complex decorative narratives that embellish the silverwork are fully described in Chapter 4. Figure 3.2 illustrates the permanent display of the Noble Silver Collection in Singapore.

The provenance and authenticity of each artefact in the collection are assessed using the following five-stage process:

1. An examination and translation of all inscription information

2. A scrutiny of the technical and artistic quality of the workmanship

3. A deciphering of the visual narratives

4. An internet and literature search for comparative information

5. A holistic and comprehensive analysis based on experience

The approximate year of completion is estimated for many artefacts. Two artefacts (S43 and S149) in the collection are attributed to the documented silversmith Maung Yin Maung, based on strong comparative evidence. All age estimates and attributions are built on a foundation of research, published and oral information, and accumulated hands-on experience examining Burmese silverwork of all ages, style, quality and authenticity.

Betel Boxes and Food Platters

Betel Boxes

'Betel chewing' is the colloquial term for the habitual social custom of chewing a betel quid – a tradition practised by men and women across all socio-economic classes in Southeast Asia for over 2,000 years. The presentation of a betel quid to a guest expresses hospitality and friendship. The quid (Fig. 3.3) consists of three basic ingredients: an *Areca catechu* palm nut; a bright green leaf from the *Piper betle* pepper plant; and 'lime' paste. This white paste, known as slaked lime, is made by mixing calcium oxide (CaO) with water. Other minor ingredients of the betel quid include tobacco, tree bark, black pepper, ginger and other exotic spices.

The quid is prepared in two stages: in the first stage, slices or cut pieces of the nut and other ingredients are placed on a flat betel leaf smeared with lime paste; and in the second stage, the aggregation is rolled into a bite-size packet. Chewing a betel quid produces blood-red saliva that needs to be frequently discharged in the direction of a spittoon or the ground! There are many claims to the positive effects of chewing the areca nut, including a sense of euphoria and well-being, a stimulant to communication, an energy boost, alertness, improved digestion, increased salivation and a host of other medicinal benefits. There are also serious negative effects not limited to stained red teeth and a carpet of unhygienic red sputum on the

3.4 Gilded areca nut scissors

ground. The World Health Organization classifies the areca nut as a carcinogen.

Preparation of the betel quid required a set of functional items: scissors to slice the nut (Fig. 3.4); a handheld piston device to fragment the nut into small pieces (Fig. 3.9); boxes to hold the slaked lime (see pages 98 to 103); and highly decorated containers, or betel boxes, to hold the ingredients and the completed quids. These items together constitute a traditional betel set, which varied enormously in material composition, artistic style, quality and sophistication, according to the wealth and status of the owner.

A ceremonial silver betel box (Fig. 3.1) is the largest and most elaborate of all the pieces in a betel set. The boxes were often displayed in private as stand-alone table centrepieces. The typical components of a ceremonial box are a rounded or tripod pedestal, a cylindrical container holding up to three trays, a friction lid and a cast silver finial on the apex of the lid. However, many surviving betel box containers from the Silver Age are not paired with a pedestal, either by design or due to the separation of the two pieces over time or when custody changed. Stand-alone cylindrical containers also functioned as general storage boxes for cheroots, cigars and other items. Owning a silver ceremonial betel box conferred status in Burmese society, and it is was not uncommon in the 19th and early 20th centuries to place boxes on the ground in front of

3.3 Betel quid ingredients: Areca nut, betel vine leaf and slaked lime

3.6 Decoration on lid

3.5 Betel Box (S40), c. 1910
Shan
Astrological
Wt 338 g ▪ D 10.5 cm ▪ H 10.5 cm

3.7 Decoration on hidden base

3.8 Betel Box (S130), c. 1910
Lower Burma
Sama Jataka
Wt 1,242 g ▪ D 18.5 cm ▪ H 17.5 cm

3.9 Elephant tusk cylinder for crushing areca nut

formal portrait photographs of the last Konbaung kings, Shan Saohpas and high-ranking Burmese families (Fig. 3.10).

Figure 3.11 is an example of a masterpiece ceremonial betel box. The two-tray box comprises five independent components: a two-section support stem soldered to a flared pedestal with five talon-like feet; a flanged base with a strongly serrated edge; two individual circular trays; and a friction lid surmounted by a soldered cast finial. These stacked components are schematically illustrated and described in Fig. 3.12. All the components of the betel box are intricately decorated with either scenes or figures from the Sama Jataka. This exceptionally large box contains about 2.6 kilograms (5.7 lbs) of silver and measures 0.5 metres (1.6 ft) in height.

3.10 Sao Shwe Thaike, Saohpa of Yawnghwe (Nyaungshwe), Shan States, with family and retinue

Betel Box (S58), 1909
Lower Burma
Sama Jataka
'Myanmar Calendar Year 1271.
Silver container'
Wt 2,589 g ■ D 33 cm ■ H 49.5 cm

A lotus bud **finial** in cast silver.

Upper tray lid decorated with repoussé figures from the Sama Jataka. An outer and inner band of chasing in the shape of lotus buds. Floral design wraps around the medallions.

Upper tray lid and **two stacked trays** for betel vine leaves and areca nuts. The repoussé figurines in the medallions are characters from the Sama Jataka. Bands of lotus bud chasing above and below each tray and floral decoration between the medallions.

A **skirting** decorated with fine and detailed repoussé work illuminating scenes from the Sama Jataka. Extravagant floral work and medallion frames. Iconic deer figures alternate with the Jataka scenes.

Upper stem of the pedestal decorated with figures from the Sama Jataka. The character visible is King Piliyakka holding a hunting bow. Open and pierced workmanship.

Lower stem of the pedestal decorated with figures from the Sama Jataka. The character visible is Sama carrying an iconic water bowl. Open and pierced workmanship.

Pedestal base decorated with fine and detailed repoussé work illuminating scenes from the Sama Jataka. There are five feet in the form of bird claws.

3.12 Betel box components

Pickled Tea-Leaf Salad Platter

Tea is both a beverage and a food in Burma. A pickled tea-leaf salad (*laphet-thoke*) is a traditional food delicacy, either served as a simple side pickle with everyday meals, or Mandalay-style on a tray accompanied by fried garlic flakes, roasted peanuts and peas, fried beans, dry fish and shrimp, pickled ginger, coconut, sesame seeds, tomatoes and chili oil (Fig. 3.13). More exotic ingredients are added depending on the locality, including fried grubs and insects. The traditional salad is often served to guests during Buddhist ceremonies and secular festivals. Historically, pickled tea-leaf salads represented a symbolic peace offering. In more recent times salads were exchanged and consumed in settlement of civil disputes.

Everyday Burmese salad platters are traditionally and most commonly made of lacquer. Silver platters are rare and would have been used more for ceremonial and display purposes. The three main components of this ceremonial piece (Fig. 3.15) are a circular platter raised on tripod legs, a truncated dome-like cover and a tall, multi-element finial. The salad illustrated in Fig. 3.13 would fit comfortably on the platter beneath the ornate cover (Fig. 3.14).

3.13 Mandalay-style pickled tea-leaf salad

3.14 Decorative detail on platter cover and base of Pickled Tea-Leaf Salad Platter S8

3.15 Pickled Tea-Leaf Salad Platter (S8), c. 1910
Lower Burma
Vessantara Jataka
Wt 2,089 g ▪ D 38.5 cm ▪ H 43 cm

3.16 Treasure Box (S86), c. 1910
Lower Burma
Vessantara Jataka
'Po Kyaw's box'
Wt 2,207 g ▪ L 33.5 cm ▪ W 20 cm ▪ H 15 cm

3.17 Lid detail (S86) – Prince Vessantara gifting a sacred white elephant

Cheroot, Treasure and Dried Food Boxes

Rectangular, cylindrical and elliptical silver boxes were used to store a variety of important items in wealthy Burmese homes, including jewellery, cigars, cheroots, special dried foods and other personal valuables. Smoking is a traditional habit enjoyed by men and women alike from all social classes. Cigars were made from Burmese tobacco and cheroots from a mixture of crushed mild tobacco and dried wood seasoned with tamarind pulp. The filter was made from a dried corn husk, while the size of the cheroot varied from the equivalent of a long cigarette to a Churchill cigar. Offering a cigar or cheroot to a guest was a social custom of equal rank to offering a betel quid or a pickled tea-leaf salad. Ornate silver boxes in the home symbolized status and wealth.

The landscape orientation of the planar lid on rectangular storage boxes served as an ideal canvas for the silversmith's decorative work. Large box lids commonly feature a single panoramic scene from either a Jataka tale or the Ramayana poem. Other framed scenes from the same narrative typically wrap around the vertical sides of the box in a storyboard fashion. These visual narratives were an effective and joyful means of teaching and reinforcing Buddhist scriptures and values in the home, especially for children in a time prior to the advent of illustrated books, comics and the internet!

The silver box S86 (Fig. 3.16) combines art, function and storytelling. It is a near-airtight container for treasured items, documents, cheroots or high-value dried foods. All the outer surfaces of the box are decorated with finely detailed scenes from the Vessantara Jataka. The hinged lid of the box is adorned with one of the best-known events in the Jataka – Prince Vessantara giving away his kingdom's auspicious white elephant (Fig. 3.17). Scrolling around the sides of the box in a chronological sequence are a series of vignettes, or scenes, that provide an abridged visual narration of the entire Jataka. Each scene differs in width according to the specific story episode and is typically framed by a tree and floral bands. Vignettes also wrap around the curved corners of the box. The Vessantara Jataka is an allegorical story teaching the moral value of charity – arguably the most important virtue in the Buddhist religion.

Storage box S56 (Fig. 3.18) is an exceptionally fine example of Burmese silver art. It is well-proportioned, aesthetically refined and the embodiment of traditional Burmese decorative style. The composition, perspective and sense of realism of the scene portrayed on the lid's landscape-oriented surface are superb (Fig. 3.19). The scene is an artistic rendition of a pivotal event from the Vidhura-Pandita Jataka – a dice competition between King Dhananjaya and his adversary Punnaka. The drama is set in a magnificent gaming room in the king's palace, filled with 22 men and women wearing a variety of lavish costumes and headdresses. These figures include the king's sage Vidhura-Pandita, a host of visiting kings, military personnel, ladies in waiting and the king's guardian deity. A floral frame around the scene features narrow bands of small lotus buds and entwined acanthus. The four side panels of the box portray other events from the Jataka in high fidelity. The Jataka is an allegory on the virtue of truth and equanimity.

S111 (Fig. 3.20) is an unusual set of six small pie-shaped storage boxes that surround and interlock with a central cylindrical box. The hinged lid of each box is decorated with exceptionally high-relief repoussé work. Scenes from the Burmese royal court during the Konbaung dynasty adorn the pie-shaped boxes and feature images of the king, his chief wives, his concubines, a newborn child, a wet nurse and a courtier holding a large snake. The central box is embellished with a stunning, almost three-dimensional, rendition of a dynamic horse and demon rider (Fig. 3.21). The horse is portrayed with flared nostrils and a gaping jaw, which reveals all the ugliness of the animal's teeth. The master silversmith has also added the precise details of the horse tack – bridle, reins and stirrups.

An inscription on the underside of the cylindrical container records that the seven-piece box set was made from 100 coins. This information cannot be precisely correlated to the current weight of the set (688 grams) and the weight of contemporary silver coins. One hundred half-kyat denomination Konbaung Peacock coins would have weighed about 600 grams. This is the closest correlation, and it assumes that all the coins used to make the box set were of the same denomination, which may not have been the case.

3.18 Treasure Box (S56), c. 1910
Lower Burma
Vidhura-Pandita Jataka
Wt 1,066 g ▪ L 24 cm ▪ W 11.5 cm ▪ H 11.5 cm

3.19 Lid detail (S56) – Punnaka and King Dhananjaya play a game of dice

3.20 Dried Food Box (S111), c. 1880
Lower Burma
Royal family at court
'Mr Tinh and Madam Hmon. Kyan Khin Shin Than.
Weight 100 silver coins'
Wt 688 g ■ D 21 cm ■ H 5 cm

3.21 High-relief horse
on lid of central box

3.22 Cheroot Box (S145), 1911
Lower Burma
Ramayana
'Burmese year 1272,
15th Day of August, Full moon.
Madam Pu Sein's silver box'
Wt 1,040 g ■ L 22 cm ■ W 12.5 cm ■ H 15 cm

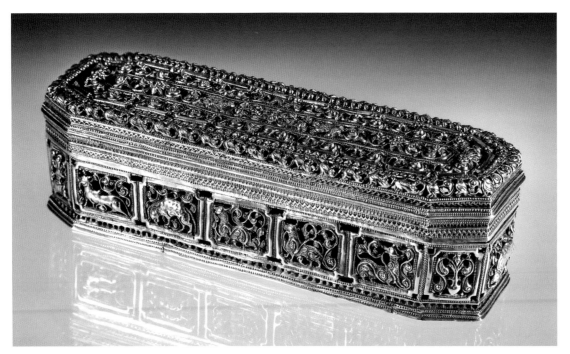

3.23 Cheroot Box (S66), 1928
Lower Burma
Floral and faunal
*'This piece was made by silversmith
Shine Hlae and Mu weight to 20 Kyats.
It was finished in 1290 Burmese year,
Thidingyut month and 7th day.'*
Wt 344 g ■ L 20.5 cm ■ W 6.5 cm ■
H 6 cm

3.24 Treasure Box (S54), 1860
Shan State
Mythological animals
'Burmese year 1222'
Wt 367 g ■ L 20 cm ■ W 8 cm ■ H 8.5 cm

The uncommon design of the silver treasure box S145 (Fig. 3.22) features 'floating' decorative panels on the lid and the four largest faces of the octagonal box. These panels were made independently from the box and soldered into prepared frames. The panels are slightly raised above the structure of the box and appear to 'float' in space, creating an attractive sense of depth and dimension. High-relief repoussé and pierced-style decoration were added before the panel was mated with the box.

A provenance letter dated 15 June 1925 (Fig. 3.26) and a 'First Prize' ticket accompany the storage box S132 (Fig. 3.25). The silver box was a gift from the Bishop of Rangoon, Rollestone Sterritt Fyffe (R.S. Rangoon), to a gentleman named Weston who had helped the Rangoon Diocese for four years before returning to England. R.S. Rangoon explains in the letter that the box had won first prize at the Rangoon Arts and Crafts Exhibition and was considered the best piece of Burmese silverwork in 1925. The bishop also quips: 'I do not suppose you would smoke Burma cheroots if I were to fill the box with them.'[1]

---

1. A note of thanks to Veronica Parry of the UK for revealing the identity and church rank of R.S. Rangoon.

3.25 Storage Box (S132), 1925
Lower Burma
Sama Jataka
Wt 681 g ▪ D 14.5 cm ▪ H 18 cm

3.26 Letter from the Bishop
of Rangoon, 15 June 1925,
enclosed with his gift of the
storage box S132

3.27 Offering Bowl (S115), c. 1880
Maung Shwe Yon
Lower Burma
Patacara Therigatha
'M.S.Y.'
Wt 1,754 g ▪ D 26 cm ▪ H 17.5 cm

Master Silversmiths (c. 1880–1910)

Maung Shwe Yon was a highly acclaimed 19th-century master silversmith from Rangoon. Harry L. Tilly, the aforementioned British expert on Burmese art, was effusive in his praise for Maung Shwe Yon. He described one of his pierced bowls as 'the best example of this kind of work ever produced' in his 1902 monograph, *The Silverwork of Burma*. The Patacara offering bowl S115 (Fig. 3.27) dated c. 1880 is a sublime example of his exceptional mastery of form, composition and the rare ability to imbue human faces with the suggestion of personality and emotion. The bowl is inscribed on the underside with the silversmith's initials, 'M.S.Y.', and a seated deer motif inside a 16-point star – the unofficial trademark of Maung Shwe Yon.

Tilly records that Maung Shwe Yon died in 1889 shortly after finishing a magnificent trophy for the headquarters' mess of the Corps of Royal Engineers in Chatham, England (Fig. 3.28). This one-metre-high trophy commemorated the active service of the Royal Engineers in Burma from 1885 to 1887. It was presented to the Corps by Major General Sir H. Prendergast, the commander-in-chief of British forces during the Third Anglo-Burmese War (1885).

Maung Shwe Yon's three sons – Maung Shwe Bin, Maung Thu Hlaing and Maung Yin Maung – were all accomplished silversmiths. After the death of their father in 1889 they formed a commercial enterprise named MSY Bros on Godwin Road, Rangoon. This prestigious enterprise, also known as Mg Shwe Yon Bros after about 1899, was famous for exceptional-quality work, and it consequently served the political, military and business elites of Rangoon. Surviving work by the company includes presentation, trophy and collectible silverwork.

The offering bowls S142 and S119 (Figs. 3.29 and 3.30) are examples of the company's finest presentation work. The rims of both bowls are inscribed with the names of the eminent donors and recipients. Robert Simpson, the recipient of bowl S119, was a celebrated maker of golf clubs and the club professional at Carnoustie, Scotland. The Simpson's Carnoustie business continues to this day. Captain Sinclair M.P., Lord Pentland, Secretary for Scotland, was the donor. The exceptionally high-relief repoussé figures on S119 create tensile

forces that have weakened the strength and integrity of the silver over a long period, resulting in small tears and perforations in the bowl. This is not uncommon on old Burmese silverwork.

Maung Yin Maung is lauded as the finest Burmese silversmith of the early 20th century. He was imaginative, prolific and gifted with superb artistic and technical skills. H.L. Tilly praised his work more than any other master silversmith. His 1904 monograph features 13 photographic plates of the best contemporary Burmese silverwork, of which five illustrate the work of Maung Yin Maung. A significant number of high-quality pieces by Maung Yin Maung survive today because they were originally taken to Britain during the colonial period and held in private family collections. In recent years, a number of these pieces have been offered for sale by London art galleries and auction houses.

3.28 Trophy for the Corps of Royal Engineers, by Maung Shwe Yon, c. 1886

3.29 Offering Bowl (S142), 1896
MSY Bros
Lower Burma
Canda-Kinnara Jataka
*'Presented to the officers, 74th Fd. By.
Royal Artillery, by Major G.P. Owen,
R.A. Jany 1891–Decr 1896'*
Wt 873 g ■ D 19 cm ■ H 12.5 cm

3.30 Offering Bowl (S119), 1899
Mg Shwe Yon Bros
Lower Burma
Ramayana
*'To Mr. and Mrs. Robert Simpson on
October 4th 1899. With hearty good
wishes from Captain Sinclair M.P.
Lord Pentland Secretary for Scotland'*
Wt 560 g ■ D 14.5 cm ■ H 10 cm

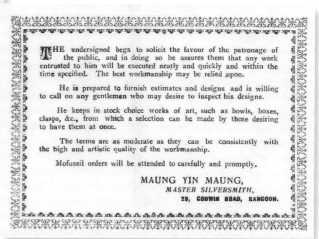

3.31 Maung Yin Maung marketing document, c. 1905
Photo: Gilles de Flogny, France

3.32 Maung Yin Maung marketing document, c. 1905
Photo: Gilles de Flogny, France

3.33 Silverwork for sale by Maung Yin Maung, c. 1905
Photo: Gilles de Flogny, France

Maung Yin Maung was also an astute businessman. Figures 3.31 and 3.32 are professional-quality pamphlets used to advertise and illustrate his work in English. The language of the advertisement is representative of a bygone and more polite age: 'The terms are as moderate as they can be consistently with the high and artistic quality of the workmanship. Mofussil orders will be attended to carefully and promptly.' A wide range of traditional Burmese artefacts are sketched on the busy illustration of Maung Yin Maung's work (Fig. 3.33).[2] It is not recorded if he worked alone or with the support of other silversmiths and apprentices. Evidence suggests that Maung Yin Maung did produce anonymous work. Silverwork inscribed with the Mg Shwe Yon Bros company name is commonly unsigned by the silversmith.

---

2. The author wishes to thank Gilles de Flogny for permission to use the three marketing documents. They were discovered inside a Maung Yin Maung bowl he recently purchased.

Figure 3.34 is a fine old photographic image of Maung Yin Maung. It is a detail from a group photograph of eight Burmese master silversmiths taken by the German photographer P. Klein and was first published in Tilly's 1904 monograph, *Modern Burmese Silverwork*. Maung Yin Maung appears as an artist in the prime of his life and career. He is proudly wearing a medal that may be the Gold Medal won for his silver table centrepiece at the 1903 Indian Art Exhibition in Delhi.

The offering bowl S43 (Fig. 3.36) is a glorious example of aesthetic Burmese silver art. Its form is elegant and wonderfully proportioned, the composition of the different decorative elements is harmonious and, above all, the artistry and fidelity of the repoussé and chasing work are peerless. Each of the six attractively framed vignettes portrays a narrative episode from the early life of Prince Siddhartha Gautama, from his conception to his first meditation. This exceptional-quality bowl has been attributed to the master silversmith Maung Yin Maung

3.34 Portrait of Maung Yin Maung, c. 1904
From H.L. Tilly (1904)

3.35 Offering bowl by Maung Yin Maung, c. 1911
Photo: Sworders Fine Art Auctioneers, England

based on the workmanship quality, signature decorative style and remarkably close resemblance to a signed bowl by the silversmith that was exhibited at the 1911 Indian and Colonial Exhibition (Fig. 3.35). Both bowls feature a distinctive *kala* face motif between the vignettes and near-identical ornamentation in the style of twisted silver fillet bands wrapping around the *kala* face and arching over the narrative scene.[3]

S149 (Figs. 3.37 and 3.38) is an ornate betel box that showcases all the skills and attributes of a master silversmith, including bold artistic imagination, a flair for exuberant style, a full repertoire of technical skills and the passion to create extraordinary silverwork. The artist who created this betel box did not sign his work. However, a photograph of a betel box with a remarkably similar design and style (Fig. 3.39) occupies a full page in Tilly's *Modern Burmese Silverwork*. This piece shared first prize for a betel box at the 1904 Rangoon Arts and Craft competition. Tilly comments on this event in his inimitable style: 'The prize was offered for the best betel box made by a master of a shop himself … In each design the box itself is a very creditable piece of work and in each the stand is inadequate and neither can be carried about without hurting the fingers. … the last thing of which the modern Burmese

silversmith thinks is the adaptability of the object to its use.' This might be sarcasm or a genuine criticism of the utility of the boxes. The silversmith who made the betel box was Maung Yin Maung.

The near identical size, design and quality of the betel box S149 compared to the piece by Maung Yin Maung leads to the conjecture that S149 is either a template or a copy of Maung Yin Maung's prize-winning work. S149 may also be a copy made by another equally gifted and anonymous silversmith for commercial rather than competitive reasons. There are many specific design similarities between the two betel boxes, including the four double-pairs of protruding, vertical silver ribs that divide the friction lid, cylindrical box and pedestal stand into four separate decorative sections. The profile of these unique ribs is triangular in the box and flat on the lid and stand. They appear to have been soldered to the betel box before the ornamentation was added. Another similarity is the scalloped design and sharply serrated edges of the pedestal and the form, but not the subject, of the finial. The four talon-like pedestal feet on S149 are absent on the Maung Yin Maung betel box.

There is evidence that Maung Yin Maung reproduced close versions of his prize-winning work. His grand, almost ostentatious, centrepiece currently exhibited in the Silver Room of the Victoria and Albert Museum in London is similar in size and style to his famous centrepiece that won the Gold Medal at

---

3. The author wishes to thank Sworders Fine Art Auctioneers of the United Kingdom for permission to use the photograph of the Maung Yin Maung offering bowl illustrated in Fig. 3.35.

3.36 Offering Bowl (S43), c. 1905
Maung Yin Maung (attributed)
Lower Burma
Early life of the Buddha
Wt 874 g ▪ D 21 cm ▪ H 12 cm

3.37 Centrepiece Betel Box (S149), c. 1905
Maung Yin Maung (attributed)
Lower Burma
Sama Jataka
Wt 2,011 g ■ D 39 cm ■ H 34 cm

3.38 Decorative detail of S149: Two *kinnari* protect Sama as a child

3.39 Centrepiece betel box by Maung Yin Maung, 1904
From H.L. Tilly (1904)

3.40 Concealed decoration below betel box S149

3.41 Offering Bowl (S141), 1905
Maung Yin Maung
Lower Burma
Jataka
*'Maung Yin Maung Master Silversmith,
29 Godwin Road Rangoon Burma 1905'*
Wt 487 g ▪ D 17 cm ▪ H 10 cm

3.42 Offering Bowl (S138), c. 1905
Mg Shwe Yon Bros
Lower Burma
Mahajanaka Jataka
'Mg. Shwe Yon Bros.'
Wt 620 g ▪ D 13 cm ▪ H 8 cm

3.43 Offering Bowl (S139), c. 1905
Mg Shwe Yon Bros
Lower Burma
Jataka
'Mg. Shwe Yon Bros.'
Wt 620 g ▪ D 13 cm ▪ H 8 cm

the 1903 Indian Art Exhibition in Delhi. Furthermore, the reproduction of acclaimed and commercially successful work is not uncommon in the world of visual art.

Figure 3.40 shows the exquisite decoration on the surface of the pedestal stand, which is only revealed when the cylindrical box is removed. This fine attention to 'hidden' detail differentiates the work of the finest prize-winning silversmiths from other highly gifted but less inspired silversmiths.

Maung Yin Maung did not craft only virtuoso and prize-winning silverwork. A small, delicately pierced and delightfully proportioned bowl (Fig. 3.41) is an example of his more commonplace work. An inscription on the underside identifies the silversmith by name, his Rangoon address and the date of completion. The lower price of these smaller pieces no doubt attracted more sales compared to his more prodigious and exceptional work.

The small bowls S138 and S139 (Figs. 3.42 and 3.43) were made by Mg Shwe Yon Bros. The similar size, form, decorative style and high quality of the two bowls suggest they were both

3.44 Portrait of Maung Po Kin From H.L Tilly (1904)

made by the same silversmith, perhaps Maung Yin Maung himself or another under his supervision in the company workshop. Unfortunately, no corporate records or catalogues from Mg Shwe Yon Bros are known to exist, although there may be traces of the company's history buried deep in British colonial or Burmese archives that have yet to be found.

Maung Po Kin belonged to the remarkable generation of gifted Burmese silversmiths who created exceptional work in the late 19th and early 20th centuries. He sits in the front row of the classic 1904 group photograph of eight acclaimed master silversmiths (Fig. 3.44). The medal worn on his chest is perhaps the First Prize with Silver Medal awarded to him at the 1903 Indian Art Exhibition in Delhi for the best silver bowl (Fig. 3.45). This large, ceremonial receptacle is in the form used at the Konbaung court before 1885 for carrying rice or other food offered to a monk or a pagoda.

Figure 3.61 (see page 78) illustrates an offering bowl by Maung Po Kin, which is decorated in his characteristic 'tapestry' style. The narrative flows around the bowl unconstrained by sharply defined frames and the only demarcation of individual scenes is provided by the silversmith's insertion of trees and other natural motifs. This style of decoration is more a feature of early 20th-century silverwork. The two small bowls by the Mg Shwe Yon Bros company (Figs. 3.42 and 3.43) are decorated in this style.

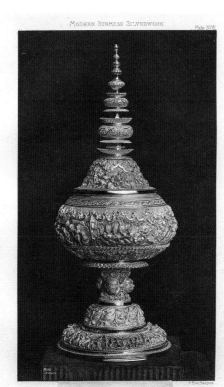

MODERN BURMESE SILVERWORK

BY MAUNG PO KIN 1903.

3.45 Centrepiece by Maung Po Kin, 1904. From H.L. Tilly (1904)

3.46 Offering Bowl (S1), 1853
Lower Burma
Sama Jataka
'1215, 7th July. Mr Lon Thar's silver bowl'
Wt 684 g ◾ D 20.5 cm ◾ H 16.5 cm

Ceremonial Offering Bowls

Silver offering bowls are the quintessential art form of the Burmese Silver Age. They also embody the ancient Burmese tradition of silversmithing that dates to the Pyu civilization in the early first millennium. The common form of the offering bowls is a likeness of the alms bowls carried by Buddhist monks to receive daily food offerings from the lay population. The original basis for this practice is unclear, although some believe it symbolizes a pivotal episode in the early life of Gautama Buddha, when he accepted a bowl of milk-rice from a young woman named Sujata. This scriptural event took place at the end of a 49-day fast, when Gautama Buddha realized that extreme austerity was not the right path to enlightenment. Thereafter, the bowl offered by Sujata became symbolically associated with the Buddha, his disciples and eventually the Buddhist monastic order.

To this day, the alms bowl remains a powerful symbol of the monk's way of life, and the historical texts of Theravada Buddhism contain detailed rules concerning the making and use of alms bowls. Importantly, a monk is prohibited from making bowls from gold or silver, although he is permitted to touch a silver bowl owned by a layperson or the community. There are also no rules against donating silver bowls or other silver artefacts to a monastery or pagoda, and this form of 'merit making' has been widely practised in Burma up to the present. The famous Shwedagon Pagoda in Yangon includes a considerable collection of donated silverwork.

The bowls in the Noble Silver Collection are all ceremonial offering bowls and were not used by Buddhist monks to collect alms. Most of the bowls were commissioned and owned by lay Buddhists, although bowls decorated with stories from the Ramayana were no doubt also purchased by Indian and Indo-Burmese Hindus, who comprised a significant proportion of the nouveau riche in colonial Burma. The most important function of the silver bowls for the majority Buddhist population was to hold and present ceremonial offerings to the Buddha. Common offerings included rice, food, water, flowers and items of practical necessity for Buddhist monks. The offering ritual was made according to the cycle of daily, monthly and annual sacred days and festivals. The location could be a pagoda, a monastery or in the privacy of a home shrine. In most cases, the underlying reason for making frequent offerings to the Buddha was to earn 'merit' and thereby improve the donor's karmic existence in the long cycle of life, death and rebirth.

An offering made in a silver bowl was especially meritorious because the merit earned was proportional to both the money spent on the offering itself and the monetary value of the receptacle used to make the offering. Accordingly, a donation offered in a ceremonial silver bowl is believed to earn more merit compared to the same donation offered in an earthenware or lacquer bowl. To capture this 'receptacle merit', wealthy owners would lend their silver bowls to their extended family and the local community. This sharing tradition may explain why many owners inscribed their name on the underside of the bowl. It was a statement of title and some insurance on the return of the valuable bowl.

Silver offering bowls decorated with Buddhist religious narratives also served important devotional and educational functions in the home and within the community. They taught and reinforced the precepts and values of Buddhism in an age before mass communication and the internet. Silver bowls also served a secular role in the home as visual art and as a status symbol of a family's wealth. This dual religious and secular value of a traditional bowl is delightfully described in the book *Burmese Family* by Mi Mi Khaing – the recollections of a Burmese woman growing up in the early 20th century:

> We had silver bowls, *ngway-balas*, of all sizes, smaller ones for drinking, bigger for pouring the bath water, and enormous ones about twelve inches across for holding gifts to the monks on festival days. Sometimes my mother used these to hold *taik-pan*, the flowers of the Honolulu creeper, for the drawing room, but she always preferred a religious use for such noble and valuable objects.

The 'gallery' of ceremonial offering bowls that follows is chronologically arranged according to the actual or estimated completion year of the bowl. Age estimates are based on a systematic comparison to dated bowls in the Noble Silver Collection, other private collections and the available reference literature.

3.47 Offering Bowl (S148), 1880
Lower Burma
Five of final ten Jataka
'Year 1242. Completed sixth day of the first week of May'
Wt 756 g ■ D 20 cm ■ H 16.5 cm

1850–1899

The Noble Silver Collection began with the spontaneous purchase of the offering bowl S1 (Fig. 3.46) in 2013. Visual delight and intrigue induced the rather impulsive purchase. There was also a mysterious tactile pleasure from holding the bowl in both hands and sensing the heaviness and value of the silver metal. The unknown decorative iconography was also the subject of curiosity. An interest in deciphering and understanding the visual narratives has sustained the continuing passion for collect Burmese silverwork. Figure 3.47 illustrates a ceremonial offering bowl dated 1880. It was added to the collection in 2018.

The bowl is an example of the highest-quality silverwork from the 19th century. It is a work of artistic imagination and impressive technical skill. The bowl is especially noteworthy for the variety, detail and charm of the ornamentation.

Shan State silverwork is dissimilar in general form and decorative style to the body of work crafted in Lower and Middle Burma during the Silver Age. Shan silversmiths preferred to embellish their work with designs taken from nature and mythology. Popular motifs include bamboo, cherry and plum trees in blossom, small and large mammals, snakes and

3.48 Pierced Offering Bowl (S11), 1895
Shan State
Signs of the Burmese zodiac
'1257. 1st week, 2nd day of January. Chaudakha Township
Mr Hlaing's bowl. 180 tola. Wishes for safety and to avert danger'
Wt 2,625 g ■ D 40 cm ■ H 23.5 cm

zodiac signs. Religious narratives are uncommon. As a result, the decorative style commonly portrays a more cheerful and sunny aspect compared to Burmese work.

Figure 3.48 exemplifies Shan-style silverwork. The imposing spherical bowl is decorated with the 12 signs of the zodiac. Each sign is enclosed within a scalloped frame of silver fillet. The delicate floral patterns that decorate much of the bowl are created using the pierce-work technique. When sunlight catches the bowl, it creates a beautiful play of reflections and internal shadows. An informative inscription on the underside of the bowl records its date in full, the owner's name and residence, the weight, and a safety wish – the wish, perhaps, alluding to the risk of travelling in the late 19th century during the 1885–95 British 'pacification' campaign against anti-colonial forces and dacoits.

The contrasting styles of ethnic Burmese and Shan silverwork is evident in the illustrations of the offering bowls S148 (Fig. 3.47) and S11 (Fig. 3.48). A late 19th-century Lower Burma decorative style is also discernible on the bowls S128 (Fig. 3.49) and S125 (Fig. 3.50). This style is generally understated compared to later work and is characterized by more restrained repoussé work, especially in the rendition of the narrative. The form, dimensions and weight of these Lower Burma bowls also tend to be more variable. S146 (Fig. 3.53) is another example of this more restrained Lower Burma decorative style of the late 19th century. The repoussé work is executed in low relief and the visual narrative, the Sama Jataka, competes for attention with the more dominant floral decoration. Also, the format of the Jataka scenes is more static and less intricate compared to the more exuberant work of the 20th century.

**3.49 Offering Bowl (S128),
c. 1890**
Lower Burma
Taungpyone folk tale
'Miss Nyine Tha's bowl.
Weight equivalent to 1500 grams'
Wt 1,526 g ▪ D 27 cm ▪ H 18 cm

**3.50 Offering Bowl (S125),
c. 1890**
Lower Burma
Ramayana
'Madam Saw Hla's silver bowl'
Wt 1,095 g ▪ D 27 cm ▪ H 16.5 cm

3.51 Offering Bowl (S151), c. 1890
Lower Burma
Ramayana
'Madam Khine Myint's silver bowl.
It was donated to a monastery'
Wt 1,585 g ▪ D 26 cm ▪ H 16.5 cm

3.52 Offering Bowl (S129), c. 1890
Lower Burma
Ramayana
'Broker Ko Bo Thar'
Wt 1,330 g ▪ D 23.5 cm ▪ H 14.5 cm

3.53 Offering Bowl (S146), c. 1890
Lower Burma
Sama Jataka
Wt 1,230 g ▪ D 26 cm ▪ H 17 cm

The offering bowls S151 (Fig. 3.51) and S129 (Fig. 3.52) are early examples of the turn-of-the-century transition towards bolder, high-relief decoration. This is manifest in the rich tapestry-style narrative scenes from the Ramayana poem. Silversmiths used the tapestry style to embellish their work with more challenging and complex narrative scenes that were free of the constraints imposed by equal-size ornamental frames. The artistic quality of the repoussé decoration on both bowls is superb. Also, the configuration and style of the concentric decorative bands became a model for many bowls made in the 20th century. This model typically comprises the following layer-cake design: a lower floral band, typically portraying lotus buds or flowers; a narrow parting featuring a simple geometric pattern; a broad central storyboard layer to illustrate the narrative; and an upper floral band, often bordered by multiple, thin horizons of geometric design. The upper floral layer commonly forms a protruding convex band below the unadorned, polished rim of the bowl.

1900–1909

Most of the offering bowls in the core of the collection weigh less than 1.5 kilograms. S147 (Fis. 3.54) is an especially fine example of a large and artistically well-decorated bowl. It weighs almost 2 kilograms. Its physical form and embellishments are grand and imposing. Ten detailed figures from the Ramayana stand out in high relief from a pierced floral background. Each figure is framed between floral pillars and narrow bands of silver fillet. It is easy to identity the figures because the silversmith has carefully detailed faces, costumes, headdresses, symbolic accoutrements and dynamic body forms. For example, Rama carries a powerful bow and is dressed in

3.54 Pierced Offering Bowl (S147), c. 1905
Lower Burma
Ramayana
Wt 1,922 g ■ D 32 cm ■ H 21 cm

3.55 The sage Vishwamitra (left) and Sukrit, the king of the monkey race (centre)

3.56 Offering Bowl (S46), 1901
Lower Burma
Taungpyone folk tale
'Madam Mya Yan's silver bowl'
Wt 1,278 g ■ D 29 cm ■ H 14 cm

3.57 Offering Bowl (S81), 1901
Lower Burma
Vidhura-Pandita Jataka
'Mr Saw Marn's silver bowl. Year 1263'
Wt 1,175 g ■ D 30 cm ■ H 15 cm

3.58 Pierced Offering Bowl (S55), 1907
Rakhine or Middle Burma
Floral and human figures
'Mr Karin's bowl. 1269'
Wt 546 g ■ D 21 cm ■ H 12 cm

3.59 Offering Bowl (S42), 1909
Lower Burma
Sula Than Pwar folk tale
'1271. Madam Pwar Oos silver bowl'
Wt 1,314 g ■ D 30.5 cm ■ H 14 cm

3.60 Pierced Offering Bowl (S22), 1900
Middle Burma
Bhuridatta Jataka
'1271. Mr Ba Kyaing's silver bowl'
Wt 245 g ▪ D 14 cm ▪ H 8.5 cm

3.61 Offering Bowl (S140), c. 1905
Maung Po Kin
Lower Burma
Tataka from the Ramayana
'M.P.K.'
Wt 1,120 g ▪ D 23 cm ▪ H 14.5 cm

3.62 Offering Bowl (S106), 1918
Lower Burma
Ramayana
'Mr Pa Lor. 1280'
Wt 3,967 g ▪ D 48.5 cm ▪ H 25.5 cm

the costume of a Konbaung king, whilst Sita, his wife, wears the robes of a queen and carries a symbolic apple that was offered in innocence to the demon king Ravana disguised as a wandering ascetic. Sukrit, king of the monkeys, is identified by his curled tail. These large, high-quality silver offering bowls are rare, perhaps reflecting their relatively high price and low demand in the early 20th century.

In contrast, the offering bowl S88 (Fig. 3.60) is one of the smallest bowls in the collection, weighing only 245 grams. It is a typical Middle Burma-style pierced bowl with a flat polished surface. The two-dimensional visual narrative is cleverly and skilfully created by an interplay of the pierce-work lattice and the detailed chasing. The central scene from the bowl includes the chased image of a turtle measuring only six millimetres

from head to tail. He sits on a small table to address King Dhatarattha, in a scene from the Bhuridatta Jataka.

1910–1919

The 1918 ceremonial offering bowl S106 (Fig. 3.62) is exceptionally large. It weighs 4 kilograms and measures nearly half a metre in diameter. The superb ornamentation portrays the iconography of the epic Ramayana poem. Scenes from the poem are interwoven and overlaid, creating a complex storyboard with non-linear timelines. Dome-shaped tree motifs are scattered within and between narrative events. The leaf shape and weeping crown of these large trees are characteristic of the angsana (*Pterocarpus indicus*) species, a tree native

3.63 Offering Bowl (S104), 1914
Lower Burma
Sama Jataka
'U Po Hlaing's silver bowl 1276.'
Wt 1,243 g ■ D 26 cm ■ H 16.5 cm

to Southeast Asia and known as the Burmese rosewood tree. The sweeping tapestry-like storyboard is set between a lower band of lotus bud motifs and an upper band that resembles scrolling acanthus stems and flowers. It is noteworthy that the silversmith did not sacrifice the quality of the decorative workmanship in crafting this remarkably large and heavy bowl. As a result, this is a tour-de-force of Burmese silverwork.

Sacred scriptures from the Buddhist canon are the primary source of the narratives that embellish Lower and Middle Burma-style offering bowls. The allegorical Jataka tales are the silversmith's most popular group of stories used to decorate all Burmese artefacts from the Silver Age. The essence of each story and its message are typically revealed in a series of framed or tapestry-style scenes in the central decorative band of the bowl.

S84 (Fig. 3.64) is an example of the framed decorative style. It features one representative scene from each of the last 10 Jataka, also known collectively as the Mahanipata Jataka. The name of the individual Jataka is inscribed on the face of the bowl beneath the scene. S143 (Fig. 3.65) illustrates the most common variant of the framed Jataka storyboards. This variant portrays scenes from one Jataka tale only in a chronological sequence that summarizes either the Jataka in its entirety or a shorter, well-known segment of the tale. The bowl is embellished with eight small-scale but detailed scenes from the Sama Jataka. This is an allegorical story that teaches the virtue of loving-kindness and it adorns more offering bowls in the Noble Silver Collection than any other Buddhist scripture.

It is difficult to classify the style of the attractive offering bowl (S110) illustrated in Fig. 3.66. The decoration seems to

3.64 Offering Bowl (S84), c. 1915
Lower Burma
Mahanipata Jataka
'Madam Shan Ma's silver bowl'
Wt 1,349 g ▪ D 28.5 cm ▪ H 15 cm

3.65 Offering Bowl (S143), 1918
Lower Burma
Sama Jataka
'Year 1280. Mr Hla's bowl'
Wt 651 g ▪ D 20 cm ▪ H 11.5 cm

3.66 Offering Bowl (S110), c. 1915
Lower Burma
Vessantara Jataka
'Mr Ba Hlaing's silver bowl'
Wt 1,304 g ■ D 29 cm ■ H 14.5 cm

Offering Bowl (S103), c. 1915
Lower Burma
Ramayana
Wt 1,660 g ■ D 32 cm ■ H 19 cm

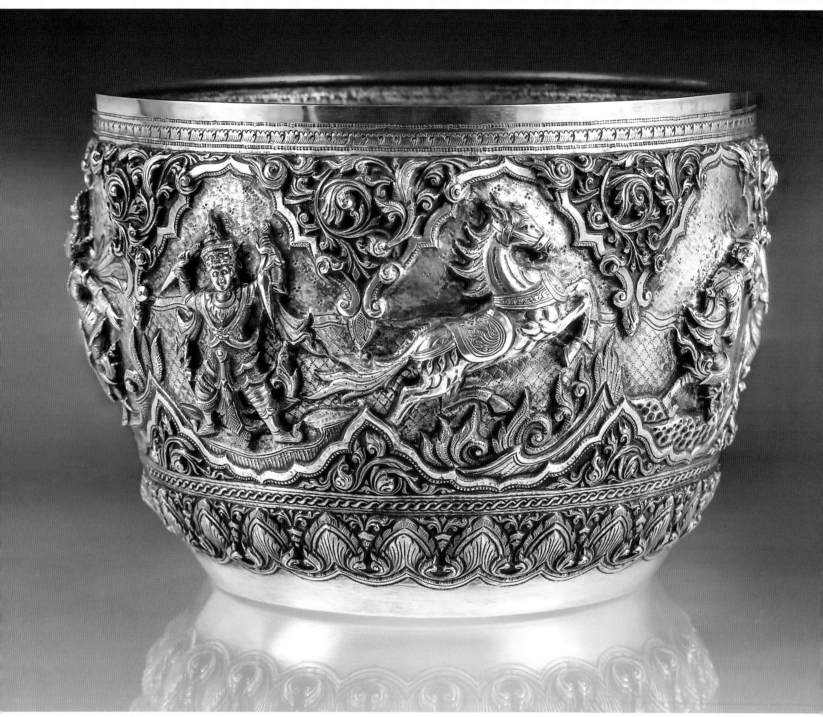

3.68 Offering Bowl (S112), c. 1915
Lower Burma
Vidhura-Pandita Jataka
'Mr Paw Sein's silver bowl'
Wt 1,596 g ▪ D 26.5 cm ▪ H 19 cm

3.69 Pierced Offering Bowl (S150), c. 1915
Lower or Middle Burma
Ramayana
Wt 1,131 g ■ D 29 cm ■ H 14.5 cm

incorporate both Shan and Lower Burma styles in approximately equal measure. The arched bamboo stems and fronds, the abundance of exotic birds and the playful deer are the natural motifs most commonly, but not exclusively, associated with Shan silverwork. Conversely, the Jataka iconography, the storyboard design and the style of the upper and lower decorative bands all express a Lower Burma style of workmanship. This is perhaps an example of Shan-Lower Burma 'cross-cultural' decoration.

S103 (Fig. 3.67) is a large offering bowl decorated with an eclectic collage of artistic styles and two unrelated, but interwoven, visual narratives – the Ramayana poem and the Taungpyone legend about a virtuous weaver and a spirit tiger. The lower, or first, decorative band features a series of individual images of the spirit tiger carrying away the helpless weaver in its open jaw. An unusual style of repoussé decoration that appears and feels similar to interleaved fish or snake scales forms a pyramidal shape that alternates with the tiger images. A seated or crouching tiger image is also represented in the third decorative band. The second, or middle band, of decoration portrays figures and scenes from the Ramayana within elongated scalloped frames. The motif repeated around the rim band is the upper jaw and face of a *kala*, a protective Indian deity that represents the threshold between time and eternity and is often carved above temple entrances. The height-to-width ratio of the bowl and the slightly concave rim gives it a distinctive shape that resembles an inverted bell.

The bold-looking offering bowl S112 (Fig. 3.68) features a magnificent caparisoned horse from the Vidhura-Pandita Jataka. This is a supernatural Sindh horse owned by Punnaka, a *yakka* general. It is portrayed leaping boldly into the air with its mane and tail flowing behind in the wind. Muscles ripple on its haunches and loins. This is a powerful and artistic portrayal of a horse by a silversmith – perhaps the best in the collection.

The offering bowls in the collection made between 1910 and 1930 have a wider range of form and decorative style compared to older work. Silversmiths continued to make variants of the archetypal offering bowls with classical Buddhist and Hindu iconography, but they also experimented with new and non-traditional designs in an imaginative fashion. There is a sense of the silversmiths finding more freedom of expression in the waning years of the Silver Age.

3.70 Offering Bowl (S85), c. 1915
Lower Burma
Ramayana
'Mr Aung Maung's silver bowl'
Wt 1,133 g ■ D 28.5 cm ■ H 15 cm

3.71 Pierced Offering Bowl (S12), c. 1915
Shan State
Floral and faunal
Wt 600 g ■ D 18 cm ■ H 15 cm

3.72 Pierced Offering Bowl (S107), c. 1915
Middle Burma
Vidhura-Pandita Jataka
'Grandmother Saw's silver bowl'
Wt 1,304 g ■ D 28 cm ■ H 15.5 cm

S150 (Fig. 3.69) is an example of a new technical style of work on an exquisite offering bowl made from an alloy with above-average silver content. It is estimated that the bowl was made between about 1910 and 1920. The style integrates high-volume pierce work with scalloped frames containing high-relief repoussé figures and narrative scenes. This work is technically difficult and unforgiving of error, but the effect is stunning.

Figure 3.70 illustrates a one-of-a-kind bowl (S85) in the collection. The common decorative band featuring visual narratives is replaced by a wide, unadorned band of polished silver. The simplicity of the burnished silver contrasts effectively with the high-relief figures from the Ramayana that repeat and fill the decorative bands around the base and rim of the bowl. S12 (Fig. 3.71) is a classic Shan-style bowl featuring a decorative menagerie of birds, snakes and small mammals in a forest of bamboo. The flora and fauna are all formed using high-volume pierce work and minimal chasing. The offering bowl S107 (Fig. 3.72) juxtaposes Middle and Lower Burma-style ornamentation. The main narrative horizon features the

3.73 Offering Bowl (S105), c. 1915
Lower Burma
Mythological animals
'Mr Pa Gee's silver bowl'
Wt 1,377 g ■ D 27.5 cm ■ H 15.5 cm

3.74 Pierced Offering Bowl (S121), 1911
Middle Burma
Vessantara Jataka
'1273. Mr Saw Hla's silver bowl.'
Wt 524 g ■ D 19 cm ■ H 12.5 cm

3.75 Pierced Offering Bowl (S144), c. 1915
Middle Burma
Sama Jataka
'Mr Ba Kyaw's silver bowl'
Wt 593 g ■ D 19 cm ■ H 12.5 cm

3.76 Offering Bowl (S126), 1918
Lower Burma
Vidhura-Pandita Jataka
'Mr Po Ni's silver bowl. 1280'
Wt 1,893 g ▪ D 34 cm ▪ H 17 cm

3.77 Offering Bowl (S39), c. 1915
Lower Burma
Sama Jataka
'Mr Ba Khine's silver bowl'
Wt 1,320 g ▪ D 29.5 cm ▪ H 14 cm

3.78 Pierced Offering Bowl (S57), 1918
Middle Burma
Pyu Saw Htee folk tale
'1280. Mr Pho Saung's silver bowl'
Wt 614 g ▪ D 20 cm ▪ H 12 cm

3.79 Offering Bowl (S51), 1916
Shan State
Floral and faunal
'Mr Mya Maung's silver bowl. 1278'
Wt 650 g ▪ D 18.5 cm ▪ H 15 cm

3.80 Offering Bowl (S131), 1916
Shan State
Mythological animals
'1278. Mr Thar Aung's silver bowl'
Wt 788 g ▪ D 19 cm ▪ H 15 cm

3.81 Offering Bowl (S127), c. 1925
Lower Burma
Sama Jataka
'Mr Hla Taung's silver bowl'
Wt 1,497 g ▪ D 32 cm ▪ H 16.5 cm

Vidhura-Pandita Jataka in Middle Burma style, while the base and rim bands are raised floral designs in the fashion of Lower Burma.

1920–1930

Many offering bowls in the collection from the 1920s display common characteristics, including the height-to-diameter ratio, the ellipsoidal shape, the tapestry-style visual narrative and the adherence to a uniform style of concentric banded ornamentation featuring similar upper and lower floral designs and geometric patterns. The bowls S37, S44, S120, S82 and S109 (Figs. 3.88–92) demonstrate these characteristics. These five offering bowls are probably the last expression of exceptional-quality Burmese silver art from the Silver Age. There are no traditional 'domestic' style bowls in the Noble Silver

Collection with an inscribed or estimated date of completion later than 1928. This is a function of market availability and not an arbitrary selection criterion based on age.

S127 (Fig. 3.81) is a fine example of an ornate bowl from the late Silver Age. There is much detail to admire on this bowl: the imposing scale; the beautifully proportioned ellipsoidal shape; an exceptional number of concentric decorative bands featuring lotus buds, forest deer, scrolling acanthus motifs and fine geometric patterns; and 10 detailed scenes from the Sama Jataka. All the individual narrative scenes are framed and rich with contextual images, including representations of Himavat forest, Sama's hermitage, the serpent that blinded Sama's parents, wild deer, stupas, rolling terrain, rocks, tree stumps and a towering forest canopy. Two entwined serpents supporting a praying deity separate each narrative scene and complete the artistic vision of the silversmith.

3.82 Offering Bowl (S59), 1921
Shan State
Floral and faunal
'1283. Madam Than Myaing's bowl'
Wt 1,253 g ■ D 29 cm ■ H 14.5 cm

3.83 Pierced Offering Bowl (S14), 1921
Shan State
Floral and faunal
'1283. Mr Shwee Ba's silver bowl'
Wt 655 g ■ D 21 cm ■ H 12 cm

3.84 Pierced Offering Bowl (S7), 1928
Middle Burma
Bhuridatta Jataka
'1290. Madam Khin Chai's silver bowl'
Wt 546 g ■ D 20 cm ■ H 11.5 cm

3.85 Offering Bowl (S47), 1928
Lower Burma
Sama Jataka
'Madam Kyin's silver bowl. 1290'
Wt 1,162 g ■ D 30 cm ■ H 14 cm

3.86 Pierced Offering Bowl (S38), c. 1925
Lower Burma
Sama Jataka
'Mr Thar Hla's silver bowl'
Wt 1,178 g ■ D 29 cm ■ H 14.5 cm

3.87 Offering Bowl (S60), c. 1925
Lower Burma
Vessantara Jataka
'Mr Aung Kyi's bowl'
Wt 1,269 g ■ D 29 cm ■ H 14.5 cm

3.88 Offering Bowl (S37), c. 1925
Lower Burma
Mahajanaka Jataka
Wt 1,242 g ■ D 30 cm ■ H 13.5 cm

3.89 Offering Bowl (S44), 1928
Lower Burma
Life of the Buddha
'Madam Ma's silver bowl. Year 1290'
Wt 1,908 g ▪ D 34 cm ▪ H 17 cm

3.90 Offering Bowl (S120), 1928
Lower Burma
Mahajanaka Jataka
'1290. Mr Pa Tyint's silver bowl'
Wt 1,638 g ▪ D 30 cm ▪ H 16 cm

3.01 Offering Bowl (S82), 1928
Lower Burma
Vidhura-Pandita Jataka
'Mr Kham Lon. Year 1290'
Wt 1,262 g ■ D 30 cm ■ H 15 cm

3.92 Offering Bowl (S109), c. 1925
Lower Burma
Cullahamsa Jataka
'Madam Pwa Zar's silver bowl. A Shan lady'
Wt 1,373 g ■ D 27.5 cm ■ H 15 cm

Food Storage Jars

Large food storage jars are a rare form of Burmese silverwork. This may reflect their limited practical utility for religious, ceremonial and food storage purposes. The clean condition of the rice and salted fish storage jars in the collection suggests these jars were used primarily for ornamentation and wealth display in the home.

Figure 3.93 illustrates an attractive pair of full-moon-shaped rice storage jars (S5 and S6) decorated in one of the classical themes of the Shan States – old plum trees weighed down with spring blossom. The Shan affection for nature is reflected in the variety of large birds perched on the branches of the trees. This springtime floral iconography suggests Chinese influence on Shan art. The plum tree in bloom is one of a trio of floral subjects that constitute the classical Chinese 'Friends of Winter' artistic theme. Pine trees and bamboo complete the trio. These ceremonial rice storage jars may have been

3.93 Rice Storage Bowls (S5 and S6), c. 1925
Shan State
Floral and faunal
Wt 1,585 g ▪ D 26 cm ▪ H 25.5 cm

3.94 Salted Fish Jar (S152), c. 1890
Lower Burma
Ramayana
Wt 1,735 g ■ D 25 cm ■ H 25 cm

3.95 Decorative detail on the cover and lid of S152

owned by the traditional rulers – the Saohpas – of the Shan States. The indigenous Shan people are ethnically Thai and their artistic and cultural traditions are distinct from ethnic Burmans.

The large salted fish storage jar (*na pi o*) displayed in Fig. 3.94 is an example of the very best quality of work from the Silver Age. It features an inverted bell-shaped body surmounted by an attached two-tier cover with a narrow-diameter opening for a raised friction lid. The seven decorative panels portray figures and scenes from the Ramayana in high relief on a flat textured background. Each panel is enclosed by an intricately designed floral pendant and interwoven ribbons of silver fillet.

Figure 3.95 reveals the exquisite artwork on the attached cover and the removable lid of the jar. The beautiful floral embellishments on the cover comprise a wide outer ring featuring flower buds, stems and leaves, and a narrow inner ring with a simple leaf pattern. The top of the jar's lid is crowned with a pretty eight-petalled flower surrounded by leaf and stem motifs. Four narrative figures framed by a floral pattern surround the central flower. This jar is a comprehensive masterpiece of Burmese silver art.

3.96 Lime Box (S74), 1894
Lower Burma
Mythological animals
'Weight 10. 1256'
Wt 114 g ■ L 7 cm ■ W 4.5 cm ■ H 6 cm

Lime Boxes

Silver lime boxes were the most popular and most affordable pieces of silverwork owned by the Burmese during the Silver Age. They would have been made in village, town and city workshops throughout the country. Most of the boxes were sized to fit inside a pocket or small bag that contained the ingredients of a betel quid. Silversmiths made lime boxes in a variety of shapes, including elliptical, octagonal, circular, square and half-moon. Each box had a detachable friction lid, which was either flat or raised. Lime boxes were popular birthday and wedding gifts due to their affordability and the prestige attached to owning silver. There are many Silver Age and reproduction lime boxes for

sale in markets and souvenir shops in modern Myanmar. The quality of the boxes varies from crude to exquisite.

Lime boxes were used to store the white slaked lime (calcium hydroxide $CaOH_2$) paste that is an essential ingredient of the betel quid. Slaked lime is made by mixing pulverized lime (calcium oxide CaO) with water. The common sources of lime were clean limestone ($CaCO_3$), coral and shellfish. The insides of many old boxes are coated with residual paste. A small silver spatula was used to smear the paste on the betel leaf. Figure 3.96 illustrates the only box and spatula set in the collection.

Silversmiths invariably decorated the lid and sides of lime boxes with charming and imaginative designs, despite the

3.97 Lime Box (S67), 1880
Lower Burma
Floral
*'Ta Lote. 1242. Completed after the full moon of
the month of War-Kaung. Silver weight 7.5'*
Wt 114 g ■ L 7 cm ■ W 4.5 cm ■ H 6 cm

3.98 Lime Box (S68), 1908
Lower Burma
Human figure
'Year 1270. Sin Pyet Leit'
Wt 218 g ■ L 10 cm ■ W 6 cm ■ H 8 cm

3.99 Lime Box (S73), c. 1900
Lower Burma
Chintha and floral
Wt 66 g ■ L 6 cm ■ W 4.5 cm ■ H 4.5 cm

3.100 Lime Box (S91), c. 1900
Lower Burma
Floral and human figure
'Mr Bo Htet'
Wt 102 g ■ L 8.5 cm ■ W 5 cm ■ H 5 cm

3.101 Lime Box (S75), 1914
Lower Burma
Floral
'1276. Completed at the end of the month of Taw Tha Lin'
Wt 84 g ■ L 6.5 cm ■ W 3.5 cm ■ H 6 cm

3.102 Lime Box (S69), c. 1900
Lower Burma
Ramayana
Wt 135 g ▪ L 8.5 cm ▪ W 5.5 cm ▪ H 6.5 cm

3.103 Lid decorative detail (S69) –
Šukrit, Monkey King

3.104 Lid decorative detail (S124) –
Konbaung king, queen and minister

3.105 Lime Box (S124), c. 1910
Lower Burma
Royal family at court
Wt 176 g ▪ D 8 cm ▪ H 8 cm

3.106 Lime Box (S123), c. 1910
Lower Burma
Royal family at court
Wt 173 g ▪ D 8.5 cm ▪ H 7.5 cm

3.107 Lid decorative detail (S123) –
Konbaung royal family

3.108 Lime Box (S62), c. 1910
Lower Burma
Mythological animals
'Ma Shin'
Wt 136 g ▪ L 10 cm ▪ W 4.6 cm ▪ H 4.5 cm

3.109 Lime Box (S118), c. 1910
Lower Burma
Royal family at court
'Let Pan Dan Township. 30th Street. Trade clerk
Mr San De. Husband of trade clerk Madam Mya Yi.
Wedding present. Wish you wealthy'
Wt 206 g ▪ D 10.5 cm ▪ H 8 cm

3.110 Lime Box (S70), c. 1910
Lower Burma
Royal family at court
Wt 176 g ■ D 6.5 cm ■ H 8 cm

3.111 Side view to show high-relief lid (S70)

3.112 Lid decorative detail (S70) –
Konbaung king and queen

3.113 Lid decorative detail (S61) –
Sama and his parents

3.114 Lime Box (S61), c. 1910
Lower Burma
Sama Jataka
Wt 142 g ■ D 8.5 cm ■ H 6.5 cm

3.115 Lime Box (S153), c. 1910
Lower Burma
Vidhura-Pandita Jataka
Wt 204 g ■ D 10 cm ■ H 7 cm

3.116 Lid decorative detail (S153) – Punnaka
and Vidhura-Pandita on Black Mountain

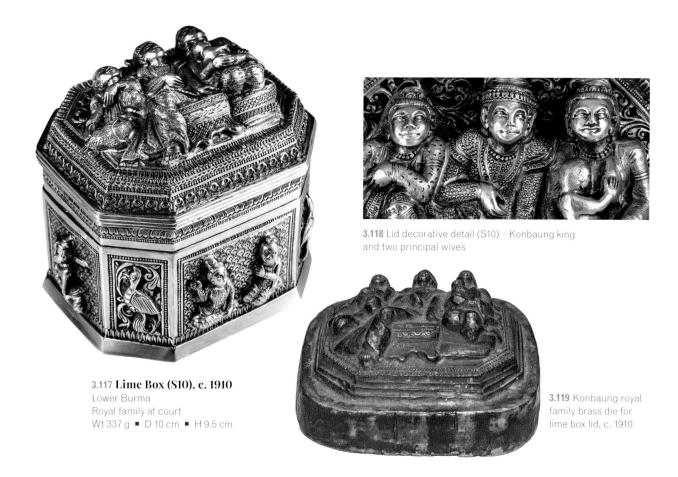

3.118 Lid decorative detail (S10) – Konbaung king and two principal wives

3.117 Lime Box (S10), c. 1910
Lower Burma
Royal family at court
Wt 337 g ▪ D 10 cm ▪ H 9.5 cm

3.119 Konbaung royal family brass die for lime box lid, c. 1910

simple, functional purpose of the box. An intimate portrait of a Konbaung king at court with one or two of his principal wives was one of the most popular lid designs. Figure 3.118 is a detail of the lid of the lime box S10 (Fig. 3.117). It portrays the king, assumed to be King Thibaw, the last Konbaung king, seated informally between two wives. A baby suckles at the breast of one of the wives. This figure most likely represents Queen Supayalat, who gave birth to four daughters. No doubt this warm family image reminded the Burmese of their historical royal heritage and former sovereign independence. Mechanical presses and brass dies were sometimes used to efficiently form an imprint of popular lid designs on silver sheet before the box was hand-finished. Figure 3.119 is a well-used brass die for the portrait of the Konbaung royal family. Other designs include figures from the Ramayana and the Jataka tales, mythological creatures, floral motifs and geometric patterns.

Drinking Vessels and Vases

The repertoire of the Burmese silversmith included a wide assortment of vases, spittoons, water cups, beakers, chalices and goblets. Much of this work was either influenced by Western style or made directly according to the functional requirement and taste of foreign customers. The decorative styles and motifs range from traditional Burmese through Burmese-European cross-cultural, to classic European and Greco-Roman compositions. Traditional Burmese forms include temple vases for flower offerings to the Buddha and small water cups with both a secular and religious utility.

S134 (Fig. 3.120) is an elegant and fine-quality drinking beaker that was awarded to a Brigadier 'Bob' who presumably won the Great Eastern Handicap horse race in Mandalay in 1889, just four years after the third and final Anglo-Burmese war. The physical form and decorative style of the beaker are fundamentally Burmese, whereas the well-executed galloping horses suggest the beaker may have been commissioned

3.120 **Beaker (S134), 1889**
Lower Burma
Horses
'Mandalay. Nov 89 Great Eastern
Handicap BR C.B.P. "Bob"'
Wt 336 g ■ W 9.5 cm ■ H 15 cm

specifically for the occasion of an entirely British horse race. The silversmith, perhaps unfamiliar with British horse racing, portrayed the jockeys in traditional Burmese dress. Unusually, this beaker is gilded on the inside – a rare attribute of Burmese silverwork.

Figure 3.121 illustrates a delightful hand-sized water cup embellished with a tapestry of detailed scenes from the Mahajanaka Jataka. The decoration is executed with precision and artistry at a miniature scale. A 6-centimetre-wide panel displayed in the centre of the photograph portrays the melee of a head-to-head battle between war elephants, cavalry horses, fighting dogs and an array of opposing soldiers. Tiny cast-silver tusks are soldered to the elephants to add realism and a sense of depth to the scene. This charming water cup is the work of the master silversmith Maung Kywet Ni of Moulmein.

3.121 Water Cup (S117), c. 1880
Maung Kywet Ni
Lower Burma
Mahajanaka Jataka
'A cup made by Maung Kywet Ni of Moulmein'
Wt 264 g ▪ W 8.6 cm ▪ H 8.3 cm

3.123 Niello Cup with Lid (S135), c. 1900
Lower Burma
Faunal and human figures
Wt 323 g ■ W 9.5 cm ■ H 11 cm

3.122 Water Cup (S15), 1908
Shan State
Faunal
'1270'
Wt 143 g ■ W 8.5 cm ■ H 7 cm

3.124 Wine Goblets (S34 and S35), 1870
Lower Burma
Mythological and floral
'76th Regiment (India) 1870'
Wt 420 g ■ W 9.5 cm ■ H 15.5 cm

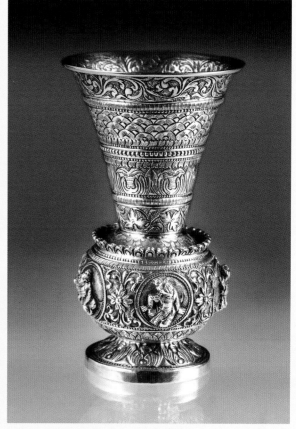

3.126 Vase (S133), c. 1915
Lower Burma
Floral and human figures
Wt 143 g ■ W 7 cm ■ H 12 cm

3.125 Vase (S108), c. 1915
Lower Burma
Vessantara Jataka
Wt 409 g ■ W 10 cm ■ H 23.5 cm

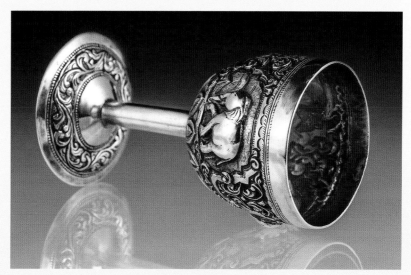

3.127 Goblet (S77), c. 1915
Lower Burma
Elephants
Wt 79 g ■ W 5 cm ■ H 10 cm

Variety Silverwork

Variety silverwork is a diverse selection of less common forms of Burmese silverwork. The selection includes work made for 'domestic' and 'export' customers with either a secular or religious use.

Artefacts commissioned by foreign patrons often display cross-cultural design elements and decorative styles. Figure 3.136 illustrates a European tea and coffee service embellished with a Burmese version of the Indian Ramayana poem. The small-scale stupa model (Fig. 3.133) and the cast figure of a Buddhist monk (Fig. 3.135) are Burmese religious artefacts in form, but were most likely sold as curios and souvenirs to foreigners. The silver document holder (Figs. 3.129–31) is a traditional design first used by Burmese kings and high-ranking court officials. Silversmiths probably reproduced these artefacts for private, ceremonial and display purposes after the overthrow of the Konbaung royal dynasty in 1885.

There are many other varieties of Burmese silverwork that are not represented in the Noble Silver Collection. These include commemorative trophies, tiffin boxes, pedestal fruit bowls, spittoons, pipes, card trays, Buddha images, secular cast figurines, and scabbards and sheaths for swords and daggers. Burmese silversmiths were imaginative and versatile

3.128 Milk Pitcher (S116), c. 1910
Lower Burma
Human figures, faunal and floral
Wt 450 g ■ D 10 cm ■ H 14.5 cm

3.129 Document Holder (S4),
c. 1910
Shan States
Faunal and floral
Wt 281 g ■ L 33 cm ■ D 6.5 cm

3.130 Document Holder (S96),
c. 1910
Lower Burma
Ramayana and faunal
Wt 342 g ■ L 32 cm ■ D 6 cm

3.131 Document Holder (S83),
c. 1910
Lower Burma
Faunal and floral
Wt 342 g ■ L 32 cm ■ D 6 cm

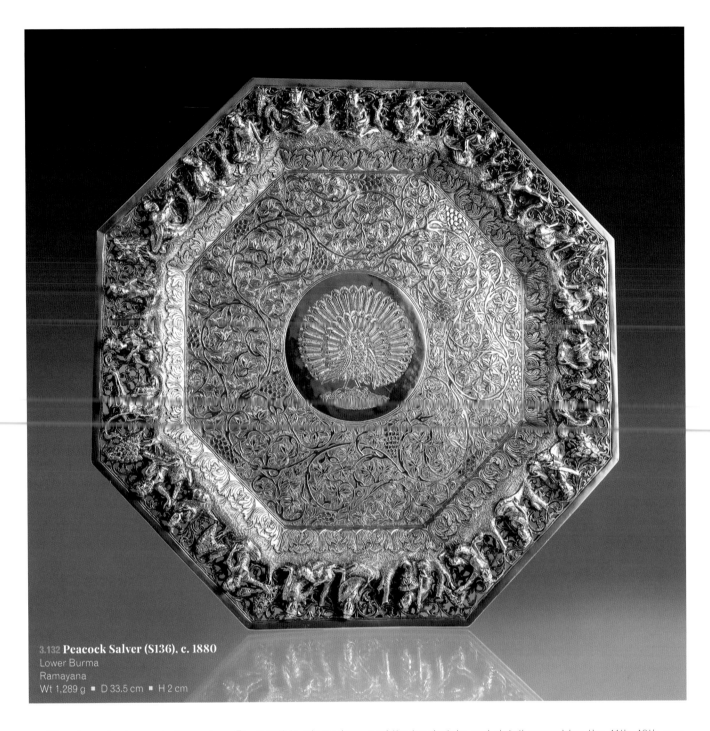

3.132 Peacock Salver (S136), c. 1880
Lower Burma
Ramayana
Wt 1,289 g ▪ D 33.5 cm ▪ H 2 cm

The elegant octagonal silver salver (Fig. 3.132) is adorned with both Burmese and European decorative elements. The peacock occupying the central medallion is a motif closely associated with the Burmese Konbaung kings, whereas the delicate floral design surrounding the medallion portrays vines and hanging grapes, which reflect an ancient European artistic theme. The raised rim of the platter is embellished with traditional high-relief repoussé figures from the Burmese version of the Indian Ramayana poem. The near-pristine condition of the salver suggests it has only been used for display purposes.

Figure 3.133 presents a high-fidelity small-scale model of a Buddhist stupa made from cast and formed sheet silver. Its architectural style and detail resembles the 11th–13th century Shwezigon Pagoda in Nyaung-U near Bagan (Fig. 3.134). The old stupa and the model have many common design elements: the rectangular base plinth; four guardian *chinthas* at the corners of the base; four 16-sided terraces; an inverted bowl-shaped dome decorated with lotus petal bands; a banana bud surmounting the roof of the dome; a delicate multi-tiered umbrella, or *hti*, crowning the stupa; 12 tiny bodhi leaves hung from the umbrella of the *hti*; a stylistic fragrant screwpine; a big spoon; a wind vane; and finally, a diamond bud at the pinnacle of the stupa. Remarkably, all these detailed design elements have been scaled to a model only 18 centimetres in height.

3.134 Shwezigon Pagoda in Nyaung-U near Bagan, 11th–13th century

3.133 Buddhist Stupa (S64), c. 1910
Lower Burma
Wt 180 g ▪ H 18 cm ▪ D 9 cm

3.135 Buddhist Monk (S122), c. 1900
Lower Burma
Wt 86 g ▪ H 7.8 cm ▪ D 3.5 cm

3.136 Tea and Coffee Service on Salver (S137), 1903
Lower Burma
Ramayana
'Presented to F.C. Kennedy C.I.E.
General Manager Irrawaddy Flotilla Co. Ltd.'
Wt 7,300 g ■ L 59 cm ■ W 38 cm

3.137 Coffee pot with *hintha* duck spout (S137)

3.138 Sugar bowl with cast handles and finial (S137)

3.139 Irrawaddy Flotilla Company engraving on salver (S137)

Silverwork can occasionally be linked by inscriptions to specific figures and events in Burmese history. These links stimulate the collector's historical imagination and attach a special intangible value to the work. The finest example in the collection of this type of silverwork is displayed in Fig. 3.136. It is a grandiose, five-piece silver tea and coffee service with a documented history. It was presented to Frederick Charles Kennedy, the general manager of the venerable Irrawaddy Flotilla Company, as a retirement gift on 6th December 1903. The service weighs 7.3 kilograms and comprises a scalloped rectangular salver (Fig. 3.139), a tea and coffee pot (Fig. 3.137), a milk pitcher and a sugar bowl (Fig. 3.138) – all the components of a formal English tea service. The design and decoration are extravagantly cross-cultural: curvaceous female Burmese dancers are used for the finials and handles; the spouts model the mythological *hintha* duck; and the decorative repoussé figures on all the components are from the Indian Ramayana epic.

A raised oval medallion in the centre of the salver lists the names of 28 flotilla commanders who served under Kennedy. Two of these commanders played small but significant roles in the Third Anglo-Burmese War. J.J. Cooper commanded the PS *Ashley* paddle steamer and personally delivered the British military ultimatum to King Thibaw in Mandalay in 1885. Cooper received a gold watch from the British government for his services, a seemingly paltry compensation for a civilian who had risked his life on such a critical and unpredictable government mission. Captain W.N. Beckett, the last name engraved on the salver, commanded the PS *Palow* in the war of 1885 and led

3.140 Ensign of the Irrawaddy Flotilla Company
Photo: National Maritime Museum, Greenwich

his ship in a vanguard action that captured the Minhla fort on 17 November 1885. This attack effectively ended Burmese military resistance and ensured the defeat of King Thibaw. A third name on the list, Captain P. de La Taste, commanded the large Siam-class steamship PS *Japan* when it served as the royal steamer for the Prince and Princess of Wales on a visit to Burma in 1906. The prince was later crowned King George V on 22 June 1911.

The Irrawaddy Flotilla Company operated 622 vessels on the Irrawaddy, Chindwin and other rivers during the heyday of the company in the early 20th century. Most of these vessels were scuttled in 1942 to deny their use to the advancing Japanese invasion forces. The fascinating history of the company parallels the history of British colonial rule in Burma from the Second Anglo-Burmese War of 1852 until World War II.

3.141 Belt Buckle (S102), c. 1910
Lower Burma
Human figures and elephants
Wt 116 g ▪ L 22 cm ▪ H 8.8 cm

Silversmiths' Marks

Burmese silversmiths commonly inscribed text information and/or whimsical marks on the underside of their work. These engaging inscriptions sometimes provide insight into the contemporary world of the silversmith and his patrons. Burmese silversmith's marks are not comparable to the legal system of hallmarks used in Britain since the 14th century. In some cases, they do represent a type of 'trademark' that identifies a documented silversmith, although in most cases the marks are anonymous. The elite and commercially astute master silversmiths were the most likely to sign their silverwork, especially items made for international art competitions and foreign patrons. Domestic silverwork made for Burmese customers was rarely signed by the silversmith.

The completion year of the artefact is the most useful text information for the collector in the absence of the silversmith's name. The year is typically inscribed in Burmese script and according to the Burmese Era calendar, which starts in the year 638 of the Common Era. The date relationship to the Common Era is calculated on the authority of a complex conversion from an earlier Buddhist calendar used in Gandhara in present-day northern Pakistan and Afghanistan. The conversion to Common Era is made by adding 638 years to the Burmese date inscribed on the silverwork – although this is not always precise, since the Burmese calendar is based on the lunar cycle and the international calendar uses the solar cycle.

Burmese silverwork is rarely inscribed with the fineness of the silver content. It is unlikely that the source silver was independently assayed and certified. Silversmiths who used Burmese and British India rupee coins would have relied on the official and regulated silver content of the coins – about 92 per cent silver. Otherwise, the silversmith relied on his experience to control the silver content when blending silver bullion with copper wire, plates and scrap in a workshop furnace. Simple scratch testing with a hard black touchstone rock, with or without acid, provided a crude determination of the silver and copper content of the finished silverwork.

Inscriptions and silversmiths' marks from 52 artefacts in the Noble Silver Collection are illustrated below in a photographic catalogue. Most of the inscriptions are positioned on the base of offering bowls and are hidden when the bowl is displayed on a flat surface. The inscriptions and marks are categorized into seven broadly defined groups, according to the dominant subject or style of the mark. Many of the marks are a composite of text and motifs from two or more groups.

The seven groups are as follows: (1) Burmese text information; (2) Documented silversmiths; (3) Jataka and Ramayana; (4) Mythology and astrology; (5) Faunal; (6) Human figures; and (7) Floral and geometrical.

A separate category of customized text information in English is sometimes inscribed on the rims of offering bowls and drinking vessels, on polished medallions and on the base of the silverwork. The inscriptions generally document the award of a prize or gift for a specific event or service rendered, either in the private sector, the military or the colonial administration. This category of inscription is not illustrated in the following catalogue.

One Burmese offering bowl in the Hermitage collection in St Petersburg is inscribed with the coat of arms of the German Mecklenburg family – a shield below a crown with a cross on the top. The provenance of this bowl based on documented research is fascinating. Duke Johann Albrecht Mecklenburg likely visited Burma in 1909 and solicited a silversmith to inscribe his coat of arms on a souvenir bowl. On the way home he visited his sister, Grand Duchess Maria Pavlovna, in St Petersburg and gifted her the Burmese bowl. The sister was married into the Romanov family and the bowl became a part of her private collection, until it was confiscated by the state following the 1917 communist revolution that overthrew the Romanov Tsar Nicholas II.

Burmese Text Information

The format of Burmese text information on ceremonial offering bowls is often standardized. This is surprising, given the wide regional extent of silversmithing and presumed independence of the many silversmiths. A typical text inscription begins with the bowl's completion date and the name of the owner. The information is ordered with either the date or name first. Occasionally, the exact month, day and moon phase of the completion date are provided, suggesting this was an auspicious date. An honorific always precedes the owner's name.

3.142 1853 Offering Bowl (S1)
'1853 7th July. Mr Lon Thar's silver bowl'

3.143 1928 Offering Bowl (S7)
'1928. Madam Khin Chai's silver bowl'

3.144 1921 Offering Bowl (S59)
'1921. Madam Tan Myain's bowl'

3.145 1909 Offering Bowl (S88)
'1909 Mr Ba Kyaing's silver bowl'

3.146 1880 Offering Bowl (S148)
*'1880. Completed sixth day of the
first week of May'*

3.147 1894 Lime Box (S74)
'1894. Weight 10'

3.148 c. 1895 Lime Box (S70)
*'Madam Ma Seh Nyo's box.
Weight in silver rupees 146'*

3.149 c. 1900 Water Cup (S117)
'A cup made by Maung Kywet Ni'
(tamarind-seed script)

3.150 1880 Lime Box (S67)
*'1242. Completed after the full moon day of
the month of War Kaung. Silver weight 7.5'*

3.151 1928 Treasure Box (S66)
*'Made by silversmith Shine Hine.
The weight is 20 kyats. Finished 1290 Burmese year
Thidingyut month, 7th day'*

3.152 c. 1905 Lime Box (S118)
*'Let Pan Dan Town, 30th Street. Trade clerk
U San De. Husband of Trade Clerk Daw Mya Yi.
Wedding present. Wish you wealthy'*

3.153 c. 1880 Offering Bowl (S115)
Seated deer within 16-point star
'M.S.Y.' (Maung Shwe Yon)

3.154 1896 Offering Bowl (S142)
Seated deer

3.155 1899 Offering Bowl (S119)
Seated deer
'Mg. Shwe Yon Bros. Gold &
Silversmith Rangoon'

3.156 c. 1900 Offering Bowl (S138)
Seated deer
'Mg. Shwe Yon. Bros. Gold &
Silversmith Rangoon'

3.157 1905 Offering Bowl (S141)
Maung Yin Maung Master Silversmith
29 Godwin Road, Rangoon.
Burma. 1905'

3.158 c. 1905 Offering Bowl (S140)
'M.P.K' (Maung Po Kin)

3.159 1937 Offering Bowl (S20)
'Sun Co Rangoon'

3.160 c. 1910 Offering Bowl (S16)
'Coombe's Company Ltd. Rangoon'

This information can establish the owner's gender, maturity, seniority, ethnicity, military rank and other measures of social status. A simple description of the artefact is often the last inscription on the bowl. '1873. 7th July. Mr Lon Thar's Silver Bowl' is an example of the typical format of a Burmese text inscription. Other information added to a small number of inscriptions includes the number of coins used, the weight of the silverwork, the occupation of the owner, a wedding gift inscription, a thoughtful message and, rarely, the silversmith's name. Figures 3.142–152 illustrate a selection of text information inscriptions.

Documented Silversmiths

A small number of artefacts in the Noble Silver Collection are inscribed in English with information that identifies the silversmith and/or his company (Figs. 3.153–160). This information is either in the format of the silversmith's full name, his initials or a trademark. It is most often found on exceptional silverwork made for international art competitions or the finest-quality work made for foreign customers in Rangoon or Mandalay. The silversmith's name in Burmese is only inscribed on two pieces of silver in the collection. Some well-established British- and European-owned art and curio galleries also inscribed their company name on more standard-quality silverwork.

One of the most recognized trademarks of a documented silversmith is a small deer seated in a circular medallion within a surrounding 16-point double-star. This is the mark of the acclaimed master silversmith Maung Shwe Yon. He also chased his initials 'M.S.Y.' over the deer on some bowls. Maung Shwe Yon's three sons later adopted their father's deer motif as the trademark of their new company, Mg Shwe Yon Bros. The precise style of this deer motif varied over time and the inscription on the bowl S141 (Fig. 3.157) suggests that the corporate name may have changed to Maung Yin Maung Master Silversmith by 1905. Perhaps this change recognized the supremacy of Maung Yin Maung's work and the departure of his two brothers from the company. Burmese silverwork inscribed with the name, initials or trademark of a documented master silversmith is rare and highly valued.

Jataka and Ramayana

Silversmith's marks rarely feature figures, scenes or motifs from the sacred Buddhist Jataka or Hindu Ramayana, although these are the sources of most of the visual narratives on Burmese silverwork. The reason for this dichotomy is unknown, although it might reflect the view that it was disrespectful to conceal religous motifs or marks on the hidden underside of silverwork.

Mythology and Astrology

Mythology and astrology are important elements in Burmese culture and life. They are also a popular source for a wide variety of strange and exotic silversmiths' marks. Many of the mythological animals and motifs also embellish the visible surface of the silverwork.

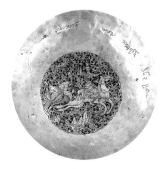

3.161 1901 Offering Bowl (S81)
Scene from the Vidhura-Pandita Jataka
'Mr Saw Marn's silver bowl.
Burmese year 1263'

3.162 1928 Offering Bowl (S82)
Coiled *naga* or serpent
'Burmese year 1290'

3.163 c. 1915 Offering Bowl (S12)
A human form with the head
of an ogre or monkey

3.164 c. 1910 Lime Box (S10)
Mythological winged elephant

3.165 c. 1910 Treasure Box (S86)
Makara, a mythological
hybrid creature
'Po Kyaw's box'

3.166 1914 Lime Box (S75)
Chintha or lion-dog
'1276. Completed at the end of the
month of Taw Tha Lin'

3.167 1907 Offering Bowl (S52)
Animals representing the eight
Burmese days of the week
'1269'

3.168 1984 Offering Bowl (S23)
Astrological chart

3.169 c. 1910 Offering Bowl (S41)
Two mythological creatures and
two human figures

3.170 c. 1915 Treasure Box (S32)
Mythological winged creature

3.171 c. 1910 Offering Bowl (S63)
Galloping horse in the countryside

3.172 c. 1915 Offering Bowl (S147)
Deer with antlers

3.173 1918 Offering Bowl (S106)
Deer kneeling to graze
'Mr Pa Lor. Burmese year 1280'

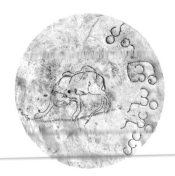

3.174 c. 1890 Offering Bowl (S129)
Fanged tiger
'Broker Ko Bo Thar'

3.175 c. 1910 Treasure Box (S53)
Two-tusked elephant marching

3.176 c. 1910 Offering Bowl (S50)
Ox in a field under an open sky

3.177 1914 Offering Bowl (S14)
Bird in flight
*'Mr Po Hlaing's silver bowl.
Burmese year 1276'*

3.178 c. 1910 Offering Bowl (S150)
Two standing deer in the forest

**3.179 c. 1920 Covered Rice
Storage Bowl (S5)**
Cherry tree in blossom with
two birds in the branches

Faunal

Natural and abstract animal forms are commonly used as a silversmith's mark (Figs. 3.171–188). Some of the more common examples include deer, tigers, birds, horses, fish and elephants. Many of these animals would have been well-known to the silversmith in nature or from Buddhist scripture and mythological tales.

The 'tiger mark' is distinctive and well-documented by collectors. It is assumed that most of the work inscribed with a tiger mark was made by one silversmith or his workshop. Few animal trademarks can be attributed to the name of a specific silversmith. A peacock was the exclusive symbol of the Konbaung royal court in Ava and Mandalay before British colonization. Thereafter, the peacock became a powerful national symbol and was used widely as a decorative motif. It is a common silversmith's mark, often depicted with its tail feathers in full display.

3.180 c. 1890 Offering Bowl (S36)
Peacock in display

3.181 c. 1910 Offering Bowl (S33)
Peacock in display

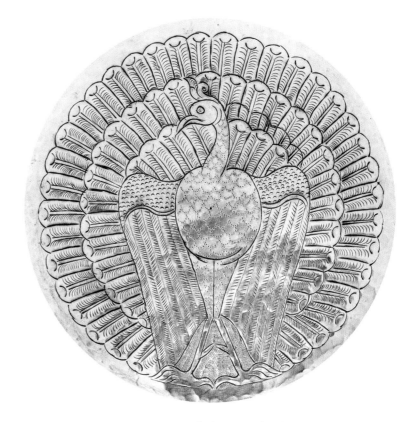

3.182 c. 1910 Offering Bowl (S48)
Peacock in display

3.183 c. 1910 Offering Bowl (S90)
Four fish circling a deer

3.184 c. 1925 Betel Box (S97)
Leaping tiger

3.185 1918 Lime Box (S17)
Juvenile deer
'1918. Weight 8.5'

3.186 1908 Water Cup (S15)
Bird of prey
'1908'

3.187 1909 Betel Box (S58)
Two tropical birds in a fruit tree
'1909. Silver container'

3.188 c. 1900 Offering Bowl (S65)
Eagle perched in a tree

3.189 c. 1910 Offering Bowl (S49)
Burmese man

3.190 1904 Lime Box (S89)
Burmese man
'1266'

3.191 c. 1915 Betel Box (S40)
Burmese man surrounded
by floral design

Human Figures

A silversmith's mark featuring a seated, or squatting, well-dressed Burmese man with a top-knot hairstyle is inscribed on three pieces of silverwork in the collection (Figs. 3.189–191). It is only possible to deduce the significance of these men. The dress style suggests some rank in society, although the lack of an identifying style of headdress minimizes the possibility that these men are royal court officials. It is perhaps more fanciful to deduce that the figures are self-portraits of the silversmith!

Floral and Geometrical

Natural and stylized floral designs are another popular style of silversmith's mark. These designs are strongly influenced by the traditional *kanote* floral motifs that adorn many forms of ancient Burmese artwork, including silverwork, lacquer work, wood and stone carving and stucco work. Stylized *kanote* designs feature lotus buds, acanthus leaves and flowers, cabbage plants, chrysanthemum flowers and other varieties of local flowers. Marks on work from the Shan States often feature bamboo stems, fruit trees in blossom and birds.

Pure geometric patterns without a stylized floral element are uncommon in the collection. Burmese text information commonly wraps around a central floral design or garland.

Figure 3.200 is an example of a few special marks that are more detailed and artistic. This mark portrays a scene from the Vidhura-Pandita Jataka and pictures the demon Punnaka flying on his supernatural horse with Vidhura-Pandita clinging to the horse's tail. A detailed *kanote* floral pattern symbolizes the background sky and mountain peaks emerge below the flying horse. This more decorative style of silversmith's mark required extra time and skill to execute compared to the common inscriptions.

Figure 3.201 pictures a decorative medallion inscribed on the concealed underside of a tray from a ceremonial betel box. It features a large fruit tree, long-tailed exotic birds and background mountains. A near identical mark is inscribed on a second tray from the betel box. The motivation or reason for adding this detailed decoration to the concealed base of two trays is unclear. It is certainly the work of a silversmith with a focus on every detail of his work.

3.192 c. 1890 Offering Bowl (S128)
Eight-petalled floral design
'Miss Nyine Tha's bowl.
Weight equals 1,500 grams'

3.193 1911 Treasure Box (S145)
Kanote floral design
'Burmese year 1272. 15th day of August.
Full moon. Madam Pu Sein's silver box.'

3.194 c. 1915 Offering Bowl (S21)
Acanthus floral design surrounded
by geometric pattern

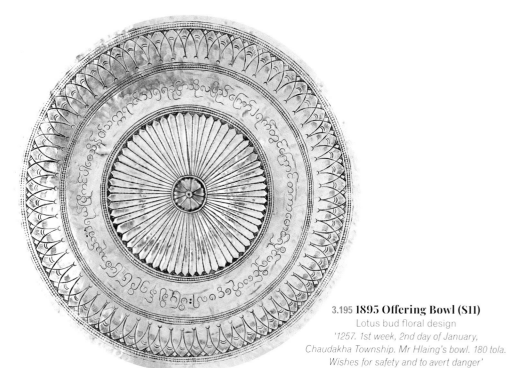

3.195 1895 Offering Bowl (S11)
Lotus bud floral design
'1257. 1st week, 2nd day of January,
Chaudakha Township. Mr Hlaing's bowl. 180 tola.
Wishes for safety and to avert danger'

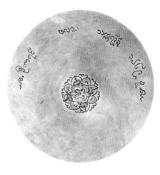

3.196 1901 Offering Bowl (S46)
Eight-peacock floral design
'Madam Mya Yan's silver bowl.
Burmese year 1263'

3.197 1928 Offering Bowl (S47)
Eight-petalled flower
'Madam Kyin's silver bowl.
Burmese year 1290'

3.198 1907 Offering Bowl (S55)
Open flower with eight outer petals
'Mr Karin's bowl. 1269'

3.199 c. 1910 Cylindrical
Storage Container (S31)
Bamboo stems and leaves

3.200 S81 Offering Bowl – Detail
Vidhura-Pandita Jataka

3.201 S58 Betel Box – Tray Detail
Two long-tailed birds in a fruit tree

CHAPTER FOUR

Understanding the Decorative Narratives

The unique allure of Burmese silver art lies in the complex and allegorical iconography that embellishes the silverwork. It is difficult to fully appreciate the character and artistic value of the silverwork without understanding this iconography and its religious and cultural origins. No other traditional silverwork from East or Southeast Asia is so overwhelmingly adorned with such a diverse collection of visual narratives. The most important sources of these narratives are sacred Buddhist scripture, the epic Ramayana poem from India, Burmese folk legends and the world of mythology and astrology.

4.2 360-degree storyboard of the early life of the Buddha on Offering Bowl S44

This chapter illuminates and interprets a selection of the most interesting visual narratives, or storyboards, that adorn silverwork in the Noble Silver Collection. The most common stories are Buddhist Jataka tales and episodes from the Burmese version of the long Ramayana poem. Each storyboard typically illustrates an abridged version of a full Jataka or select episodes from the Ramayana. These episodes are commonly some of the most dramatic and well-known stories in the Ramayana. The broad range of stories and small narrative details used to decorate Burmese silverwork indicate that many silversmiths were well-educated in Buddhist theology, Hindu tradition and Burmese legend. Most silversmiths would have received a monastic education in their youth and lived at least a short period of their life as an ordained Buddhist monk.

The interpretation of the visual narratives presented in this chapter largely relies on two published reference works: *The Jataka*, edited by Professor E.B. Cowell and first published by the Pali Text Society of London in 1895; and *Burmese Ramayana* by Ohno Toru – a translation of a palm-leaf manuscript dated 1871 and published in English in 2000. *The Jataka* translates all 547 Jataka tales from the original Pali language and is the source of all Jataka quotations used in this chapter. *Burmese Ramayana* is the only available English translation of the Burmese version of the Indian Ramayana poem. The daunting task of this chapter is to condense each of the long and complex text narratives into a coherent synopsis that integrates with the illustrated visual narratives on the silverwork.

4.1 Offering Bowl S44

4.3 360-degree storyboard of the early life of the Buddha on Offering Bowl S43

Early Life of the Buddha

The 'Buddha' is, strictly speaking, a title and not a name. The Indo-Aryan root of the word is *buddh*, meaning to be 'awake' and 'enlightened'. In common usage the title 'Buddha' refers to the historical Indian sage whose life and philosophy is the historical foundation of the Buddhist religion. He is referred to as the Gautama Buddha in his afterlife in deference to his family's clan name.

The Buddha was born in about 563 BCE near the city of Kapilavastu in the northern plain of the Ganges river, now Tilaurakot in the Terai region of southern Nepal. The Buddha's father, King Suddhodana of Kapilavastu, was a descendent of the Brahmic line of Gautama and a scion of the ancient Shakya clan that traces its roots to the Later Vedic Period (c. 1100–c. 500 BCE) in northern India. His mother was Queen Mahamaya (also known as Queen Maya), the daughter of a neighbouring king of the Koliya clan. The child Buddha was named Prince Siddhartha Gautama five days after his birth – 'Siddhartha' meaning 'one who has accomplished his goal'.

Prince Siddhartha was a Bodhisattva at birth and did not achieve Buddhahood until he attained enlightenment in Gaya at the age of 35. The word 'Bodhisattva' means a being seeking enlightenment, or an 'Awakening Being', whereas 'Buddha' translates as one who is already an 'Enlightened Being'. Prince Siddhartha was also known as 'Shakyamuni' during the six years he wandered as an ascetic in northern India in the quest for enlightenment. Shakyamuni means 'the sage of the Shakya clan'. The Buddha died at Vaishali in about 483 BCE at the age of 80. This was the Buddha's final death.

His karmic cycle of death and rebirth, also known as *samsara*, was extinguished.

Today, there are about 500 million worldwide adherents of the Buddha's teachings, mostly located in South, Southeast and East Asia. In Myanmar, about 90 per cent of the 55 million population follow the Theravada school of Buddhism. The designation 'Theravada' denotes that this form of Buddhism is the 'Tradition of the Elders', or the pure and orthodox tradition of the religion. Mahayana Buddhism – known as the 'Greater Vehicle' – is a second major school of Buddhism, which is practised more widely in Tibet, Japan, Korea and China.

The many cycles of the Buddha's life are described in a variety of both Pali and Sanskrit language texts and religious scriptures that constitute both Buddhist canon and extra-canonical narrative. Three of the most important sources are the Mahavastu, the Pathamasambodhi and the Jataka. These works largely describe the incarnations of the Buddha prior to his last life on earth. There is no complete biography of the Buddha, and details vary between sources and vernacular versions.

The early life of Prince Siddhartha from his miraculous conception to his renunciation of the protected life of a prince at the age of 29 is portrayed in a series of framed scenes on the offering bowls S43 and S44. All the decorative scenes are illustrated in a panoramic storyboard format in Figs. 4.2 and 4.3. Eleven of these scenes are presented below in chronological order to illustrate important and formative events in the first 29 years of the Prince's life.

4.4 Offering Bowl S43

Figure 4.5 is the first of the 11 scenes. The setting is the Buddhist heavenly realm known as Tusita, the ninth plane of Buddhist existence. This is the abode of many god-like figures, known as *devas,* and the temporary resting place of the Bodhisattva destined to be the future Gautama Buddha. The Bodhisattva had transmigrated to Tusita heaven after his penultimate human existence as Prince Vessantara of the Sivi kingdom, a life described in the last Jataka. In the radiant image on the offering bowl, the Bodhisattva appears wrapped in a golden cloth immediately prior to his final rebirth in the world

of human beings. Four heavenly *devas* surround and support the baby Bodhisattva. The silversmith has chased symbolic rays of celestial light emanating from the Bodhisattva's head. According to the scriptures, these rays illuminated the world and dispelled darkness when the Bodhisattva left heaven and descended to earth for the last time. This journey ended with his supernatural conception in the womb of Queen Maya.

The scriptures recall that the ground trembled and was shaken by six earthquakes at the significance of this conception. Queen Maya remained asleep throughout these events

4.5 The Buddha-to-be in Tusita heaven before descending to earth

4.6 Queen Maya visualizes her Bodhisattva child

and dreamt of a white elephant, which court astrologers later interpreted as a sign that she would give birth to either a world sovereign or a Buddha. She had been selected by the Tusita gods to be the mother of the Bodhisattva because she was pure, of good birth, gracious and destined to die seven days after the end of her pregnancy. This destiny was essential to the gods because they considered it unfitting for the mother of the Buddha-to-be to ever again indulge with her husband in the pleasures of love and sensuality.

Figure 4.6 portrays Queen Maya kneeling on a round dais in her bed chamber during her pregnancy. The enraptured mother visualizes an image of the baby Bodhisattva sitting cross-legged on the right side of her womb. King Suddhodana, her husband, kneels to the right of the queen with his hands clasped and raised in respect to the image of the Bodhisattva. The female figure behind the king is either a secondary queen or one of the thousands of heavenly figures who visited the queen during her confinement to venerate the Bodhisattva and protect his health. The male figure to the queen's left is either a principal court minister or perhaps Sakka, the lord of all the *devas* and a recurrent figure in many of the Jataka tales.

Figures 4.7 and 4.8 illustrate the birth of Queen Maya's baby in Lumbini park. The setting is a beautiful grove of flowering sal trees (Dipterocarpaceae family – *Shorea robusta*). Lumbini park was located midway between her hometown of Devadaha and Kapilavastu, the ancestral home of her husband's Shakya clan. Figure 4.7 pictures Queen Maya holding a lowered sal tree branch and Indra, the god of the heavens, holding the Bodhisattva soon after the child emerged from her right side – a scriptural detail not forgotten by the silversmith. Four other deities attend the queen, one supporting a golden curtain to protect the queen and her newborn child. The child

Bodhisattva was born on the full-moon day of the month of Visakha (May–June) in about 563 BCE.

The miraculous Bodhisattva child could walk and speak immediately after his birth. Figure 4.8 portrays the child taking seven mighty strides on lotus flower leaves placed under his feet by the gods. His steps are first towards the north cardinal point. The scripture then records that he turned to face the other cardinal points and surveyed the regions of the world, proclaiming:

> I am chief in the world: I am supreme, I am the eldest.
> There is no one higher than me.
> This is my last birth, there will be no more re-becoming.
> (Pathamasambodhi, verse 2.1)

The Bodhisattva child is issuing this proclamation in the centre of the image. He is standing with his right hand raised on the last and the largest of the supporting lotus leaf pads. Queen Maya extends her arm towards the child in a gesture that perhaps recognizes his destiny or her imminent death. A golden net has been provided by the gods to catch the child at birth and the queen is surrounded by five *devas* who have come to honour the peerless child. A heavenly *kinnari*, the female version of a mythical bird-human creature, observes the Bodhisattva from the heavens in the top right corner of the scene. The curled, cloud-like motif below the *kinnari* is a common decorative motif used to delineate the boundary between the realm of the heavens and the earthly world below.

The luxuriant trees in the background with dense leaves on weeping branches are sal trees. These trees are common in northern India and Burma and many narrative scenes from the life of the Buddha and the Jataka tales feature this style

4.7 Queen Maya gives birth to Gautama Buddha in Lumbini park

4.8 Gautama Buddha takes his first steps on seven lotus leaves

4.9 Gautama Buddha is carried to Kapilavastu by the Four Heavenly Kings

of tree in the background. Another small detail of note in this birth scene are the small, scattered flowers in the foreground. They symbolize the thousands of fragrant flowers and garlands brought in baskets by the *devas*, *deva* maidens and *apsaras* (celestial nymphs) in honour of the newborn Bodhisattva.

After his birth the Bodhisattva was taken from the Lumbini grove to Kapilavastu in a jewelled palanquin carried by the Four Heavenly Kings: Kubera, Virudhaka, Dhrtarastra and Virupaksa (Fig. 4.9). Buddhist scripture records that Queen Maya also travelled in the palanquin, although this detail is omitted by the silversmith. And, as foretold, the queen dies seven days after the birth of her son. Thereafter, she is reincarnated in Tusita heaven and never reborn again into the world of human beings. Her newborn child was subsequently named

Prince Siddhartha Gautama by King Suddhodana and raised by Queen Mahapajapati, the king's second wife and Queen Maya's sister.

Figures 4.10 and 4.11 illustrate the story of Asita, a young brahmin and a celebrated sage. He lived in a hermitage in the Vindhya mountains and witnessed the quaking of the earth and heard the thunder when the Bodhisattva was born. He also possessed magical powers – a *deva* eye that allowed him to see from a distance that a powerful and virtuous child had been born in Kapilavastu, and the supernatural ability to fly at great speed. These two powers brought Asita to Kapilavastu to witness and examine Prince Siddhartha soon after his birth. Figure 4.10 portrays Asita's first meeting with King Suddhodana – he kneels before the king and requests to see

4.10 The sage Asita requests permission to see the child Siddhartha Gautama

4.11 Asita and King Suddhodana observe Siddhartha in the royal court

4.12 Siddhartha's first meditation under a rose apple tree

4.13 Siddhartha competes in an archery competition

Siddhartha, while a court servant on the right holds an honorary white parasol over the king to protect him from the sun.

Figure 4.11 is a formal palace scene with King Suddhodana seated on a raised platform and Asita – with clasped hands to symbolize respect – kneeling to the left of the king. The smaller figure to the left of Asita is most likely his nephew Nalaka, who accompanied the sage to Kapilavastu according to some historical accounts. The attention of everyone in the palace is focused on the child Siddhartha, who is striding across a large round lotus leaf with his right hand raised high. A servant, or perhaps a heavenly *deva*, holds a large parasol over the infant and another waves a fan to cool Siddhartha's face. The scene portrays the moment described in the Pali Canon when Asita confirms that Prince Siddhartha is blessed with the 32 marks of a Great Man. Asita also foretells that the prince will not become a universal king as predicted by the court astrologers, but instead become a Buddha during his life on earth. Asita weeps before the king at this prophecy because he knows that he would not live long enough to hear the Buddha preach or see his great work.

The last illustration of Prince Siddhartha as a child (Fig. 4.12) is a skilled work of art from the beautiful offering bowl S43. It pictures Siddhartha's symbolic first meditation. The prince is sitting in a cradle suspended by ropes from the bough of a rose apple tree. The tree provides cool shade for the child and his three attendant nurses kneel before the prince and rock his cradle. Siddhartha's eyes are closed and his expression is serene and peaceful. Legend tells that the shade cast by the rose apple tree did not move during Siddhartha's meditation. King Suddhodana is seen in the background performing the traditional annual ploughing ritual to mark the beginning of the rice season. The two oxen drawing the golden royal plough are rendered in wonderful perspective and anatomical detail. A flock of birds in the sky follow the plough in life-like detail and provide subtle depth to the pastoral image.

The last three scenes in the chronology (Figs. 4.13–15) picture important events during Prince Siddhartha's life as a young man. At the age of 19 he fell in love with the beautiful Yasodhara and soon proposed marriage. However, her father refused to give away his daughter, because he believed that Siddhartha had only grown up amongst women and did not know the manly arts of archery, elephant riding, boxing and the use of a bow and a sword. In fact, Prince Siddhartha was raised exclusively within the confines of three palaces – one for each of the cold, warm and rainy seasons – and was always surrounded by luxury, music, dancing and the close company of beautiful young maidens.

To refute the charge that he was unqualified to marry Yasodhara, Siddhartha asked his father to organize a tournament of the manly arts and invite all the eligible young men in the kingdom to compete for the hand of Yasodhara. Figure 4.13 illustrates the decisive moment in the tournament – Siddhartha successfully draws the great bow of his grandfather after all the other contestants had failed. And, according to scriptural history, Siddhartha further proved his strength and prowess at archery by shooting an arrow through the trunks of seven palm trees. With this last feat Siddhartha was acclaimed the tournament winner and soon married Yasodhara.

'The Great Departure', or 'Renunciation', is a pivotal event in the life of the Bodhisattva. The iconography of the Great Departure is featured on many genres of Buddhist art. A short introduction to the events that preceded the Great Departure is valuable as context to the departure scene portrayed in Fig. 4.14.

4.14 The Great Departure from Kapilavastu

Prince Siddhartha was 29 when he decided to renounce his worldly life of sensual pleasures to become a wandering ascetic in search of the true meaning of life. He reached this life-changing decision after travelling four times in his chariot to an amusement park in Kapilavastu, and each time encountering one of the 'Four Signs' – an old man, a sick man, a corpse and finally, an ascetic. After the last encounter Siddhartha returned to the palace and vowed to leave that night on the full-moon day of Uttarasalha (June–July). He first took one final look at his wife and newborn son and then summoned his equerry Chandaka to prepare his favourite horse Kanthaka for the departure. Prince Siddhartha then quietly and secretly left Kapilavastu through a door in the city walls that had been magically unlocked by a heavenly *deva*. At the same time, 'Four Great Lords' from heaven held Kanthaka's hooves aloft to muffle their noise and avoid waking King Suddhodana.

Fig. 4.14 illustrates the Great Departure soon after Prince Siddhartha passed beyond the city walls. He is riding Kanthaka while Chandaka follows behind, holding up the horse's tail. There is also a scriptural detail in the lower right-hand corner of the image. The small figure blocking Siddhartha's path by stooping in front of his horse and raising his hand is the evil Mara, whose goal is to prevent Siddhartha achieving enlightenment. Mara first tries to entice Siddhartha by offering him power over four continents and 200 islands in exchange for not pursuing the goal of enlightenment. Siddhartha refuses this offer and then Mara threatens to follow him like an evil shadow until he finally succumbs to the temptation of malevolence and lust. Siddhartha, however, is unafraid and continues his journey towards a new life of asceticism. Other scriptural detail added by the silversmith are the background *devas* and

three *kinnaya* who shower the Bodhisattva with fragrant flowers, garlands and celestial sandalwood powder. Note again the silversmith's repeated use of the cloud motifs to outline the symbolic boundary between heaven and earth.

Fig. 4.15 is the last of the 11 scenes from the early life of the Buddha. It takes place soon after the Great Departure and is set 30 leagues (166 km) south of Kapilavastu. Siddhartha has just crossed the river Anoma and now begins his preparation for the life of an ascetic. The silversmith's image shows Siddhartha cutting off his long hair with his sword and throwing a lock up into the air. He performed this act believing that he would become a Buddha if the lock of hair miraculously stayed aloft. Sakka, the lord of the *devas*, is visible above Siddhartha, waiting to receive the lock of hair in heaven and thereby confirm Prince Siddhartha's destiny.

This episode ends with Siddhartha giving all his jewels to Chandaka and commanding him to return them to his father in Kapilavastu. Kanthaka is broken-hearted at leaving Siddhartha and dies of grief beside the river. The horse is portrayed by the silversmith lying on his side with his head lowered. The four deer in the foreground represent the animals of the forest, which recognize the Bodhisattva and have no fear of his presence. Historical accounts of this event describe *deva* gods who come to witness Siddhartha cutting his hair. These gods represent the many sacred figures that watched over and protected the Bodhisattva in all his previous lives. They also remind the observer that existence occurs on many planes in which beings can be reborn during their long journey towards enlightenment. Two witness *devas* are visible in the scene above the symbolic line of clouds that define the boundary of heaven.

4.15 Siddhartha cuts his hair in preparation for the life of an ascetic

4.16 Glazed plaques depicting the Jataka tales at the 12th-century Ananda Temple in Bagan

Jataka Tales

The Jataka tales are the best-known source of Buddhist religious knowledge in Southeast Asia. Jataka are 'birth stories' of Gautama Buddha as narrated by himself and recorded by his disciples. They describe his many previous lives in other incarnations as a human, animal, spirit or deity, according to his karmic cycle of life, death and rebirth. In each of these lives the Buddha-to-be was referred to as a Bodhisattva, one who is on his way to becoming a Buddha. Each Jataka tale also illustrates moral lessons, the workings of karma, or the 'perfections' required to achieve enlightenment and become a Buddha.

Jataka tales are the most popular narrative theme used to decorate Burmese silverwork from the late 19th and early 20th centuries. The tales remain an important element of the living tradition of Buddhism – they are included in the core of the monastic curriculum, and the visual representation and retelling of the narratives are central to the modern-day practice of Theravada Buddhism throughout Burma. Also, many of the stories are written in the style of allegorical parables, which makes the complex teachings of the Buddha more accessible to lay Buddhists. They also encourage the individual to pursue the great virtues of Buddhism and help to reinforce the morals of the scriptures.

Jataka stories are wonderful works of imaginative literature and many combine drama, adventure, charm and emotional appeal. They are commonly illustrated on silverwork, lacquerware, manuscripts, temple murals and wood carvings. Theatrical versions of popular Jataka are also performed at certain annual Buddhist and secular festivals. Cartoons, films and children's books have also been used to illustrate the Jataka tales. Any artistic characterization of the Jataka, or the sponsorship of a Jataka performance, earns the artist or sponsor great merit, since any representation of the former lives of the Buddha serves to popularize his teachings and promote the values of Buddhism.

The sacred Theravada Buddhist canon is written in the Pali language of ancient India and includes 547 Jataka tales. These are the oldest and largest extant collection of stories in the world and the only stories with one central figure – the Bodhisattva who became the Gautama Buddha. They date from the 5th century BCE and were originally transmitted as an oral form of literature. Some Jataka verses may also be adaptations from texts that predate Buddhism.

In the earliest nine-fold division of the Theravada Buddhist canon, the Jataka tales comprised the seventh 'limb'. Later, the Pali Canon incorporated the teachings of the Buddha into three baskets, known as the Tripitaka. The Jataka are found in the tenth section of the fifth division, the Khuddaka Nikaya, of the second basket – the Sutta Pitaka. Each Jataka typically consists of four parts: a tag or mnemonic device for the monk to recall the first few words; a story from the present for context; a story from the past in verse with accompanying commentary; and finally, a short description of who all the story participants were in their earlier lives and a confirmation of the part played by the Bodhisattva. The 547 Jataka in the Pali Canon are arranged according to the number of verses in each Jataka, with the first being a simple one-verse work.

Many of the Jataka stories are set in the Ganges river basin in northern India and take place in or around the ancient city of Benares, now known as Varanasi. The earliest stone relief and painted depictions of the Jataka tales are found at Ajanata, Bharut and Sanchi in central and northern India. These reliefs date to about the 1st century BCE. Jataka narratives also adorn 2nd-century CE Gandharan stupas in the Peshawar region of northern Pakistan and Afghanistan. Glazed terracotta plaques illustrating one scene from all 547 Jatakas are found on the roof terraces of the 12th-century Ananda Temple at Bagan in central Burma (Fig. 4.16). King Mindon (r. 1853–78), the penultimate king of Burma, encouraged his ministers to behave like their forebears described in the Jataka tales.

Mahanipata Jataka

The final 10 birth stories of the Bodhisattva are called the Mahanipata Jataka. These are the stories wherein he perfects each of the 10 virtues required to achieve enlightenment and fulfil his goal of becoming the Buddha. The stories are numbered 538 to 547 in the popular Theravada chronology of Jataka tales. The names of the Jataka and their allegorical moral perfections are tabulated below:

The Ten Virtues of the Mahanipata Jataka

Temiya (538) – *Renunciation*
Mahajanaka (539) – *Vigour or Energy*
Sama (540) – *Loving-kindness*
Nimi (541) – *Resolve or Determination*
Mahasoda (542) – *Wisdom or Insight*
Bhuridatta (543) – *Good conduct or Restraint*
Canda-Kumara (544) – *Forbearance or Patience*
Narada (545) – *Equanimity*
Vidhura-Pandita (546) – *Truthfulness*
Vessantara (547) – *Generosity or Charity*

Scenes from the 10 Mahanipata Jataka embellish more Burmese silverwork than all other Jataka. The archetypal ceremonial offering bowl is typically embellished with up to 10 separate scenes from one familiar Jataka. These scenes are normally displayed in a chronological sequence to create a Jataka storyboard that illustrates either a synopsis of the entire story or highlights from a discrete section.

The offering bowl S48 (Fig. 4.17) is decorated with a single scene from each of the 10 Mahanipata Jataka, thereby providing the owner of the bowl with a powerful visual reminder of the 10 most important moral virtues of Buddhism. This is not a common form of Jataka decoration. The visual narrative on most offering bowls in the Noble Silver Collection consists of multiple scenes from a single Mahanipata Jataka. Figures 4.18–27 detail each of the 10 Mahanipata Jataka scenes on bowl S48. In each figure, the title of the Jataka is inscribed in Burmese script on a silver band below the image. Trees, shrubs and architectural features serve as narrow vertical dividers between each Jataka illustration. A scalloped cornice of burnished silver fillets crowns each image and a rosette of acanthus leaves fills the arch between the adjacent cornices.

A short interpretation of the iconography accompanies the illustration of each Mahanipata Jataka. More complete and detailed accounts of the most popular Jataka stories are provided in the next section, which illustrates and deciphers offering bowls decorated with chronological storyboard scenes from one Jataka only. This is the most common form of Jataka decoration on Burmese silverwork. The most popular narratives on silverwork in the Noble Silver Collection are five Mahanipata Jataka – Sama, Mahajanaka, Bhuridatta, Vidhura-Pandita and Vessantara. However, no two artefacts

4.17 Offering Bowl S48

4.18 Temiya witnesses his father condemn a robber to death

4.19 Mahajanaka is pronounced King of Mithila

are decorated with identical scenes from the same Jataka. Each individual Jataka illustration adds detail to the story and a deeper understanding of the content and meaning of the narrative.

Temiya Jataka

The allegorical tale of Prince Temiya reveals the Buddhist virtue of renunciation. Temiya was the first-born son of King Kasiraja of Benares and a Bodhisattva. The Jataka describes why Temiya renounced his royal birthright to become an ascetic. As a young child, Temiya watched his father make many weighty life-and-death decisions and realized that kingship was no path towards enlightenment. Therefore, he pretended to be crippled, deaf and mute to disqualify himself as the future king of Benares. He also steadfastly refused all his father's enticements to accept his birthright. Finally, the exasperated King Kasiraja decided to kill his son when he reached the age of 16. However, Temiya escaped execution by using his Bodhisattva powers and fled into the forest. He lived the remainder of his life as an ascetic searching for the right path towards enlightenment.

Figure 4.18 portrays a radiant one-month-old Temiya and his father sitting in a lotus position on a magnificent winged throne. A court minister kneels to the left of the throne to honour Temiya, whilst two robbers on the right side await the king's judgement for their crimes. The Jataka describes the sentencing of four robbers – two receive 'dreadful' punishments and two receive a death penalty. Temiya is terrified by his father's decisions and thinks to himself: 'Ah, my father through his being a king, is become guilty of a grievous action which brings men to hell.' The next day. a goddess from Tusita heaven advises Temiya to pretend to be deaf, dumb and a cripple to escape his royal karma.

Mahajanaka Jataka

The Mahajanaka Jataka dramatizes the Buddhist virtues of vigour and energy. It is the story of Prince Mahajanaka's long life and his recovery of his father's throne of Mithila. Figure 4.19 portrays the prince sitting on a ceremonial rock inside a mango grove in Mithila. He was recently rescued from a shipwreck and flown to the grove by the goddess Manimekhala. Four court ministers surround Mahajanaka and proclaim him to be the new king of Mithila based on the four signs of royalty found on his feet. After this event, he marries a beautiful princess and rules the kingdom wisely for many years. Later in life King Mahajanaka realizes that all his possessions only bring sorrow and he abandons his kingdom for the life of an ascetic.

Sama Jataka

The story of Sama is an allegory of loving kindness. Sama is the miraculous child of two ascetics living in a remote forest.

4.20 Sama's dying words to King Piliyakka

He behaves with exceptional filial devotion towards his parents after they are blinded by a venomous snake. Each day he joyfully fetches water and collects food to sustain the family. Sama is assisted by wild deer who carry heavy water jars. The deer have no fear of Sama because they realize he is a Bodhisattva.

Figure 4.20 illustrates a pivotal event in the Jataka. Sama is lying on a rock in the forest with a poisoned arrow embedded in his right side. Two deer stand behind him and view the scene with astonishment. On his left is King Piliyakka of Benares, who has just shot and mortally wounded Sama. Sama then addresses the king and speaks these words without anger or blame: 'Thou canst not take my flesh for food, thou canst not turn to use my skin. Why couldst thou think me worth thine aim; what was the gain thou thought'st to win?'[1]

Nimi Jataka

The Nimi Jataka illustrates the virtues of resolve and determination. The main character, Prince Nimi, was also named Prince Hoop after the hoop of a chariot wheel. He received this name after soothsayers recognized that he was a Bodhisattva and destined to complete the Buddhist wheel of life that cycles through birth, death and rebirth. Nimi was an inspirational king and ruled virtuously and faultlessly, although he was always troubled by one spiritual question: 'Was it more fruitful to live a holy life as an ascetic or to be faithful in giving alms?' The great God Sakka in Tavatimsa heaven answered, 'It is more fruitful to live a holy life.' At the same time, the other gods in heaven heard of the pious Nimi and persuaded Sakka to bring him before them to hear his words of wisdom. Sakka agreed

and sent a royal chariot to carry him to heaven. On the journey, Nimi was shown both the fearsome levels of hell and the glories of heaven. He stayed with the gods for seven days discussing moral precepts and then returned to his subjects on earth.

Figure 4.21 depicts Nimi in a discourse with three gods in Tavatimsa heaven. He is sitting on a royal throne and the gods kneel before him with their heads bowed in respect to the Bodhisattva. Back on earth, Nimi speaks to his subjects and describes the horrors he witnessed in hell and the wonders and happiness of heaven. He also exhorts them 'to give alms and do good, for so they should be born in that divine place'. Much later in life, Nimi finds a white hair on his head and decides to renounce the world and live the life of an ascetic. When he passes away of old age, he ascends to Brahma's heaven and finally completes the wheel of life.

Mahasoda Jataka[2]

This Jataka is a long saga about the life and exploits of the sage Mahasoda. It is an allegory to illustrate the virtues of wisdom and insight. Mahasoda was a Bodhisattva, a gifted architect and engineer, and the principal sage to King Vedeha of Mithila. The Jataka narrative describes his birth, his adoption by the king and his military prowess in defending the kingdom against the combined armies of 101 Indian princes. These armies fought under the banner of King Culani and were commanded by the evil sage Kevatta. The drama of the Jataka includes the construction of defensive palaces and a secret underground tunnel, the abduction of King Culani's beautiful daughter, the machinations of fierce sage rivalry and, finally, the reconciliation of the two warring kings.

1. A more complete account of the Sama Jataka accompanies the illustration and interpretation of multiple scenes from the Jataka on the offering bowl S148 (see pages 152 to 155).

2. Also titled the Maha-Ummagga Jataka (546) in the classical Jataka order.

4.21 King Nimi in a discourse with three gods in Tavatimsa heaven

4.22 The Battle of the Law – Mahasoda defeats Kevatta

The scene in Fig. 4.22 illustrates how Mahasoda uses his wisdom and insight to humiliate Kevatta. This is the Battle of the Law. Kevatta's armies have failed to capture Mithila and he now proposes a new stratagem to King Culani: 'Sire, no army shall fight. The two sages of the two kings shall appear in one place, and one of these, whichever shall salute the other shall be conquered. I am older and he is younger, and when he sees me, he will salute me. Thus, we shall conquer Mithila.' However, Mahasoda quickly understood the ruse and was prepared to thwart Kevatta in the Battle of the Law. When the two sages met, Mahasoda first pretended to offer his rival a sparkling gemstone and then dropped it on the ground. Kevatta, overwhelmed by greed, immediately stooped down at the feet of Mahasoda to seize the gemstone. By this act he effectively saluted Mahasoda and lost the Battle of the Law. Kevatta is picking up the gemstone in Fig. 4.22 and Mahasoda holds down his head to emphasize Kevatta's humiliation. Mahasoda then cries out: 'Rise teacher, rise. I am younger than you, young enough to be your grandson; do no obeisance to me.' Kevatta has been outwitted and conquered by the young sage Mahasoda. Two princes from King Culani's army are shown fleeing the battlefield on the right side of the scene.

Bhuridatta Jataka

The Bhuridatta Jataka illustrates the universal virtues of good conduct and restraint. It is a complex narrative set in the underworld of the *nagas* and the earthly domain of humans. *Nagas* are supernatural serpents with the ability to assume the form of humans. Bhuridatta is a Bodhisattva and the son of the *naga* King Dhatarattha and a human princess. This marriage took place following a deception perpetrated by a talking tortoise named Cittacula.

Figure 4.23 illustrates a key event that leads to the conclusion of the Jataka – the end of Bhuridatta's enslavement by an old brahmin named Alambayana who had forced the *naga* to perform and dance for money throughout the kingdom of Benares. Alambayana had earlier purchased Bhuridatta in exchange for a magical *naga* gemstone. In Fig. 4.23 Bhuridatta is in the form of a serpent facing the shirtless Alambayana. His bejewelled and cramped snake basket is placed behind the brahmin. The king of Benares observes the performance from a platform in the centre of the scene. The identity of the figures flanking him is uncertain. They may represent Sudassana and Accimukhi, the brother and sister of Bhuridatta who had threatened to destroy Benares if Alambayana did not free their brother. In the conclusion to the Jataka, Bhuridatta returns to the underground realm of the *nagas* having maintained good conduct and restraint throughout his ordeal on earth.[3]

Canda-Kumara Jataka

Prince Canda lived in the kingdom of Pupphavati near Benares. He patiently and fairly served his wicked father, King Ekaraja. The prince was also a Bodhisattva and in the Jataka he demonstrates the virtues of patience and forbearance. The story begins with King Ekaraja dreaming of the celestial heaven, occupied by 33 gods, and filled with magnificent buildings, streets of gold, lakes, forests and a multitude of heavenly beings. After the dream, he longed to enter this world and asked the brahmin Khandahala, his principal advisor, to show him the path to heaven. The brahmin was an evil man and quickly realized that the king's request for counsel

---

3. A full synopsis of the intriguing Bhuridatta Jataka accompanies the multiple illustrations from offering bowls S88 and S7 on pages 156 to 159.

4.23 Brahmin Alambayana, the *naga* Bhuridatta and the King of Benares

4.24 King Ekaraja is beseeched not to kill Prince Canda

was an opportunity to destroy his court rival, Prince Canda. Consequently, Khandahala counselled the king to slay four each of his sons, queens, merchant princes and prize animals and sacrifice them to the gods. He also surmised that the selfless prince would plead with his father to take only his life and forgo the sacrifice of the other innocents. However, King Ekaraja paid no heed to Prince Canda and proclaimed to his people: 'By sacrificing my sons and daughters and wives I shall go to the world of the gods; you go and announce to them and bring them all here.' In response, the king's aged parents, his queens and princes all came in turn to kneel before the king and beg him not to follow the evil advice of Khandahala.

Figure 4.24 portrays two princes and princesses beseeching King Ekaraja to reject the advice of the malevolent brahmin. The king sits uncomfortably on his throne and defiantly holds aloft a long sword to symbolize his murderous intent to sacrifice his family to the gods. He is unmoved by all pleas for mercy. However, the dreadful cries of Prince Canda's queen are heard by Sakka, the king of the gods, and he intervenes to stop the slaughter. He destroys all the sacrificial preparations in a wind storm. This rouses the citizens to beat the evil Khandahala to death and it is only another intervention by Sakka that prevents the same fate befalling King Ekaraja. Instead of death, he is exiled for the remainder of his life. And, to happily conclude the Jataka tale, all the sacrificial captives are released and Prince Canda is anointed king of Pupphavati. In celebration, there is a great festival and 'a new and happy reign of plenty, peace and halcyon days' begins throughout the kingdom.

Narada (or Mahanaradakassapa) Jataka

The Narada Jataka is an allegory to illustrate the virtue of equanimity. It is set in the kingdom of Videha. Narada was a Great Brahma and a Bodhisattva in heaven who descended to earth disguised as an ascetic. His mission was to teach moral precepts to King Angati. This once-virtuous king was now under the influence of a false ascetic who had convinced the king to believe there was no right or wrong way to live, and no afterlife. In Fig. 4.25, Narada stands before King Angati, his beautiful daughter Ruja and five queens. He is giving a discourse on the right way of living and the moral conduct that will lead the king to heaven. Narada wears the symbolic headdress of a god and the simple garments of an ascetic. An alms bowl hangs from a shoulder strap. The king kneels with his head lowered and hands clasped in supplication towards Narada. This scene is described in the Pali Canon as follows:

> Having thus instructed him in the law and taken away his false doctrines, and established him in the moral precepts, he commanded him henceforth to eschew evil friends and to follow virtuous friends and to take heed how he walked.

In conclusion, King Angati became a virtuous king once again and Narada achieved the virtue of equanimity due to his calm and effective discourse on the right way to live.

Vidhura-Pandita Jataka

The Vidhura-Pandita Jataka is a powerful and important allegorical story to illustrate the virtue of truthfulness. The saga features a cast of dramatic characters including a beautiful *naga* princess from the underworld; Punnaka, a *yakka* general riding a magical horse; a king of Indapatta with a penchant for gambling; a deity guarding the king; and Vidhura-Pandita, a truthful and eloquent sage and advisor to the king in all temporal and spiritual matters.

Figure 4.26 illustrates Punnaka throwing Vidhura-Pandita to the ground on the summit of Black Mountain after failing

4.25 Narada instructs King Angati in the right way of living

4.26 Punnaka casts Vidhura-Pandita onto Black Mountain

in many previous attempts to kill the sage. Punnaka is readily identified by his demon-like face mask. The head of his magical horse, which gallops across the sky and walks on water, is visible on the left of the scene. Vidhura-Pandita is dressed in a simple gown and wears the headdress of a court minister or sage. The figure holding the sage is not clearly identified in the Jataka narrative. He may be either a guardian deity or a symbolic representation of King Dhananjaya, who had recently lost his sage to Punnaka in a game of dice. The lesson behind this scene is that truth can triumph over evil intent.[4]

Vessantara Jataka

The tale of Prince Vessantara is the longest and final Jataka in the Theravada canon. It is the story of the penultimate human birth of the Buddha-to-be, wherein he fulfils the last and most important perfection on the journey to enlightenment and Buddhahood – generosity or charity. This virtue is a central tenet of Buddhism and its practice in everyday life is the most important source of karmic merit.

Figure 4.27 portrays Vessantara making the supreme act of charity – he is gifting his two beloved children to the evil brahmin Jujaka. The scene is set outside Vessantara's forest hermitage and he is portrayed in the act of pouring water over the outstretched hands of Jujaka. This is a symbolic ritual to consummate the gift of the children, who look towards the portly brahmin with dread. Jujaka is old and poor and his young wife had ordered him to find slaves to do the housework and care for him. The Vessantara Jataka is the most popular expression of Buddhist decorative art in Southeast Asia.[5]

---

4. A full synopsis of the Vidhura-Pandita Jataka accompanies the images of the bowl S126 and cheroot box S56 on pages 160 to 164.

5. A synopsis of the complete Vessantara Jataka is found on pages 165 to 168.

4.28 Offering Bowl S148

Theh-Za-Tu-Neh-Ma Jataka

The offering bowl S148 (Fig. 4.28) is decorated with eight scenes from five of the last 10 Jataka. The hyphenated name of the bowl is derived from the Burmese mnemonic used to help remember the names of the five Jataka – Theh-Za-Tu-Neh-Ma.

The illustration of this group of five Jataka and their sequential arrangement on the offering bowl is unusual. The scriptural explanation is unknown. The Jataka stories are illustrated below in the Theh-Za-Tu-Neh-Ma sequence and not according to their scriptural number.

Figure 4.29 illustrates two different episodes from the first Jataka in the Theh-Za-Tu-Neh-Ma sequence – the Temiya Jataka. There is no decorative device separating the episodes, although they occur many years apart. A double-wide

Theh-Za-Tu-Neh-Ma

Theh – Theh-mi / Temiya (538)

Za – Mahanaradakassapa (?) / Narada (545)

Tu – Thuwannashan / Sama (540)

Neh – Nehmi / Nimi (541)

Ma – Mahajanaka (539)

4.27 Prince Vessantara gifts his two children to Jujaka

4.29 Two scenes from the Temiya Jataka

4.30 Scenes from the Sama Jataka (left) and the Narada Jataka (right)

scalloped frame encloses the two scenes. The scene on the left portrays the Bodhisattva Prince Temiya as a one-month-old baby sitting on his father's lap on a high throne in the Benares royal palace. He is looking towards a robber who kneels on the ground before the king. Two guards stand over the robber, who is to be judged and condemned by the king for his crimes. One guard holds a thick rope that binds the robber and forces his arms behind his back. Both guards and the king are armed with long swords. Two courtiers on the left side of the scene kneel and bow in respect before Temiya and the king. This event illustrates Temiya's first realization that a king must perform cruel duties and therefore be assuredly condemned to hell.

The scene inside the right half of the frame takes place after the king finally realizes that his 16-year-old son can never succeed him as king of Benares and must be killed. Therefore, he ordered his charioteer Sunanda to 'yoke some ill-omened horses to an ill-omened chariot, and having set the prince in it, take him out by the western gate and dig a hole with four sides in the charnel-ground; throw him into it, and break his

head with the back of the spade and kill him'. The beginning of this episode in pictured on the offering bowl. Temiya is sitting on the horse-drawn chariot during the journey to his own grave. His demeanour is calm and Sunanda dutifully leads the royal chariot forward. Temiya's mother, knowing her son's fate, is portrayed in the background looking into the distance and waving farewell.

Moments later Temiya reveals himself as a Bodhisattva to Sunanda, who then agrees to release Temiya and maintain the falsehood of his death to his parents. Temiya now begins a new life as an ascetic in the forest. Many years later, the king and queen of Benares visit their son and embrace the ascetic life themselves after listening to Temiya's discourse on the impermanence of life.

The second pair of Theh-Za-Tu-Neh-Ma Jataka scenes are pictured in Fig. 4.30. These scenes are from the Narada Jataka (right) and the Sama Jataka (left). An ancient sal tree separates the two illustrations.

Narada is a Bodhisattva and a Great Brahma. He has flown to earth disguised as a venerable ascetic so that his words will

4.31 Two scenes from the Nimi Jataka

be counted as worthy to be received. He carries a large yoke on his shoulders, which supports two baskets: one containing a golden begging bowl and the other a coral water pot. Narada has come to earth in response to princess Ruja's supplications to the gods. She has solicited help in persuading her father, King Angati, to renounce his heretical views and decadent lifestyle and follow a righteous path to heaven. Narada is welcomed by King Angati as an ascetic and permitted to give a long discourse on the law, good conduct, the nature of hell and the moral precepts of a pure and righteous life.

Figure 4.30 portrays King Angati kneeling before Narada at the end of the discourse. The king begs the Great Brahma for forgiveness and beseeches the deity in the following words:

Teach me, O seer, the sacred text and its meaning; verily the past has been all sin; teach me, Narada, the path of purity, so that I may not fall into hell.

Ruja kneels behind her father and raises a hand in reverence and gratitude to Narada for redeeming the king. The standing figure behind the king is most likely a heavenly deity who witnesses the redemption of King Angati.

The episode from the Sama Jataka takes place in the great Himavat forest in front of a simple wooden hut belonging to two ascetics – Dukulaka and his wife Parika. The god Sakka, identified by his symbolic anvil-shaped headdress, stands at the entrance to the hut addressing the ascetics, who are preparing to collect water and food in the forest. Dukulaka supports a large water pot on his right shoulder. Sakka has foreseen a great danger facing Dukulaka and Parika – they will both be blinded by a snake while gathering their daily food – and has come to earth to advise them to have a child who can care for them when they are blind. Dukulaka and Parika, not wanting to have a natural-born child, follow Saka's instructions

and Parika miraculously conceives a Bodhisattva son who is named Sama. The Jataka tells the story of Sama's loving-kindness towards his parents.[6]

Figure 4.31 illustrates two episodes from the tale of Nimi, the noble king of Mithila. This Jataka is an allegory on the virtue of resolve. A resplendent Sakka, the king of the gods from Tavatimsa heaven, stands in the centre of the left scene. He is wearing the full costume and regalia of a Burmese king and the headdress of a deity. Sakka faces the virtuous King Nimi, who sits on a throne in a palace chamber. A court minister kneels on the ground in reverence before Sakka and the king. Sakka is surrounded by cloud motifs to confirm that he is from the heavenly realm of the gods. He is visiting Nimi to resolve a spiritual question: 'Which is more fruitful – holy life or giving alms?' The scene on the bowl depicts Sakka answering King Nimi in the following words:

But, great king, although holy living is more fruitful by far than almsgiving, yet both of these are the thoughts of great men; do you be watchful in both, give alms and follow virtue.

The event depicted on the right side of Fig. 4.31 takes place after Sakka's visit to Nimi. The king of the gods has returned to heaven and reported to his brother deities on the virtuous King Nimi. Roused by these reports, the gods all wish to meet Nimi in Tavatimsa heaven and listen to his discourses. To fulfil this wish, they persuade Sakka to quickly send his divine royal chariot and charioteer to earth and to return with the king.

Figure 4.31 portrays King Nimi sitting inside the winged chariot as it races through the sky towards heaven. The charioteer Matali leans forward and directs his two magical

---

6. There is a full synopsis of this popular Jataka on pages 152 to 155.

4.32 Two scenes from the Mahajanaka Jataka

thoroughbred horses with outstretched arms. Heavenly cloud icons surround the chariot and two protective deities in the sky watch over the king. The decorated palace in the sky above Matali's head may represent one of the seven golden mansions of the god Sonadinna. The Jataku asserts that King Nimi viewed these mansions during his flying tour of Tavatimsa's heavenly delights. Nimi stayed seven days in heaven to speak with the gods before declining Sakka's offer to remain. His departing words were as follows:

> I'll go and do much good to men, give alms throughout the land, will follow virtue, exercise control and self-command: he that so acts is happy, and fears no remorse at hand.

After King Nimi returned to earth, he described the happiness of the gods to his people and exhorted them to give alms and do good. Years later, when his barber found the first white hair in his head, the king renounced the world and became an ascetic, living in a simple hut within a mango grove. The noble King Nimi entered Brahma's heaven at the end of his long life.

Figure 4.32 illustrates two episodes from the Mahajanaka Jataka. This is the last pair of framed scenes from the Theh-Za-Tu-Neh-Ma sequence. They are divided in the frame by a luxuriant sal tree.

Mahajanaka is the exiled and rightful heir to the kingdom of Mithila. The illustrated episodes are from his journey home to reclaim the throne. The detail on the left scene pictures different events that occurred over a 14-day period. These events begin when Mahajanaka's ship is sunk in violent seas, drowning all the animals and passengers aboard except for Mahajanaka. Knowing the ship was doomed, Mahajanaka smeared himself with water-resistant fats and oil and climbed to the top of the ship's mast so that he could dive as far away as possible from the ship before it sank. His dive is dramatically

portrayed by the silversmith. Mahajanaka then floated for seven days in the open ocean under the protection of female deities. One of the deities is depicted in the water with her arms outstretched like a dancer. After the seventh day, Manimekhala, the guardian of the sea, found Mahajanaka and lifted him in her arms to safety. She then realized that he was a Bodhisattva and questioned him about his power and resolve to survive in the water. Mahajanaka responded eloquently with words that speak to the eternal values of courage and personal responsibility:

> He who thinks there is nought to win and will not battle while he may, Be his the blame whate'er the loss, 'twas his faint heart that lost the day.
>
> So I will ever do my best to fight through ocean to the shore; While strength holds out I still will strive, nor yield till I can survive no more.

On hearing these inspiring words, Manimekhala praises Mahajanaka's bravery:

> Thou who thus bravely fightest on amidst this fierce unbounded sea. Nor shrinkest from the appointed task, striving where duty calleth thee, Go where thy heart would have thee go, nor let nor hindrance shall there be.

The events portrayed on the right-hand side of Fig. 4.32 occurred seven days after Mahajanaka's rescue. The sea guardian has flown with Mahajanaka in her arms to a mango grove in the kingdom of Mithila, where she lays him down asleep on his right side on a ceremonial rock. Three figures in the grove examine his feet for the signs and marks of royalty whilst he continues to sleep. One of the figures, dressed in the costume of a court minister, is making a statement to acclaim that Mahajanaka is both a royal being and a deity. Another figure pours water over his feet in recognition of his heavenly status. The figure behind Mahajanaka is probably a military general.

The silversmith has also squeezed the detail of a charioteer and his magical chariot into the image. The Jataka tells that this chariot had been dispatched by the royal court to find someone of royal and holy merit to occupy the empty throne of Mithila. King Polajanaka had died without a son or brother on the same day that Mahajanaka was forced to dive into the ocean from his sinking ship. The late king was Mahajanaka's uncle, who had earlier deposed his father in a great battle between elephant armies. In the conclusion to this episode in a mango grove, the sleeping Mahajanaka is awoken by the sound of musicians and the court minister speaks these words to him: 'Rise, my lord, the kingdom belongs to thee.' Finally, Mahajanaka has recovered the kingdom of Mithila lost by his father.[7]

Canda-Kinnara Jataka and Takkariya Jataka

The source of the visual narratives on the offering bowl S142 (Fig. 4.33) by Mg Shwe Yon Bros of Rangoon is deduced to be two unrelated Jataka – the Canda-Kinnara Jataka (No. 485 of the Jataka tales) and the Takkariya Jataka (No. 481). The only common link between these two stories is the key role played in each Jataka by *kinnaya* birds. These mythical birds typically possess a human head and torso, and large, bird-like wings and feet. A lovely rendition of two *kinnaya* is shown in Fig. 4.34. The male *kinnara* on the right wears the costume and headdress of a Burmese king. The headdress of the female *kinnari* on the left suggests she is a celestial *deva*. S142 is the only bowl in the collection to illustrate the Canda-Kinnara and Takkariya Jatakas. Furthermore, several of the scenes are difficult to decipher because details are inconsistent with the original Jataka narrative. Perhaps the silversmith exercised 'artistic licence' in his interpretation of the stories.

4.33 Offering Bowl S142

The central character in the Canda-Kinnara Jataka is a Bodhisattva named Canda who was born as a *kinnara* in the Himalayan mountains. His *kinnari* wife is named Candā, and they both lived together on Canda-pabbata mountain, or 'Mountain of the Moon' – a rather confusing similarity of names! One day, the king of Benares visited the mountain and discovered Canda and his beautiful wife enjoying an idyllic existence in a secret place in the forest. The king observed the *kinnaya* from a distance for a short while and immediately fell in love with Candā. This attraction to Candā was so strong that he quickly decided to kill her husband with a poisoned arrow. Then he planned to marry her and live forever on the Mountain of the Moon.

Figure 4.35 portrays the king shooting Canda. He is accompanied by two female courtiers and a hunter. These three figures are not described in the original Jataka. The next image (Fig. 4.36) is a detail of Candā supporting her dying husband, who lies on his side with the king's poisoned arrow in his chest.

4.34 Mythological *kinnaya* in Himavat forest – a mixed human and bird form

4.35 The King of Benares shoots Canda

Each *kinnaya* wears a headdress in the design of a bird's neck with a beaked head at the top. They both display the articulated wings of their bird-like form.

There are only two scenes from the Canda Kinnara Jataka on the bowl S142. The silversmith does not reveal the fate of the injured Canda or the story's conclusion. In the original Jataka narrative, the joyful conclusion is as follows. The evil king of Benares, believing that he has killed Canda, has the impudence to propose marriage to his widow. Candā, the recent widow, understandably curses the king and adamantly refuses the king's audacious proposal. As a result, he quickly loses interest in the *kinnari* and eventually leaves the mountain and returns home. Candā then realizes that her husband is not dead at all and immediately summons help from the god Sakka.

4.36 The dying Canda supported by his wife

He arrives disguised as a brahmin and sprinkles a magical elixir on Canda's wound to save his life. After Canda recovers, Sakka advises the *kinnaya* to never again go down among the paths of men, but to stay high on the Mountain of the Moon. Candā echoes this advice in a charming poetic stanza spoken to her fully recovered husband:

> To the mountain let us go,
> Where the lovely rivers flow,
> Rivers all o'ergrown with flowers:
> There forever, while the breeze
> Whispers in a thousand trees,
> Charm with talk the happy hours.

The second *kinnaya* narrative portrayed on the offering bowl S142 is the Takkariya Jataka. Figures 4.37 and 4.38 illustrate two significant scenes from this Jataka. In the first scene, the king of Benares is sitting on a magnificent dais and dressed in the sumptuous and traditional costume of a Burmese king at court. The extravagantly flared legs of the dais are in the style of a *kinnara*'s wings. The king is peering towards a captive female figure, who kneels plaintively before the king with her hands held together in a gesture of supplication. The female's headdress identifies her as a *kinnari*. She is one of two *kinnaya* captured by a hunter in the Himalayan mountains and gifted to the king because of their musical nature and delight in dancing. The background to this scene is as follows. The king had commanded the *kinnaya* to perform their traditional songs and dances, but they repeatedly refused and remained silent and motionless. Consequently, the king lost his patience and ordered the *kinnaya* to be killed and cooked for dinner that night. Now, fearful for their lives, the *kinnaya* finally explained to the king the reasons for their

4.37 A *kinnaya* explains her silence to the king of Benares

4.38 A *kinnaya* is returned home in a golden cage

silence and spoke these words: 'If we are not able to convey the full sense of song, the song will be a failure, they will abuse and hurt us; and then again, those who speak much speak falsely.' This scene is portrayed in Fig. 4.37. The figures from left to right are the queen of Benares, the king, the *kinnari* and two court minister witnesses.

The just conclusion to this Jataka is revealed by the scene in Fig. 4.38. The *kinnaya*'s words spoken to explain their silence pleased the king and he immediately ordered them returned in a golden cage to their home in the Himalayas. This cage is portrayed in the centre of Fig. 4.38. It contains a musical drum to emphasize the artistic nature of the *kinnaya*. And, the once-captive *kinnari* now stands proudly outside the cage to symbolize her freedom and homecoming. The figure on the left is deduced to be the hunter who first captured the *kinnaya* and then returned them to the Himalayas. His headdress and costume are clues to his role in the narrative. In conclusion, the moral of this Jataka is that controlled speech at the appropriate

time is beneficial, whereas speaking ill at the wrong moment can lead to great misery.

Cullahamsa Jataka

The endearing story of the elephant Nalagiri decorates the offering bowl S109 (Fig. 4.39). This story comprises a short introduction to the longer Cullahamsa Jataka (No. 533 of the Jataka tales), which describes the life of a Bodhisattva when he was the king of a flock of geese. The Nalagiri narrative describes a fiendish plot by Devadatta to slay the Buddha while he is collecting alms in the city of Rajagaha. Devadatta is the Buddha's cousin, brother-in-law, rival and the villain of many Jataka tales.

Elephants are popular icons in Burmese silver art and silversmiths excelled in crafting the form, dynamic motion and character of the valued pachyderms. Four different images of Nalagiri decorate the bowl S109. The Nalagiri narrative begins

4.39 Offering Bowl S109

4.40 Elephant keepers instructed to intoxicate Nalagiri with arak spirit

4.41 The drunk Nalagiri goaded to stampede

4.42 Villagers flee before the charging Nalagiri

4.43 The Buddha's power calms Nalagiri

with a short account of a failed attempt by Devadatta to slay the Buddha by hurling a large stone at him from the top of a cliff. Next, Devadatta convinces the king of Rajagaha that only the king's fiercest elephant can destroy the Buddha. This is Nalagiri. Devadatta mistakenly believed that only this elephant would be immune to the influence of the virtuous Buddha.

Figure 4.40 illustrates the beginning of Devadatta's murderous plot. The king is ordering the elephant keepers to serve Nalagiri 16 pots of a fiery arak spirit, twice his normal consumption, and more than enough to intoxicate him. Three arak pots stand in the right foreground of the scene. The following morning, Nalagiri is frenzied with alcohol and the cruel elephant keepers spike and goad him to break down his stall and charge into the street. Figure 4.41 portrays the drunk elephant struggling to stand and thrashing his head and trunk towards his abusive handlers. Once in the street, Nalagiri charges towards the Buddha who is collecting morning alms with his disciples. The terrified citizens in his path flee in fear of their lives (Fig. 4.42).

The Buddha, however, is unperturbed by the raging elephant charging towards him. He faces Nalagiri directly, and calmly speaks these compassionate words:

> Ho! Nalagiri, those that maddened you with 16 pots of arak did not do this that you might attack someone else, but acted thus thinking you would attack me. Do not tire out your strength by rushing about aimlessly, but come hither.

These words immediately soothed Nalagiri and the intoxicating effects of the arak miraculously passed away. And, overcome by the spiritual power of the Buddha, he dropped his trunk, shook his ears and fell at the feet of the Buddha. This moment is portrayed in Fig. 4.43. The Buddha is standing on a lotus pad holding an alms bowl and blessing Nalagiri. Five of his disciples, including Ananda and Sariputta, stand behind him in a traditional file of monks. The citizens of the town clasp and raise their hands in praise towards the Buddha after witnessing the miraculous taming of Nalagiri. Finally, the elephant lifted dust from the Buddha's feet and blew it all over his head before quietly returning to his stall. Thereafter, Nalagiri was always tame, harming no one, and became known as Dhanapalaka, 'the keeper of treasure'.

Mahajanaka Jataka

The Mahajanaka Jataka (No. 539 of the Jataka tales) is an inspiring allegorical tale of courage and vigour centred on the life of Prince Mahajanaka, the lost prince of Mithila. It is worthy of a full account. The biographical story includes the death of his father in battle, Mahajanaka's subsequent birth and life in exile, his return to Mithila as a virtuous king, and – like many Jataka kings – his final rejection of the material world in favour of the ascetic's life. Two offering bowls from the collection illustrate pivotal events in this heroic story: S120 (Fig. 4.44) and S37

4.44 Offering Bowl S120

4.45 A battle between two elephant armies

4.46 Mounted soldiers in close combat

(Fig. 4.48). All the decorative scenes on the offering bowl S37 are illustrated in a panoramic storyboard format in Fig. 4.49.

The Jataka narrative begins before the birth of Prince Mahajanaka. There is a war in Mithila between Aritthajanaka, the legitimate king, and a challenger named Prince Polajanaka. The challenger is the king's brother and viceroy of the kingdom. The titanic war between the brothers is fought between richly caparisoned elephant armies (Fig. 4.45) and mounted soldiers on beautifully dressed ceremonial horses (Fig. 4.46). The ferocity and dynamism of these head-to-head clashes are almost tangible in the silversmith's high-relief repoussé work.

Figure 4.47 is set in the royal palace in Mithila and depicts the moment when King Aritthajanaka's wife is informed by a kneeling court minister that her husband has been killed in battle by Prince Polajanaka and the war is lost. The queen is supported by two ladies-in-waiting or relatives and there is a hint of grief on her face. Now she must fulfil a promise to her husband to flee Mithila to protect her unborn child. This child is also a Bodhisattva. Leaving the city in disguise, the queen soon encounters an old man with a carriage, who offers to take her in safety to the distant city of Campa. This old man is in fact Sakka, the king of the gods, disguised as a charioteer. He is depicted in Fig. 4.50 driving a simple two-oxen cart with the queen standing behind in the chariot. There is a nimbus over her head to symbolize the Bodhisattva child in her womb. On the crenellated city walls behind the chariot, a figure wearing a king's headdress is about to be slain with a long spear. This detail probably symbolizes the earlier death of her husband, King Aritthajanaka.

Sakka transports the pregnant queen to Campa in a miraculously short time and she is invited to live under the protection

4.48 Offering Bowl S37

4.49 360-degree storyboard of the Mahajanaka Jataka on Offering Bowl S37

4.47 The queen of Mithila learns of her husband's death in battle

of a kind brahmin. Later, the queen gives birth to a son who is named Mahajanaka after his royal grandfather. However, this royal heritage is concealed from Mahajanaka during his childhood. One day, tiring of always being called 'the widow's son' by his friends, he angrily forces his mother to name his father. Thereafter, he ceases to be angry and devotes his youth to studying the scriptures and the sciences in the firm knowledge that he is the son of the slain king of Mithila.

At the age of 16, Mahajanaka resolves to regain the kingdom that belonged to his father. To finance this mission, he uses half of his mother's wealth to purchase trading goods and sets out on a ship bound for Suvarnabhumi to earn enough money to regain the kingdom of Mithila. This quest starts badly. After seven days at sea, the ship runs into a storm and begins to sink. Realizing the danger, Mahajanaka quickly covers himself with ghee and oil for protection, and dives into the ocean moments before the ship disappears below the water.

Fig. 4.51 portrays Mahajanaka diving from the bow of a ship which has the form of a *garuda*, a mythical eagle-like bird representing wisdom, one of the Four Dignities of Buddhism. The three-deck superstructure of the floundering ship hints at a

European design. Other narrative details from this tragic event are pictured in the water along the lower edge of the scene. The Pali version of the Jataka describes the fate of the other passengers on the ship: 'The crowd on board became food for the fishes and turtles, and the water around assumed the colour of blood.' The silversmith, inspired to preserve the fidelity of this scene, crafted two fishes and the rear of a diving turtle in the waves beside the sinking ship. This is surely a rather whimsical artistic rendition of 'man-eating' sea life. The four 'dancing' figures in the water between Mahajanaka and the sea creatures are heavenly nymphs sent to protect Mahajanaka from danger. Another important event occurred elsewhere on the same day that Mahajanaka's ship sank – King Polajanaka, who had usurped his father's rightful crown, died in Mithila.

Mahajanaka floated in the ocean without food for seven days before Manimekhala, the guardian of the seas, lifted him like a child from the water. Asked by the goddess where she should carry him, Mahajanaka replied, 'To the city of Mithila.' On the seven-day journey to Mithila, Mahajanaka slept in a trance wrapped in the heavenly arms of the goddess (Fig. 4.52). He is guarded by five dancing nymphs who float in the water

4.50 The pregnant queen flees Mithila in an ox-drawn cart

4.51 Mahajanaka dives from the bow of a sinking ship

4.52 A goddess rescues Mahajanaka

4.53 Mahajanaka sleeps on a rock surrounded by Mithila court officials

4.54 Mahajanaka draws a powerful bow to win the hand of Princess Sivali

4.55 King Mahajanaka gives a discourse on courage

below. Iconic cloud motifs surround Manimekhala to confirm her heavenly nature and the presence of the Bodhisattva.

When the goddess arrived in the kingdom of Mithila, she laid the sleeping Mahajanaka down on a ceremonial rock in a mango grove (Fig. 4.53). In the meantime, the court ministers, anxious to preserve the kingdom, heeded the advice of a religious advisor and sent out a magical festive chariot yoked to four lotus-coloured horses to find a being with the merit to be the next king. The chariot passed through the palace and out of the city before entering the mango grove. Here, the chariot completed a ceremonial circle around Mahajanaka before coming to a halt. Court officials examined Mahajanaka for the signs of royalty and proclaimed him a king of many lands. Musical instruments were then sounded and Mahajanaka awoke and quickly perceived that the 'white umbrella' had come to him and he was destined to become king of Mithila. Other figures surrounding the new king include army generals, court ministers with distinctive tall, rounded hats, and numerous well-dressed courtiers with bun-like hairstyles.

Figure 4.54 portrays the new king of Mithila in the palace garden drawing the string of a powerful bow before his chief minister and courtiers. He is fulfilling one of the important qualifications required of a new king: 'He who can string the bow which requires the strength of a thousand men.' Mahajanaka then marries Princess Sivali, the beautiful daughter of the late King Polajanaka, and rules wisely and virtuously. In celebration of his rule, the people of Mithila offer him presents of food, drinks and fruit at a great festival. The pomp of this court festival is illustrated in Fig. 4.55. King Mahajanaka sits high upon a royal throne attired in the full costume of a Burmese king. A minister and a host of courtiers and subjects kneel before him in devotion and respect. Other courtiers look down from the parapet of the palace wall. In memory of his former struggles, Mahajanaka speaks these words: 'Courage is the right thing to put forth – if I had not shown courage in the great ocean, should I have ever attained this glory?'

Mahajanaka subsequently ruled for 7,000 years before renouncing his kingdom for the life of an ascetic and leaving Mithila forever. The queen attempted to follow him out of the city, but Mahajanaka was not seen again after he entered Himavat forest. The queen returned to Mithila, arranged for the coronation of their son, and then chose the ascetic's life herself. Both King Mahajanaka and Queen Sivali entered the kingdom of the gods when their earthly lives came to an end.

4.56 360-degree storyboard of the Sama Jataka on Offering Bowl S39

Sama Jataka

The Sama Jataka (No. 540 of the Jataka tales) is an allegorical story of loving-kindness and filial piety. It is a straightforward, intelligible drama that resonates to this day with the clarity of its moral lesson. The story is ideally suited to the artistic medium of silver due to the cogent linear nature of the narrative. The offering bowl S148 (Fig. 4.57) has been selected to illustrate the Jataka from many other artefacts in the collection decorated with the Sama Jataka. Each of the 10 scenes on the bowl S148 are surrounded by an ornate frame of entwined flowers, stems and leaves. Figures 4.58–67 depict details from each of the scenes. A panoramic storyboard of the Sama Jataka from the offering bowl S39 is portrayed in Fig. 4.56 for comparison.

The Sama Jataka is set in the kingdom of Benares. Two hunter chiefs who are longtime friends agreed to betroth their infant children. The two children grew up as close friends and when the time came for their arranged marriage, they refused because they shared a destiny from their former lives to only do penance in their current life. Eventually, a compromise was agreed and after the marriage the two friends travelled to Himavat forest and lived as brother and sister in separate hermit huts. They followed an ascetic life and were secretly under the care of the god Sakka. The visual narrative on the offering bowl now picks up the Jataka tale.

Figure 4.58 shows the god Sakka visiting Dukulaka and his wife Parika in their forest hermitage. Dukulaka is sitting on a tree stump in the centre of the scene and Parika kneels behind him. Sakka bows his head and raises his hands in respect towards the two devout ascetics. He offers a warning to Dukulaka: 'Sir, I foresee a danger which threatens you. You must have a son to take care of you – follow the way of the world.' Dukulaka, however, does not wish to have a 'natural child' and is depicted with his hand raised as if rejecting Sakka's warning. Sakka, not wishing to make the ascetics break their vow of celibacy, informs Parika that she will miraculously conceive a Bodhisattva child if Dukulaka touches her navel with his hand in the 'proper season'.

4.57 Offering Bowl S148

4.58 The god Sakka visits Dukulaka and Parika in Himavat forest

Parika gives birth to a son 10 lunar months later and he is named Sama. Figure 4.59 pictures the small child standing between two *kinnaya* from the forest. These mythological figures have been sent by Sakka to protect and care for Sama when his parents go into the forest to collect food and water. To the right of Sama is a male *kinnara* dressed in the magnificent style of a Burmese king and wearing a royal crown and regalia. His bird-like feet, legs and lower wing feathers emphatically identify him as a guardian *kinnara*. A female *kinnari* dressed as a Burmese queen to the left of Sama displays her lower wing and towering tail feathers. The pose and hand positions of both *kinnaya* speak eloquently of their responsibility to shelter the young Bodhisattva. A stupa icon in the background reminds the observer that Sama is a Bodhisattva, a 'Great Being'.

Sama is pictured as a young boy in Fig. 4.60. It is an image of the family together in the forest and serves to establish the strong bond between Sama and his parents. Dukulaka and Parika are both waving to Sama, either in play or before they leave him to forage for food. There is a subtle expression of mysticism or sadness on Sama's face. The anatomical and costume details of all three figures are finely rendered. This is exemplified by the many small creases and folds that create shape and dimension to the robe worn by Dukulaka.

One day, Sama's parents are caught in a storm while collecting food. They take shelter under the roots of a large tree and inadvertently stand on an anthill that harbours a venomous snake. Angered by their presence, the snake spits his venom out and instantly blinds both Dukulaka and Parika. This is their misfortune predicted by the god Sakka. Figure 4.61 is a magnified illustration of the venomous snake from the offering bowl S104. It has just blinded Parika and she holds her hand to her face in agony. Later, Dukulaka and Parika are rescued by Sama, who leads them carefully back to the hermitage. At home he both weeps and laughs at their incapacitating blindness, saying: 'I wept because your sight is gone while you are still young, but I laughed to think that I shall now take care of

4.59 Two *kinnaya* guard the young Sama

4.60 Sama and his parents in the forest

4.61 Parika blinded by a venomous snake

4.62 Sama holding a water pot, with his blind father

4.63 Sama collecting water accompanied by wild deer

you; do not grieve, I will take care of you.' Thereafter, Sama laid out directional ropes for his parents and each day collected enough water and food for all the family. Figure 4.62 portrays Sama leaving the hermitage to collect water. Dukulaka, his blind father, sits sadly on a tree stump holding a long walking stick for support.

Figure 4.63 is a portrait of Sama as a strong young man carrying two heavy water pots on a yoke that rests on his broad shoulders. It is the image of a filial son filled with loving-kindness towards his parents. Sama is accompanied in the forest by wild deer, who have no fear of him because they recognize his benevolence towards all creatures and his special nature as a Bodhisattva. Sama is an icon of compassion, conscience and humanity, and no doubt many Burmese parents have used him as an example to teach their children the value of loving-kindness.

Figure 4.64 pictures Sama calmly filling his water pots

from a stream in Himavat forest. He is surrounded by four joyful deer who will help to carry the pots home to Sama's hermitage. Unbeknown to Sama, he is being observed at the same time by the wicked King Piliyakka of Benares, who is hunting wild deer to satisfy his greed for venison. The drama and menace of this moment is wonderfully captured by the silversmith. King Piliyakka is so fascinated by Sama's behaviour and friendship with the deer that he decides to slay him. He imagines that Sama would be a unique hunting trophy to display in Benares.

King Piliyakka does not wait long to execute his plan. Figure 4.65 illustrates the king firing a poisoned arrow at Sama. He stands with his feet braced and his right arm pulls back the drawstring of a large curved bow. His costume is like the traditional robes and headdress worn by a Burmese king. A Benares court minister, identified by his iconic tall rounded headdress, kneels behind the king with one hand reaching out

4.64 King Piliyakka secretly watches Sama collecting water

4.65 King Piliyakka shoots a poisoned arrow at Sama

4.66 The dying Sama talks quietly to King Piliyakka

to his master. It is interesting to speculate on the meaning of this gesture. Is he praising the king's archery skills, or, perhaps, imploring him not to gratuitously slay Sama because he recognizes him as a sacred Bodhisattva?

Figure 4.66 pictures Sama lying on his side holding the shaft and feathers of the poisoned arrow with his right hand. King Piliyakka stoops over him and falsely claims that he mistakenly shot Sama when aiming for a deer. As blood pours from Sama's mouth he speaks aloud: 'Who, as I filled my water jar, has from his ambush wounded me … Why couldst thou think me worth thine aim; what was the gain thou thought'st to win?' King Piliyakka is taken aback on hearing these calm words and realizes that the mortally injured Sama neither reviles nor blames him for his wicked deed. Sama continues to speak, lamenting that his blind parents will perish without his care. These words fill the king with shame and cause him to make a solemn promise to Sama: 'O Sama of auspicious face, let not despair thy soul oppress. Lo, I myself will wait upon thy parents in their lone distress.' On hearing these words, Sama's mouth and eyes close and he appears to have taken his last breath. The facial expressions and bearing of both Sama and King Piliyakka seem to speak to the drama and emotion of this tragic moment.

In keeping with his immoral character, King Piliyakka quickly wavered in his commitment to care for Sama's parents when he perceived that Sama was going to die. Furthermore, he concluded there would be no consequence for killing Sama because no one in the forest knew his name and there were no witnesses, except his minister and servants. However, unbeknown to the king, a daughter of the gods witnessed the tragic events and now recognizes the peril facing Sama's parents if the king reneges on his promise. Accordingly, she intercedes and persuades the guilty king to keep his vow, with a promise

of redemption for his sins and rebirth in heaven. The king could not refuse the promises of a god, and after paying homage to Sama's body travels to his parents' hermitage to confess his crime and offer his care. Dukulaka and Parika, inconsolable with grief, hear the king speak and only ask that he should lead them to their son to await the approach of his death. The king reluctantly agrees and takes them to Sama's body lying in the forest. Thereupon the weeping Dukulaka and Parika kneel beside their son and pray for his life. The guardian daughter of the gods also prays. Finally, as the dawn approaches, Sama recovers from his wound and his parents' eyesight is also miraculously restored. Figure 4.67 superbly illustrates this joyful moment. In the silversmith's image, Parika is tenderly holding her son and Dukulaka, kneeling at Sama's feet, reaches out to help raise him from the ground.

King Piliyakka observes the miracle of Sama's recovery and is bewildered by all the unexpected events. To resolve his confusion, he asks Sama for guidance on how to better live his life. Sama replies by describing the 10 duties a king must practise if he wishes to reach the world of the gods and enjoy divine happiness. The Jataka story concludes with King Piliyakka returning to Benares to live a virtuous life before entering the world of the gods upon his death. The karmic penance attached to Sama's parents is removed and eventually they ascend with Sama to the high heaven of the great Brahmas.

4.67 Sama recovers in the arms of his parents

4.68 Offering Bowl S88

4.69 Offering Bowl S7

Bhuridatta Jataka

Nagas are magical serpents from the underworld with the power to assume human form and live on earth. The Bhuridatta Jataka (No. 543 of the Jataka tales) is a labyrinth-like story of a *naga* prince set in the world of both serpents and humans. Its underlying message is the virtue of resolution and perseverance. Episodes from the long and fascinating Jataka decorate the Middle Burma style offering bowls S88 (Fig. 4.68) and S7 (Fig. 4.69). These are openwork, lattice-like bowls created by detailed piercing and chasing of flat silver surfaces. Figures 4.70–77 depict nine episodes chosen to illustrate highlights of this narrative.

Figure 4.70 portrays an early event in the Bhuridatta story. The prince of Benares is living with a widowed young *naga* lady in a simple wooden hut in a forest beside the Yamuna river. They are both sitting on a low bench outside the hut. She is identified as a *naga* by her symbolic serpent-like head-dress. A minister from Benares kneels before the prince. He is imploring the prince to return home and be crowned king following his father's death. The prince agrees and the *naga* lady returns to the underworld, knowing that she could never live

as a queen in the realm of humans. Their children, although possessed of a *naga*'s 'watery' nature, accompany their father to Benares.

The story now continues in Benares. The new king has constructed a lake for his 'watery' children to play sports (Fig. 4.71). Four figures standing in the lake are reacting to the presence of a small turtle named Cittacula, who has surfaced in the foreground. These figures are presumed to be the king's children, although the Jataka narrative is not explicit on the number and gender of the *naga*-human children. A figure in the centre of the lake wears the regalia of a prince and is probably the king's oldest son. His hands are outstretched to protect his siblings from Cittacula. Two sisters on the right side of the prince look afraid and are leaving the lake. They fear that the turtle is a demon *yakka*. The king, angered that Cittacula frightened his children, orders the turtle to be thrown into a whirlpool in the Yamuna river, where the strong currents lead down to the realm of the *nagas*.

As soon as Cittacula reaches the *naga* world he is captured by two fierce sons of King Dhatarattha. To avoid death,

4.70 The Prince of Benares and his *naga* wife living in a forest hut

4.71 The turtle Cittacula scares the king's children in a lake he devises a ruse and tells the princes he is a messenger from the king of Benares, who wishes to betroth his daughter to the *naga* king. Figure 4.72 pictures the cheeky turtle sitting on an ornate circular pedestal in conversation with King Dhatarattha and his two sons. Each is identified by their royal attire and symbolic *naga* headdress. Cittacula convinces his audience that he is a true messenger delivering the marriage proposal. The king is overjoyed and immediately orders four *naga* youths and Cittacula to go to the human world and ask the king of Benares to set the wedding day. When this group nears Benares, Cittacula begins to fear that his ruse will soon be exposed. To avoid this calamity, Cittacula successfully tricks the accompanying *nagas* into going ahead to meet the king of Benares while he stops, supposedly to collect valuable lotus plants to give to the king. No more is heard of Cittacula, the tricky and manipulative turtle.

Figure 4.73 returns the story to the land of the *nagas* following the wedding 'arranged' by Cittacula. The *naga* king Dhatarattha is now married to Princess Samuddaja, the human daughter of the king of Benares. They live in a palace filled with humans and the new queen is deceived into believing that she is still living in the human world. In the course of time Samuddaja gives birth to four *naga* sons and eventually realizes she is married to a *naga* and living in their land. The second son is named Datta and is born a Bodhisattva. He is later named

Bhuridatta for his wisdom, following his many visits to heaven and wise discourses with Sakka, the king of the gods.

As a result of these enlightening discourses, Bhuridatta decides to fast and meditate to ensure that he will eventually be reborn among these gods. This proves difficult in the *naga* world; his devotion is constantly disturbed by *naga* maidens, who wait on him day and night with food and drink and entertain him with songs, dance and music. Five of these dancing *naga* maidens are portrayed in the foreground of Fig. 4.73. Bhuridatta looks down on the entertainment on the right side of the image. The two *nagas* facing him are deduced to be his father King Dhatarattha and his mother Queen Samuddaja. Bhuridatta is stretching out his arms and looks back towards his parents. This gesture may allude to his decision to escape from the dancing maidens at nighttime and peacefully fast and meditate under a banyan tree in the human world above. However, Bhuridatta did not wish to completely forgo the pleasures of the maidens and made a compromise. He permitted them to come to the banyan tree at dawn to wake him with perfumes and flowers and conduct him back to the *naga* world with sensual song and dance.

One morning Bhuridatta is about to return to the *naga* world with the dancing maidens when he is discovered by an inquisitive brahmin and his son named Somadatta. They ask if he is a god or a *yakka* demon. Bhuridatta, not wishing to identify

4.72 Cittacula addresses the *naga* king Dhatarattha

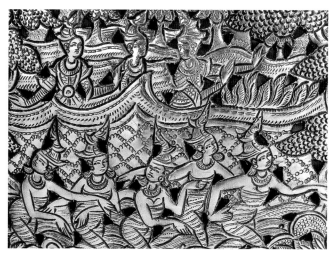

4.73 *Naga* maidens entertain Bhuridatta

4.74 A brahmin and his son feasting in the *naga* kingdom

himself as a Bodhisattva, answers truthfully that he is a serpent prince. He then reflects on this response and begins to
fear that the brahmin might betray him to a snake charmer on
earth. To prevent this outcome, he invites the brahmin and his
son to return with him to the *naga* kingdom and enjoy a divine
existence in eternity. They readily agree, and Bhuridatta uses
his great power to transport them to the underworld.

Figure 4.74 portrays the brahmin and his son enjoying the
'good life' in a sumptuous *naga* palace. The brahmins are identified by their two-feathered hats and the hunting bags slung
from their shoulders. The father is taking a piece of sliced fruit
from a low table covered in food and drink, and the son tilts his
head back as he drinks from a large vessel of wine or water.
They are surrounded by six attentive *naga* maidens, all wearing
the distinctive *naga* headdress in the form of a serpent's head.
A year later, after enjoying much pleasure, the brahmin wishes
to see his family again and asks Bhuridatta to return him and
his son to the world of humans. At first, Bhuridatta is reluctant
to agree because he is still fearful that his nightly meditation
under the banyan tree might be exposed. Therefore, he offers
the brahmin a magical jewel that grants all desires as an
incentive to not reveal his secret. To Bhuridatta's surprise, the
brahmin replies that he simply wishes to become an ascetic in
the human world and would have no use for the magical jewel.
Later, after returning home, the brahmin becomes an outcast,
because his wife is unhappy at his decision to become an
ascetic and displeased that he hasn't returned from the *naga*
world with anything of value.

The bowls S88 and S7 are not decorated with a complete
or continuous version of the Bhuridatta tale. An important set
of events that occur after the brahmin and his son return to the
land of humans is not illustrated on the bowls. These events
are narrated below to help understand the depth of the Jataka
story and to provide narrative continuity between Figs. 4.74
and 4.75.

One day in the kingdom of Benares a mythological *garuda*
bird gifts a priceless and magical spell to an ascetic living in
the forest. Alambayana, a poor brahmin in debt, wanders into
the same forest and finds the ascetic. The ascetic employs
Alambayana and later gives him the magical spell as a reward
for his good work. Alambayana now realizes that owning the
spell gives him the means to a new livelihood and he soon
fakes sickness to leave the ascetic. He then wanders in the
forest repeating the spell until he reaches the Yamuna river,
whereupon he sees a thousand *naga* maidens waiting to
escort Bhuridatta back to the *naga* world after his nightly fast.
These *nagas* are also carrying the magical jewel that grants
all desires – the same gem that was offered earlier to the
outcast brahmin and his son Somadatta. The *naga* maidens,
hearing Alambayana repeat the *garuda* spell, plunge back
into the underworld in fear because the *garuda* is their traditional enemy. In their haste they leave behind the magical
jewel, which is quickly seized by Alambayana. Later, he meets
the outcast brahmin and his son who had previously lived in
the *naga* underworld. The brahmin immediately recognizes

4.75 A brahmin receives a jewel from Alambayana for betraying
Bhuridatta

the jewel on Alambayana's hand as the one offered to him by Bhuridatta.

The narrative continues with a discourse between the outcast brahmin and Somadatta regarding the morality of cheating Alambayana out of the ring and at the same time, betraying their earlier promise to Bhuridatta. Somadatta strongly advises his father against losing his honour, but his moral advice is rejected. Later, his father learns that Alambayana will give the jewel to anyone in exchange for information on where to find Bhuridatta. Accordingly, the duplicitous father leads Alambayana to the anthill where Bhuridatta fasts and meditates at night. Figure 4.75 illustrates Alambayana giving the jewel to the outcast brahmin, who points to where the *naga* prince is meditating in the form of a coiled serpent. Bhuridatta realizes he has been betrayed by the brahmin but chooses not to be angry, thereby preserving his moral character. Instead he closes his eyes, continues his fasting duties and 'following the highest ideal of resolution, he placed his head between his hoods and lay perfectly motionless'.

As for the foolish brahmin, the jewel slips from his hand as he takes it from Alambayana and is immediately lost to the *naga* underworld. Figure 4.76 portrays Alambayana holding Bhuridatta over his shoulders as he leaves the forest. He now intends to travel from village to village, earning gold and money as a snake charmer. Bhuridatta is forced to live in a small basket and endure Alambayana's mistreatment.

Figure 4.77 is the final storyboard scene from bowls S88 and S7. It portrays Bhuridatta in the form of a serpent entertaining the king and queen of Benares. The wicked Alambayana, dressed as a poor brahmin with a feather-like headdress, stretches forward to exhort Bhuridatta to perform. A figure in the top-right corner of the scene wears a *naga* headdress and holds up his hands, perhaps in a gesture of protest or anger. This is probably Sudassana, Bhuridatta's brother.

A condensed account of the conclusion to the Jataka follows to explain this last illustration: Sudassana was searching the human world for his long-lost *naga* brother; eventually he reached Benares and soon realized that the serpent performing before the king was Bhuridatta. Sudassana confronts Alambayana and they agree to match their powers in an open contest; Sudassana reveals a poison so strong that it could destroy the kingdom of Benares; Alambayana is humbled and terrified by the poison's power and quickly concedes the contest and agrees to set the serpent free; finally, Bhuridatta emerges radiant from his basket in human form and is reunited with his brother. Soon after, the brothers return to the *naga* world, and Bhuridatta, 'having kept the precepts all his life and performed all the duties of the fast-day, at the end of his life went with a host of other *nagas* to fill the seats of heaven'. The evil Alambayana becomes a leper!

4.76 Alamabayana takes possession of Bhuridatta

4.77 Bhuridatta entertains the king and queen of Benares

4.78 Cheroot Box S56

4.79 Panorama storyboard on S56

Vidhura-Pandita Jataka

The Vidhura-Pandita Jataka (No. 546 of the Jataka tales) is an inspiring narrative that teaches the essential moral value of truth. It incorporates the drama of young love, misunderstood language, a supernatural horse, high-stakes gambling, abduction, attempted murder, reconciliation and, finally, the revelation of truth. Burmese silversmiths had a penchant for crafting majestic silver images of the supernatural horse. This popular horse was the mount of Punnaka, a *yakka* general and a demon spirit. His supernatural horse is featured in six of the seven Jataka scenes on the offering bowl S126 (Fig. 4.80) and

4.80 Offering Bowl S126

the rectangular cheroot box S56 (Fig. 4.78). The decorative scenes from all sides of the cheroot box are illustrated in a panoramic storyboard format in Fig. 4.79.

A short introduction to the Jataka is required to understand the visual narratives. Vidhura-Pandita was a wise minister and sage to King Dhananjaya in the kingdom of Kura. He had a sweet tongue and gave eloquent instructions concerning temporal and spiritual matters to hundreds of spell-bound kings at the court of King Dhananjaya. Vidhura-Pandita's fame also spread to the underworld kingdom of the *nagas*, where Queen Vimala longed to hear his discourses but knew he would never visit the underworld. This realization made the queen deeply unhappy and in her desperation she exclaimed to her husband that she desired the 'heart' of Vidhura-Pandita, otherwise she would die. Naturally, the king was unwilling to perform this dire request. Instead, he persuaded his beautiful daughter Irandati to seek a husband with the power to fulfil her mother's desire. Irandati agreed and devised a clever plan to attract such a powerful husband. She prepared a nighttime garden in the mountain spread with perfumed flowers and here she

4.81 The demon Punnaka courts the *naga* princess Irandati

danced and sang songs appealing for a powerful husband able to bring her mother the heart of Vidhura-Pandita. At the same moment Punnaka was flying above her on his supernatural Sindh horse and heard her sweet siren songs. Overcome by her voice and beauty, he descended to the garden and made a promise to Irandati in these words: 'Oh lady, I can bring you Vidhura's heart by my knowledge, holiness and calmness. Be comforted, I will be thy husband.'

Figure 4.81 illustrates this garden scene. Irandati is identified by her serpent-head *naga* headdress and Punnaka wears the face mask of a *yakka* demon. His caparisoned horse grazes and waits at his side. The garden is filled with a variety of pretty flowers, bushes and trees. A respectful distance separates the courting couple and Irandati's body language suggests both happiness and a coy allure. After the couple agree to marry, Punnaka flies Irandati back to her father's palace and asks the king for permission to marry his daughter.

The *naga* king and queen agreed to the marriage on one condition: Punnaka must first deliver the heart of Vidhura-Pandita. Punnaka, although filled with passion and desire for Irandati, dared not fulfil the marriage condition without the permission of Vessavana, his respected *yakka* uncle. To obtain this approval, Punnaka had to fly a long distance on his Sindh horse. When he eventually found Vessavana, he was already busy resolving the case of two disputants and Punnaka was required to wait patiently for an audience with his uncle. During this wait he overheard Vessavana instruct one of the disputants to 'Go thou and dwell in thy palace'. Punnaka, impatient and deceitful, seized on the words 'Go, thou' to falsely confirm his uncle's permission to bring the heart of Vidhura-Pandita to Queen Vimala. Without further ado, he mounted his magical steed and rose into the sky in search of the sage Vidhura-Pandita.

The scene in Fig. 4.82 depicts Punnaka's grand departure from his uncle's home. His majestic caparisoned horse is

4.82 Punnaka and his supernatural horse surrounded by *yakka* demons

4.83 Punnaka's supernatural horse

rearing up on its hind legs, ready to fly away. Punnaka sits confidently astride his horse, holding the reins with one hand and a raised sword in the other. Five *yakka* soldiers on the ground brandish their swords in a farewell salute. A small figure in the top right corner of the image observes Punnaka's departure. The figure wears a court minister's hat and is most likely a representation of Vidhura-Pandita, although his presence in this scene is an invention of the silversmith. The supernatural horse in Fig. 4.83 is a fine example of the silversmith's skill in rendering the dynamism and anatomy of a powerful horse.

Punnaka pondered at length on how to defeat King Dhananjaya and claim Vidhura-Pandita as his prize. Since force was not an option, he decided to exploit the king's renowned interest and skill in gambling. A game of dice on a silver board was proposed and King Dhananjaya readily accepted Punnaka's challenge. In fact, the king was so confident of winning that he offered Punnaka everything he possessed, except

his body and white umbrella, if he were beaten. In return, Punnaka agreed to give the king his supernatural horse and a magical lapis lazuli gem if he lost the game. Figure 4.84 is a splendid panoramic view of the dice competition in the gaming hall of the king's palace. This silver artwork decorates the lid of the cheroot box illustrated in Fig. 4.78. It faithfully reproduces many details of the Jataka narrative.

The focus of the panorama is the small dice box standing on a circular pedestal or table in the centre of the hall. King Dhananjaya (right) and Punnaka (left) sit on ornate benches either side of the table. A servant holds a royal fan over the king's head and Punnaka's demon facemask is raised on his forehead to reveal an underlying human face. He offers the dice to the king for the first throw. Vidhura-Pandita sits on a less ornate bench on the left of the hall. He wears the cylindrical hat and costume of a court minister and raises his left hand, perhaps to warn the king not to challenge the demon power of Punnaka. An elegant and noteworthy lady is sitting on another royal bench on the right side of the gaming hall. She is King Dhananjaya's guardian deity, who tries unsuccessfully to help the king win the game. A figure standing between the two dice players is perhaps the court referee, while a tall army general with his sword at the ready stands menacingly behind Punnaka. The other figures witnessing this high-stakes game of dice include ministers, courtiers and visiting kings.

4.84 King Dhananjaya and Punnaka play dice

4.85 Vidhura-Pandita is taken from the king by Punnaka

The narrative continues. King Dhananjaya throws the dice first and can see they are falling against him. In desperation he tries three times to magically re-order the fall of the dice with the help of his guardian deity but fails each time. Next, Punnaka throws the dice and they land in his favour. He wins the game and demonstrates that his *yakka* power is superior to the combined magic of the king and his guardian. King Dhananjaya is distraught at losing and pleads with Punnaka not to claim the famous sage as his prize. Understandably, Punnaka will not compromise and retorts with these words: 'Elephants, oxen, horses, jewels and earrings, whatever gems thou hast in the earth, Vidhura is the best of them all; he has been won by me, pay him down to me.' Vidhura-Pandita must now comply with the demon's demand because the king had made a solemn promise before he gambled. He attaches only one condition to the promise – to spend three days with his family and have a final discourse on the value of truth with all the kings assembled at the palace.

Figure 4.85 illustrates Punnaka's triumphal departure from the court of King Dhananjaya. The scene is set outside the crenallated defensive walls of the city. The great sage stands under a gnarled old tree, clinging to a rope held by Punnaka. The *yakka* now reveals his demon face and sits boldly astride his powerful horse. Vidhura-Pandita is soon to be dragged into the sky on a journey to Black Mountain. King Dhananjaya stands in the foreground beneath a large white umbrella lamenting the irresponsible loss of his great sage. He is surrounded by a mournful group of courtiers and citizens.

In a foretaste of what lies ahead, Punnaka warns the sage: 'Thou standest here as one about to cross – this is a long journey before thee. Take hold without fear, of the tail of thy noble steed, this is the last sight of the world of the living.'

Vidhura-Pandita replies: 'Of whom shall I be afraid, when I have done no evil to him by body, speech or thought, whereby I could come to misfortune?' The supernatural horse then bounds into the sky with the Bodhisattva sage clinging desperately to his long tail. King Dhananjaya then speaks these prescient words: 'The sage is wise, and learned, and skilful; he will soon set himself free. Fear not, he will be back.'

Punnaka's plan is to quickly slay the sage by dashing him against the many rocks and trees during the flight to Black Mountain. When Vidhura-Pandita miraculously survives this ordeal unscathed, Punnaka next decides to kill the sage with his own hands and take out his heart. Figure 4.86 portrays this dramatic moment on Black Mountain. Vidhura-Pandita lies on the ground looking up fearlessly at the menacing demon. Punnaka holds out a sword ready to strike and appears intent on taking the sage's heart. Punnaka's caparisoned horse rears up powerfully above the sage and his hooves threaten to crush the sage. Two *naga* ladies with serpent headdresses stand on either side of the horse in the foreground, while another observes from a building in the background in the company of a *yakka* demon.

As the narrative continues, there is a turn of events. Vidhura-Pandita is not killed by the *yakka*. Punnaka has second thoughts about murdering his captive and decides instead to try and indirectly cause Vidhura-Pandita's death by showing him frightful shapes and beings – a demon, a lion, a furious elephant and a great serpent. However, this is all to no avail and the sage remains calm and unruffled. Next, the *yakka* makes the mountain shake and conjures up tumultuous rain and wind. Again, without effect. In desperation, Punnaka 'seized the Great Being violently and whirled him around, and flung him head downwards into the sky, where there was nothing

4.86 Punnaka prepares to slay Vidhura-Pandita on Black Mountain

4.87 Vidhura-Pandita gives Punnaka a discourse on truth

4.88 Punnaka returns Vidhura-Pandita to King Dhananajaya

that he could lay hold of'. During this torture, Punnaka began to converse with the sage, and soon experienced an epiphany. He suddenly understood why his calamitous effort to slay Vidhura-Pandita had come about – it was a direct result of misunderstanding Queen Vimala's request. She metaphorically demanded Vidhura-Pandita's heart, not his physical heart and therefore his death. The queen had only desired to hear the sage's powerful discourses on holy law and to appreciate his spiritual heart.

Vidhura-Pandita then offered to take his own life if only Punnaka would first listen to a discourse on the laws of good men that had 'the power to bring light to the world and reveal absolute truths'. Punnaka, wishing to hear these laws, set Vidhura-Pandita down again on the summit of Black Mountain and brought the sage bathing water, heavenly food, clothes and perfume before the start of the discourse. He also prepared a richly decorated seat for the sage and summoned the most righteous Kurus people to hear the mountain-top discourse. Figure 4.87 pictures the discourse between the sage and the *yakka* on Black Mountain. Vidhura-Pandita sits on an ornate bench and Punnaka kneels before him on a tree stump with his hands raised in respect. His aggressive horse observes the discourse and is soothed. A *naga* lady stands in the background looking intently towards Vidhura-Pandita. This is probably a symbolic image of Queen Vimala who so desperately wished to hear the eloquent sage's holy discourse. The Jataka narrative does not place her on Black Mountain during this event.

The Black Mountain discourse had a profound impact on Punnaka. The wise and truthful words of the sage opened his eyes to the duties of a good man, and he immediately offered to free Vidhura-Pandita. The sage countered by asking the *yakka* to take him directly to the *naga* kingdom to meet King Varuna and to calm his queen's desire to hear his soft words of wisdom. Punnaka agreed and they flew directly to the *naga* underworld, whereupon Vidhura-Pandita spoke at length to the queen and her family. King Varuna was joyful at hearing the sage's words and replied: 'The heart of sages is their wisdom – we are delighted today with thy wisdom. Let Punnaka take his bride today and let him return the sage today to his land of the Kurus.' Thereupon, Punnaka placed Vidhura-Pandita on the

horse's saddle and they both rode swiftly to the great sage's home in the city of Indapatta.

Figure 4.88 illustrates Punnaka and Vidhura-Pandita arriving before the ceremonial gates of Indapatta. Punnaka gently supports Vidhura-Pandita with his hand and the sage holds the horse's neck. King Dhananjaya waits outside the city for the return of his wise counsellor, an event he'd foreseen the night before in a vivid dream. This joyful scene ends the Jataka storyboard on the silverwork. The narrative concludes as follows: Punnaka delivers the sage to the centre of the Hall of Truth in the king's palace; Princess Irandati and Punnaka are married in the *yakka*'s celestial city; King Dhananjaya organizes a month-long festival to celebrate the return of his wise sage; royal courtiers, visiting kings and all the citizens of Indapatta attend the festival; and Vidhura-Pandita, the Bodhisattva sage, having fulfilled his duties on earth to always speak the truth, completes his destiny and ascends to heaven.

Vessantara Jataka

The Vessantara Jataka (No. 547 of the Jataka tales) is the most sacred narrative in the Buddhist world. It is commonly represented on Burmese silverwork and in the art of all Buddhist countries. The tale is an allegory on the virtues of generosity – the act of giving in the literal sense. It is the last and most important of the 10 ethical standards a Bodhisattva must perfect to achieve Buddhahood. Therefore, the act of giving earns relatively more karmic merit than any other aspect of everyday Buddhist practice. The two artefacts selected to illustrate the Vessantara Jataka are S86 (Fig. 4.89) – a large treasure box; and S110 (Fig. 4.90) – a ceremonial offering bowl decorated with elements of both Shan and Lower Burma regional styles.

4.89 Treasure Box S86

4.90 Offering Bowl S110

4.91 Prince Vessantara gifts the elephant Paccaya to eight brahmins

Figures 4.91–96 portray six of the most informative and popular episodes from the Jataka.

The narrative begins in the city of Jetuttara in the kingdom of Sivi. Vessantara is the first child of King Sanjaya and Queen Phusati. He is also a Bodhisattva. An auspicious white elephant was left in the royal animal stable by a flying elephant god on the day of Vessantara's birth. This white elephant was named Paccaya because it was born for one purpose: to commemorate the birth of the Bodhisattva. Vessantara's selfless generosity was evident from birth and he continuously gifted large numbers of gold coins and ornaments to his nurses and courtiers. At the age of 16 he was appointed as the viceroy of Sivi and in the same year he married Princess Maddi. The couple had two children: Jali, a son and Kanhajina, a daughter.

Many years later there was a severe drought and famine in a nearby kingdom. The desperate citizens, realizing that the king's efforts to bring rain had failed, informed him that in Sivi there lived a generous prince named Vessantara, who owned a lucky white elephant that brought rain wherever it travelled. This valuable information prompted the king to dispatch eight brahmins to Jetuttara to ask Prince Vessantara to gift him the lucky elephant. The prince, true to his generous nature, agreed without hesitation.

Figure 4.91 is a masterful rendition of Vessantara giving the royal white elephant to the eight brahmins. Forty-one human figures and Paccaya fill the panoramic canvas on three decorative levels: a colonnaded balcony for the courtiers in the background; a mid-level throne platform for the prince and his family; and the paved foreground to parade Paccaya and his mahouts. Vessantara sits on the edge of a grand throne in the centre of the scene together with his wife Maddi and their two children. He is pouring water on the outstretched hands of a brahmin in a Buddhist ritual to consummate the gift to his starving neighbours. Paccaya is majestically proportioned and elegantly caparisoned. Two brahmins are preparing to receive Paccaya: one holds the elephant's tusk and touches his forehead and the other is pushing from behind. The eight brahmins are identified by their tall, rounded hats with a spiked finial.

The citizens of Sivi were naturally incensed that Vessantara had donated their auspicious white elephant to another kingdom. They claimed he was ruining Sivi and petitioned King Sanjaya to banish the prince to distant Crooked Mountain in the Himalayas. The king reluctantly agreed and ordered his son to leave Sivi. Vessantara accepted his fate, but first insisted on performing the ritual of the 'gift of seven hundred' – the giving away of seven hundred elephants, horses, chariots, male and female slaves, food, drink and everything of quality to the citizens of Sivi. The prince and his family then took leave of the king and queen and began their journey into exile in an everyday horse-drawn carriage. Once outside the city they were soon stopped by four brahmins who had arrived too late for the 'gift of seven hundred' ritual and audaciously asked Vessantara to gift them the carriage horses as compensation

4.92 A brahmin asks Vessantara to gift his royal carriage

4.93 Vessantara gifts his two children to the brahmin Jujaka

4.94 Jujaka leads Vessantara's captive children away

for their tardiness. Figure 4.92 illustrates this event. A brahmin raises his hand to stop Vessantara's horse-drawn carriage and asks for the horses as a gift. The large wheel of the royal carriage is decorated with a traditional floral motif and the family sits above on the ornate carriage frame. Vessantara happily grants the brahmin's request and the horses are taken away. Shortly thereafter they meet another brahmin; this time the prince gives away the carriage, leaving the family to continue their long journey to Crooked Mountain on foot. This journey and the family's arrival in a beautiful forest valley are described at length in the Jataka, but rarely feature in the visual narratives on Burmese silverwork.

Figure 4.93 is set in a spartan hermitage in a forest where Vessantara and his family live an ascetic life sustained only by wild fruits, berries and plant roots. One day, an old and deceitful brahmin named Jujaka visits Vessantara while Madi is collecting food and water in the forest. Jujaka is married to a young woman in a distant village, who is teased by the other village women due to her husband's old age. She refuses to collect water and commands Jujaka to bring her a slave. The brahmin, knowing Vessantara's reputation for generosity,

decides to travel to Crooked Mountain and ask the ascetic to gift his children so that he can provide slaves for his young wife. Vessantara agrees and is full of joy at making the perfect gift of his beloved children and utters these words: 'Omniscience is a hundred times, a thousand times, a hundred thousand times more precious to me than my son!' He then watches as Jujaka binds and beats his children before dragging them away.

The Jataka narrative describes this heartbreaking event as follows: 'Then that cruel brahmin bit off a creeper. With the creeper he bound their hands, with the creeper he thrashed them. Then, holding a rope and a stick, the brahmin led them away, beating them while the Sivi prince looked on.' This event is pictured on a side panel of the treasure box (Fig. 4.94). Vessantara stands without remorse before his hermitage, while Jujaka leads Jali and Kanhajina away.

The Jataka narrative describes two events that occurred when Vessantara gave away his children: the earth roared as high as Brahma's heaven; and the spirits who live on Mount Himavat heard the grief-filled cries of Jali and Kanhajina who were now Jujaka's prisoners. These caring spirits also realized that Maddi was collecting food in the forest while Vessantara

4.95 Wild animals block Madi's passage in the forest

was giving away her children and would suffer great anguish if she returned home to see them with Jujaka. To avoid this terrible encounter, the spirits devise a subterfuge to prevent Madi from returning home before sunset. Figure 4.95 portrays the subterfuge. Madi, balancing a tall basket of fruit on her head, is warding off the approach of a ferocious lion and tiger that block her way forward. However, she is in no danger because these animals are in fact gods in disguise who take part in the subterfuge. Later, Maddi successfully entreats the animals to let her pass and she returns home by moonlight only to discover the tragic loss of her children.

The next day Vessantara welcomed a second brahmin to his hermitage and asked the reason for his visit. His reply was direct: 'I am a very old man. I have come here to ask for your wife Maddi. Give her to me.' Vessantara, wishing to free himself of all attachments in order to achieve omniscience, did not hesitate to give his wife to the brahmin and spoke these words: 'I give what you ask of me brahmin, and I do not hesitate. I do not keep back what I have. My mind is glad at the gift.' The old brahmin then revealed himself as the god Sakka. He had tested Vessantara's generosity for the last time and promptly returned Maddi to Vessantara. The prince had now perfected the supreme virtue of generosity. Sakka then granted Vessantara eight wishes and returned to heaven.

Meanwhile, Jujaka travelled 60 leagues through the forest with Vessantara's children. During the night he would tie the children to a tree and make them lie on the ground, while he climbed a tree and slept in a fork of the branches, fearing attack by wild animals. Figure 4.96 illustrates this reprehensible behaviour. The portly Jujaka lies in the tree holding ropes attached to the wrists of Jali and Kanhajina on the ground below. The two figures guarding the children from behind the bushes on the left are divine spirits, who have taken the form of the children's parents. Each night they bathe, feed and guard Jali and Kanhajina to ease their suffering. This is the last

illustrated scene on the offering bowl and cheroot storage box, but it does not conclude the Jataka narrative. The dramatic turn of events that provide closure to this psychologically difficult Jataka are now summarized.

After a two-week journey, Jujaka and the captive children mysteriously arrive in Jetuttara and not, as intended, in his home village. Unknown to him, he is possessed by a deity in the form of a spirit. The deity leads Jujaka and the children to Vessantara's father, King Sanjaya, who ransoms his grandchildren for gold coins and gives the evil brahmin a seven-storied palace and a large retinue. A week later the king and his army find Vessantara and Maddi on Crooked Mountain and the whole family is reunited. Meanwhile, the evil Jujaka ate and drank too much in his new palace and died of indigestion. All his wealth, so recently bestowed on him as a ransom, reverted to King Sanjaya. The supremely generous Prince Vessantara returned triumphantly to Jetuttara and was crowned the new king of Sivi. The Jataka narrative concludes with these words to celebrate his return:

> At the entrance of Vessantara, the bringer of prosperity to the kingdom of the Sivis, the god made fall on that place a shower of gold.
>
> The noble king Vessantara, after so much giving, at the dissolution of his body, full of wisdom, was reborn in heaven.

4.96 Jujaka sleeps in a tree above the roped children

Therigatha Scriptural Poem

The Therigatha (also known as 'Verses of the Elder Nuns') are a collection of 73 short poems composed by the earliest Buddhist nuns in the 6th to 3rd centuries BCE. They were first passed on by oral tradition and then written down in the Pali language in about 80 BCE. The 73 poems are organized into 16 chapters of the Khuddaka Nikaya. This is a collection of short books in the Sutta Pitaka, the second of three scriptural 'baskets' in the Tripitaka. The poems recount the struggles and accomplishments of the early nuns along the path to enlightenment. These stories comprise the earliest collection of women's literature composed in India.

Patacara – Preserver of the Vinaya

The tragic yet inspirational five-verse Patacara poem is found in the fifth chapter of the Therigatha collection. It is an allegorical tale of how loving-kindness can restore mindfulness and virtue in the face of grief and great tragedy, thereby purifying the path to enlightenment.

Patacara was born in the 6th century BCE in Savatthi, India, in the present-day states of Bihar and Uttar Pradesh. She was a contemporary of the Buddha during his last existence on earth. The exceptional offering bowl by Maung Shwe Yon (Fig. 4.97) is adorned with 10 poignant scenes from her calamitous early life. Patacara was the attractive young daughter of wealthy and overprotective parents. She was effectively imprisoned in her own house and not allowed to meet any young men until her

4.97 Offering Bowl S115

marriage could be arranged with a suitor of affluence and high social status. Unsurprisingly, this approach to parenting had unintended and painful consequences. At 16, Patacara fell in love with the only young man in her life – a handsome household servant and her putative guard.

Figure 4.98 begins the gripping story of Patacara's early life. It is set in Patacara's bed chamber. The young girl is sitting comfortably on an elegant couch, which is draped in a rich, folded fabric. Patacara looks radiant. All aspects of her dress, hairstyle, pierced ears and body curves are executed in lovely detail. She gazes directly into the eyes of her servant and her body language is clearly flirtatious. The servant returns her inquiring look from a subservient kneeling position beneath Patacara's feet. His right hand rests suggestively on Patacara's couch in a gesture that symbolically expresses his desire for the young girl. This gesture was surely a breach of strict social and employment protocol. It is also a hint of the events to follow. The servant's low social status is emphasized by the traditional tattoos on his thigh, his simple *longyi* wrapped between his legs and his bare torso. A silver vase containing flowers and an empty silver bowl stand on top of a tall chest of drawers draped with a delicately patterned cloth. Also note the rich damask-like fabric on the wall behind Patacara and the intricacy of the floor design. In summary, this scene is a masterful introduction to the tale of the two 'star-crossed' lovers – the young Patacara and her adoring servant.

Patacara's story now begins. She learns that her parents have arranged her marriage to a stranger who is the scion of a wealthy family in Savatthi. Patacara is distraught and fatefully decides to follow her heart and defy her parents and convention. She elopes with her handsome servant to a remote village far from Savatthi and the reach of her parents. Figure 4.99 is a portrait of the young couple eloping. Patacara carries a few personal possessions in a bundle on her head and leans forwards towards her lover and erstwhile servant. He tenderly wraps his hand around her shoulders. They look at each other with deep affection and perhaps with some trepidation in the knowledge of the difficult life they now face. This is a tender artistic portrait of the two lovers. The superb quality of the workmanship is evident in the beautiful rendition of

4.98 Patacara looks lovingly at her servant

4.99 Patacara and her servant elope

the human forms, the body language, facial emotions, and the lavish design of Patacara's flowing costume.

The setting of the story now moves to a small village in the forest. The young couple marry and begin a new life as farmers. Patacara is soon pregnant and intent on following tradition by returning to her parents' house for the birth of the child. Unsurprisingly, Patacara's husband fears the dire consequences of returning to Savatthi and delays their departure. This ploy is successful and Patacara delivers a baby boy in the forest before they can reach Savatthi. A few years later, Patacara is pregnant again. This time she is determined to return to her parents' house for the birth and sets off with her young child while her husband is away in the forest collecting food and water. However, her timing is not propitious, and she is quickly caught in the open during a violent storm.

Figure 4.100 is set in a makeshift shelter deep in the forest during the storm. The scene takes place after Patacara's husband returned home and discovered that his wife and child had already left for Savatthi. Fearing for their safety, he tracked their path and eventually found them bedraggled and unprotected. He addressed this immediate danger by quickly constructing a makeshift shelter and searching the forest for firewood. Patacara is portrayed in Fig. 4.100 sitting on a simple bamboo bench in the shelter. She has just given birth to her second son. The baby is swaddled in a neatly wrapped cloth and suckles at his mother's breast. Her first son stands naked before her with one hand resting gently on her knee. A simple tripod cooking pot sits over a log fire in the foreground. Patacara's husband is noticeably absent from the nativity

scene. He is searching the forest again for firewood. Figure 4.101 is a statuesque portrait of him striding purposefully back to his family in the makeshift shelter. He carries a machete in his left hand and a heavy load of wood on his shoulder.

The narrative now turns tragic. Patacara's husband did not return to the shelter with the firewood. Patacara waited all night to see him again, but in the morning concluded that he had abandoned his family because he was too afraid of returning to Savatthi and facing the consequences of the elopement. Patacara's only option now is to return home alone with her children. Thus, begins a calamitous journey. Soon after leaving the shelter she discovers the body of her husband lying in the forest. He was bitten by a venomous snake while cutting a tree that stood on top of an anthill that hid the snake. Patacara weeps and laments in grief for a day and a night beside her husband and blames herself for his terrible death. Figure 4.102 illustrates Patacara's grief in poignant detail. She is kneeling behind the prostrate and lifeless body of her husband. One hand covers her tormented face and the other cradles the newborn baby. The older son gazes up at his grieving mother and mournfully lays one hand on his father's shoulder. This is a remarkable artistic rendition of this emotional event.

Figure 4.103 is an image of Patacara and her children as they begin their journey home to Savatthi. The sleeping baby is tightly wrapped in a maternity cloth and the older child stands on the ground looking up at his mother with his right hand raised. His body language suggests that he is reluctant to leave his dead father in the forest, or is just too tired to continue the long walk. Patacara's attention is clearly directed at the boy

4.100 Patacara holds her newborn second son

4.101 Patacara's husband collects wood in the forest

and she places a hand on his shoulder as if to comfort him and give him strength. Maung Shwe Yon's fine attention to detail and artistry is exemplified by his execution of the maternity cloth – the small folds of the fabric, the light polka-dot pattern and its natural cocoon-like form.

Patacara is half-way home and now faces the challenge of crossing the River Aciravati, which is swollen due to the terrible storm of the previous night. She is too weak and distraught to cross the river carrying both children and decides to take one across at a time. First, she carries the newborn to the opposite side of the river and places the child on an improvised cradle made from nearby tree branches. Next, she wades back into the river to pick up her first son who was left alone on the opposite bank. Patacara's plan now unravels. She is in the middle of re-crossing the river when an eagle mistakes the newborn baby lying in the branches as prey. It swoops down and seizes the baby in its talons, and, despite Patacara's desperate screams, flies away into the distance. And, if this is not tragedy enough, the child remaining on the near bank of the river mistakes his mother's screams as a signal to walk into the river towards Patacara and quickly drowns in the swift currents and swirling water.

Figure 4.104 details this heart-breaking scene. Patacara's clothes have been stripped off by the raging water and she reaches up in a futile effort to rescue her baby from the talons of the mighty eagle. The mother and the child look directly at each other and their hands almost touch in the final moment before the eagle flies away. In the same instant, the older son is being swept away by the river in flood. His torso is already

submerged and only his small face and hands are visible above the water. The child appears to look towards his mother for the last time and his tiny curled hands beg her to save him, but to no avail. Patacara has now lost her husband and her two young children on the ill-fated journey to her parents' home.

The portrayal of Patacara in the River Aciravati is a sublime example of Burmese silver art. It is arguably the most aesthetic work in the Noble Silver Collection. Few other Burmese master silversmiths were able to craft silver like an artist paints a picture and imbue human forms with emotion and life.

Patacara is now alone, naked and bedraggled. She is also in a state of utter shock and deep grief. On the outskirts of Savatthi she meets a traveller and plaintively asks for information about the whereabouts of her parents. The traveller's cryptic reply is that he knows her parents but will not speak of them. In desperation, Patacara asks the question a second time and he reluctantly discloses that her parents' house collapsed during the recent storm and her father, mother and brother all died. He points to smoke rising in the distance from their funeral pyre. This culmination of tragedies causes Patacara to lose her mind and she wails these words:

My children both are gone, and in the bush
Dead lies my husband; on one funeral pyre
My mother, father and my brother burn.

Figure 4.105 portrays Patacara's meeting with the traveller. She buries her head in her hand and her grief is almost palpable. The traveller looks down on her kindly, but the body

4.102 Patacara and her two children mourn their father's death

4.103 A reluctant child is led away from his father by Patacara

4.104 The tragic death of Patacara's two sons

4.105 A traveller informs Patacara of the death of her family

4.106 Two heavenly deities observe and guide Patacara

4.107 The Buddha advises Patacara on the path to enlightenment

language of his folded arms suggests sympathy but little empathy. Patacara's fate will now be determined by the gods and the Buddha.

First the gods intervene. Figure 4.106 portrays two deities in heaven staring intently down towards earth. Their hands are clasped and raised as if in prayer. Each is dressed in a sumptuous Burmese royal costume and wearing a crown-like headdress. The body language and facial expressions suggest benevolence and concern. This episode is not found in the translation of the original scriptural poem. The silversmith perhaps added the deities to the storyboard to emphasize the sacred powers of the gods to intervene in the lives of all men and women. The two deities in this scene are witnessing Patacara wandering naked around Savatthi and behaving in a demented fashion. The reaction of the cruel citizens of her former hometown is to pelt her with rubbish and clods of earth. This is the nadir of her suffering. The deities are finally moved by her deep distress and misfortune and intervene in her life for the first time. Unbeknownst to Patacara, they guide her towards the Buddha, who by good fortune was currently speaking to his disciples in the Jeta grove close to Savatthi.

When Patacara enters the Jeta grove, she is at first held back by the Buddha's disciples because she is still naked and deranged. The Buddha observes this and rebukes his disciples because he has recognized that Patacara had earned great merit in her former lives. He bids Patacara to 'recover her presence of mind' and infuses her mind with his spirit of redemption. This spirit restores her sanity and she falls to the

ground and worships at the Buddha's feet. Figure 4.107 portrays this moment of redemption. The Buddha is dressed in the simple robes of an ascetic and is identified by three unique features of Buddhist iconography: an *ushnisha*, or crown of hair; a radiant star-like nimbus surrounding his head; and a lotus leaf under his bare feet. Patacara is kneeling on the ground with her head lowered and her hands clasped in veneration of the Buddha. She tells him the reason for her grief and the Buddha explains that wasted tears shed for the loss of all things impermanent are greater than all the water in four oceans. Patacara is consoled by these words of wisdom and soon realizes that brooding and crying will not lead her to salvation. Understanding this wisdom lightens her grief and restores her state of mind.

Finally, the Buddha advises Patacara on the right path to enlightenment:

O Patacara, to one passing to another world no child nor other kin is able to be a shelter or a hiding place or a refuge. Therefore, let who so is wise purify his own conduct, and accomplish the Path leading even to Nirvana.

Thus, Patacara understood the impermanence of all things and began a new life. She was immediately admitted by the Buddha into the *sangha*, or Buddhist community, as an ordained nun and thereafter she dedicated her life to preserving the integrity of the Vinaya, the rules of conduct for Buddhist monks and nuns.

4.108 Rama is commanded by his father to slay the demon Tataka

Ramayana Epic – The Deeds of Rama

The Ramayana is an epic Indian poem that narrates the heroic life of the legendary Prince Rama. It was written in Sanskrit by the great poet Valmiki between the 4th and 2nd centuries BCE, although the poem undoubtedly has an earlier oral origin. It comprises seven Kandas, or sections, and 24,000 verses. Each Kanda describes a period in the life of Rama, from his early childhood to old age. The poem is one of the world's most important and longest literary works. It is a profound allegory on moral behaviour and duty, particularly with respect to the archetypal relationships between fathers, sons, brothers, wives and kings. The timeless value of this narrative has moulded and defined many aspects of the Hindu character over millennia and strongly influenced Indian and Southeast Asian art, culture, religion and politics.

The Ramayana most likely came to Burma from India as an oral tradition during the Pyu Period (1st to 9th centuries CE). The oldest surviving images of Rama are found at Bagan in the Abeyadana temple, built by King Kyansittha (r. 1084–1113 CE). Today, there are 13 historical Burmese-language versions of the Ramayana, all of which differ in considerable detail from the original Indian Valmiki version. Nevertheless, the underlying narrative of the Indian and Burmese versions is similar. Many of the Burmese versions were transcribed in the late 19th century from older palm-leaf scripts and printed manuscripts. The Ramayana poem is also incorporated into the Buddhist Jataka number 461, which dates from the 5th to 4th centuries BCE.

One of the most popular Burmese versions of the Ramayana is the 'Pondaw Rama', also known as the 'Palace Rama', since it was performed at the royal court of the Konbaung kings. In its original format, the Palace Rama took 65 days to present, with each daily performance lasting three to six hours! After the Buddhist Jataka tales, the Burmese Ramayana is the second most popular visual narrative found on Burmese silverwork. The abduction of Sita by Ravana, described in the third section of the Ramayana (the Aranya Kanda), is the silversmith's most favoured narrative.

Rama and the Demon Tataka

Figure 4.109 illustrates an offering bowl by the award-winning silversmith Maung Po Kin. The five scenes decorating the bowl are from a short story in the Bala Kanda, the first section of the Valmiki version of the Ramayana. The story narrates an encounter between a youthful Rama and Tataka, a beautiful *yaksha* princess who was cursed to become an ugly and evil demon.

The story of Tataka begins when Rama is 16 years old. An honoured sage named Vishwamitra asks King Dasaratha, Rama's father, for help in slaying a demon *rakshasa* named

4.109 Offering Bowl S140

4.110 Rama crosses the Ganges and enters Tataka's forest

4.111 Rama prepares to sever Tataka's hands

Tataka. The *rakshasa* had persistently tormented and harassed the sage as he performed his sacrificial rituals in a forest close to the Ganges river. King Dasaratha agrees to help Vishwamitra and decides to send Rama, his eldest son, to protect the sage from Tataka. Rama is accompanied on the mission by his devoted younger brother, Lakshmana. This is the first time that King Dasaratha has entrusted Rama to independently undertake the responsibilities and duties of a warrior prince. The king is testing Rama's character and resolve.

Figure 4.108 pictures the opening scene of the story. King Dasaratha stretches out an arm as if to command Rama to protect the sage. The youthful Rama sits on a simple bench and raises a sword in his left hand in a symbolic gesture of strength and authority. The figure kneeling to his right carries a machete and looks intently to his right in anticipation of the mission. His identity is uncertain. The tattoos on his thighs and his *longyi* drawn up between his legs discount Lakshmana. He is deduced to be the sage Vishwamitra.

Figure 4.110 depicts Rama walking towards Tataka's forest after crossing the Ganges river near its confluence with the Sarayu river. The swirling, bubbling motif on the left symbolizes the turbulent waters of the two rivers. The tree in front of Rama indicates that the party has reached Tataka's dread forest. Once inside, Rama is soon attacked by Tataka and her *rakshasa* sons Maricha and Subahu. However, Rama and Lakshmana have superior powers and combat skills and soon capture Tataka. Vishwamitra then instructs Rama to kill Tataka without delay in order to free the forest from her terror and permit him to fulfil his rituals in safety.

Rama, however, is reluctant to ignore the warrior code of conduct that forbids the slaying of females. He decides instead to cut off Tataka's hands and thereby prevent her from attacking anyone again. Figure 4.111 shows Rama, his sword raised high, poised to chop off Tataka's two hands, which are pressed to the ground. Tataka has the face of a demon, and her long hair wraps around her crouching body. Vishwamitra

4.112 Rama draws an arrow to slay Tataka

4.113 Tataka's sons descend to earth to attack Rama

observes Tataka's punishment and perhaps his face expresses some doubt as to its efficacy. A radiant sun in the sky symbolizes the new light that will now shine for the first time in Tataka's forest.

However, Tataka is a powerful *rakshasa* and after Rama spares her life she transforms into an invisible demon and simply continues her attacks. Vishwamitra again advises Rama that as a prince he has a duty to protect his people and end Tataka's reign of terror, notwithstanding his personal reluctance to kill a woman. Finally convinced, Rama draws his bow and shoots an arrow that pierces Tataka's heart. Figure 4.112 portrays the death of Tataka. She kneels before the Ganges river with her back to Rama and her head gazing up to the sky. Vishwamitra kneels on the ground and blesses Rama for finally slaying Tataka. In heaven the gods rejoice.

The scene in Fig. 4.113 takes place six days after the death of Tataka and represents the final episode in the Tataka drama. Rama, Lakshmana and Vishwamitra are still in the forest performing sacrificial rituals when they are attacked by Tataka's sons Maricha and Subahu and other demons. The *rakshasas* appear suddenly from the treetops, roaring with a thunderous sound, intent on destroying the sage and his sacrificial fire. Rama responds by firing a magical weapon that hits Maricha in the chest, throwing him far from the forest. Subahu and the other *rakshasas* are eventually slain by Rama and Lakshmana, and Vishwamitra can at long last complete his rituals in peace.

Later in the Ramayana story, Rama marries Sita following guidance given to him by Vishwamitra, while the demon Maricha, who survived the fight with Rama, helps his uncle Ravana to abduct Sita after she married Rama.

4.114 Offering Bowl S147

Key Protagonists

The imposing offering bowl S147 pictured in Fig. 4.114 is embellished with eight silver portraits of the key protagonists of the Ramayana epic. The portraits are crafted in high-relief repoussé work and are set on a pierced background to enhance visual depth and perspective. The anatomy and costume details of each figure are superb. The narrative source of these portraits is the Rama Vatthu, a Burmese palm-leaf text version of the Ramayana dated 1871. The original composition of the Rama Vatthu likely dates to the 17th century. Many of the names of the key protagonists in the Rama Vatthu version of the Ramayana are different from the classical names found in the Indian versions of the poem. Story episodes also vary in detail. These narrative variances sometimes create confusion and inconsistencies in the interpretation of the visual narratives on Burmese silverwork.

Rama (Fig. 4.115) is the central figure in the Ramayana. He is the eldest and favourite son of King Dasaratha and Queen Kosala of Ayuttaya. Rama is an avatar, or incarnation, of Vishnu, the supreme Hindu deity in the Indian version of the Ramayana. In the Burmese version of the poem, he is also a Bodhisattva from Tusita heaven. Rama's marriage to Sita is at the core of the Ramayana story. Rama also has a strong bond with his brother Lakkhana (commonly known as Lakshmana in the Indian Ramayana). The figure of Rama on the bowl is meticulously attired in the ceremonial costume and regalia of a Burmese king. The long, curved bow in his hand is an icon used to identify Rama on many silver artefacts. He is portrayed as a young, handsome man in a dynamic, regal pose.

Sita (Fig. 4.116) is the adopted daughter of King Janaka of Mithila. She is beautiful, virtuous and the avatar of the

4.115 Rama from the Ramayana epic

4.116 Sita, Rama's wife

4.117 Lakkhana, Rama's brother

deity Lakshmi, Vishnu's consort in the Valmiki version of the Ramayana. Sita is also recognized as the celestial goddess of wealth and prosperity. Rama marries Sita following a competition to find a prince who can string the Shiv Dhanush bow owned by Sita's father. Sita follows Rama into exile and is abducted by Ravana. She is portrayed on the silver bowl as a tall, attractive and shapely woman, dressed in the layered costume of a Burmese queen. In her left hand is a piece of fruit, the alms she offered to a disguised ascetic before her abduction. The ascetic was her captor Ravana.

Lakkhana (Fig. 4.117) is Rama's younger brother and married to Sita's younger sister, Urmila. He is a warrior prince and devoted to serving Rama throughout the Ramayana story.

Dasagiri (Fig. 4.118) is the Burmese name for Ravana. He is Rama's nemesis and the king of Theinkho, or Lanka island. Dasagiri is a *rakshasa,* a type of mythological creature whose character can be either good or evil. Dasagiri is an evil *rakshasa* who cannot be killed by a god, a demon or other divine being. He abducts Sita in one of the most frequently illustrated episodes from the Ramayana and flies her to Lanka island to propose marriage. Sita adamantly refuses and is eventually rescued after a long and ferocious war that ends in the defeat of Dasagiri by Rama and his monkey allies. Dasagiri is identified on the bowl by his demon-like face and arrogant, threatening posture. He wields a long, monacing sword above his head to demonstrate his strength and power.

Trighata (Fig. 4.119) is known as Maricha in the Indian version of the Ramayana. She is an evil *rakshasa* who convinces her older brother Dasagiri to abduct and marry Sita in revenge for the slaying of her two sons by Rama. Trighata is most often portrayed on Burmese silverwork in the disguise of a golden deer in the forest. This deer lured Rama and Lakkhana away from Sita and thereby facilitated her abduction by Dasagiri.

4.118 Dasagiri, also known as Ravana

4.119 Trighata, also known as Maricha

4.120 Kotampa, a sage, also known as Vishwamitra

4.121 King Janaka, Sita's stepfather

4.122 Sukrit, king of the Vanaras monkey race

Trighata is then killed in the forest by a golden arrow fired by Rama. She is easily identified by her demon-like face and a headdress comprising the head and multi-pointed antlers of a large golden deer. In Fig. 4.119 she carries a large feather-like object in each hand. These feathers are often carried by female demons, although their symbolism is unknown. Perhaps the silversmith is conflating the *rakshasa* Trighata with a demon-crow named Kakavanna and using crow feather motifs as a generic motif to identify female demons.

Kotampa is the old character holding a walking pole and fan in Fig. 4.120. He is also known as Vishwamitra in the Valmiki Ramayana. He is a great sage, wise man and a former king. Earlier in the Ramayana, Kotampa had requested Rama's help to drive away the crow-demon Kakavanna. Later he advised Rama to attend the archery competition organized by King Janaka to find a husband for his stepdaughter Sita. He also educates Rama and Lakkhana in spiritual and earthly matters.

King Janaka of Mithila, the stepfather of Sita, is portrayed in Fig. 4.121 as an elegantly dressed man writing with a quill pen on a hinged tablet. A regalia-like ring hangs from the back of his long, patterned overcoat and he wears a double-pointed headdress. Perhaps he is recording the results of the archery competition that he arranged to find a husband for his beautiful stepdaughter Sita.

Sukrit (Fig. 4.122) is the rightful king of the Vanaras, a race of magical monkeys. His name is Sugriva in the Valmiki Ramayana. Sukrit's brother Vali usurped his throne, stole his wife and exiled him to the forest. In the Burmese Ramayana, Sukrit is the only witness to Sita's abduction by Dasagiri. Later, he meets Rama and Lakkhana in the forest and agrees to serve Rama in the war against Dasagiri, on the condition that Rama slays his evil brother and restores him as king of the Vanaras. The monkey Hanuman is the chief counsellor to Sukrit and leads the Vanaras army against Dasagiri. King Sukrit is easily recognized among the portraits on bowl S147 by his long tail, monkey-like face, animal toes and royal costume and regalia.

Abduction of Sita

The 'Abduction of Sita' is a collective title for a sequence of 12 scenes from three offering bowls and one fish storage jar (Figs. 4.124–27). This sequence illustrates four events from the interwoven lives of Rama, Sita and Dasagiri (Ravana): Rama and the Archery Competition; the Death of King Dasaratha; Dasigiri Abducts Sita; and Sukrit and Rama Unite Against Dasagiri. These events span many years between the marriage of Rama and Sita, and Sita's abduction and captivity on Lanka island. The source narrative describing these events is found in the first four Kandas of the Valmiki Ramayana.[8]

---

8. This book's account of these four events is brief and incomplete by necessity. The reader is encouraged to peruse abridged translations of the Indian version of the Ramayana poem to fully appreciate and understand the depth and allegorical nature of the epic story.

4.123 Rama wins the hand of Sita at an archery competition

Rama and the Archery Competition

King Janaka has informed the princes of the world that whoever pulls the string of an ancient bow and fires three arrows will marry Princess Sita, his most beautiful and virtuous daughter. This archery competition is artistically portrayed in a detail-filled panorama in Fig. 4.123. Rama is holding up the ancient bow while Lakkhana kneels to his right and passes him an arrow. The demon Dasagiri has already failed to pull the bowstring and now stands in a posture of defeat to the left of Rama. Sita is portrayed in the upper left corner of the image. She is holding out a garland of flowers dedicated to the gods and prays for Rama's victory. The sage Kotampa stands in the

background with his arm outstretched, perhaps to encourage Rama as he pulls the bow. It was Kotampa who first alerted Rama to the competition and advised him to participate. He foresaw that Rama alone would succeed in firing three arrows and thereby win the contest to marry Sita. The Ramayana also records that three of Rama's brothers married Sita's sisters in a family wedding ceremony.

Death of King Dasaratha

A pivotal event in Rama's life occurred some years after his marriage to Sita. His father, King Dasaratha, exiled him to a remote forest for 12 years. The exile fulfilled a 'boon', or favour, made earlier to his manipulative second wife. She wickedly exercised the boon to make her own son the new heir to the kingdom of Ayuttaya. Since Dasaratha was a deeply moral man, he could not deny the boon and was obliged with extreme reluctance to exile Rama. Sita and his devoted brother, Lakkhana, chose to accompany Rama into the forest. Soon thereafter, King Dasaratha died from the grief and anguish of his loss. Figure 4.128 portrays the king's death. He is lying on an ancient tree stump in the palace garden. The three mourners observing the king are, from left to right, Kotampa the sage, Lakkhana and Rama. The silversmith has also added an unusual motif to the scene – a large crane holding a turtle in its mouth (Fig. 4.129). The symbolic meaning of this motif is unknown. Perhaps it relates to the historical story that Valmiki was inspired to write the Ramayana by his deep grief at witnessing a hunter kill an elegant male saurus crane and then hearing the mournful cries of the bird's devoted female partner.[9]

4.124 Salted Fish Jar S152

4.125 Offering Bowl S129

4.126 Offering Bowl S143

4.127 Offering Bowl S151

---

9. This interpretation may be fanciful, since there is no explanation for the unfortunate turtle in the crane's mouth.

4.128 The death of King Dasaratha

4.129 A crane holds a turtle

Dasagiri Abducts Sita

The abduction of Sita takes place during Rama's exile in a forest far from the kingdom of Ayuttaya. It is precipitated by Rama killing the two demon sons of the *rakshasa* Trighata (Maricha). To avenge their death, she devises a cunning plan to abduct Sita and force her to marry her brother, King Dasagiri. Figure 4.130 illustrates the first phase of the plan. Trighata has assumed the form of a beautiful golden deer and she quietly approaches Sita, who is resting with Rama and Lakkhana. Sita is absolutely enchanted by the wild deer and asks Rama to capture the animal alive for her pleasure. Rama reluctantly agrees.

Sita is portrayed in the scene with her hand on her heart, imploring Rama to bring her the deer, not knowing that the deer is a *rakshasa* in disguise. Trighata is easily identified by her demon face and prominent headdress in the form of a deer head with antlers. Trighata's body language clearly intimates her plan to bewitch and beguile Sita. The symbolism of the long feather-like object in her left hand is uncertain, although

4.130 Trighata disguised as a golden deer enchants Sita

4.131 Dasagiri waits for Lakhhana to leave Sita alone

4.132 Rama slays Trighata

4.133 Dasagiri disguised as an ascetic lures Sita beyond her protective circle

4.134 Dasagiri abducts Sita in his flying chariot

the feather is often carried by female demons and *rakshasas*. Rama is holding up a powerful bow and leans towards Sita as she urges him to catch the deer. Lakkhana kneels respectfully behind Rama.

Before Rama enters the forest to catch the deer, he instructs Lakkhana to faithfully protect Sita and always stay by her side. The scene in Fig. 4.131 shows Sita waiting patiently for Rama's return in a forest glade. She is under the watchful eye of both Lakkhana and a menacing figure in the background. This is Dasagiri waiting for an opportunity to abduct Sita. He carries an alms bowl and is disguised as a wizened ascetic. Meanwhile in the forest, Rama realizes that the golden deer he is chasing is the dangerous *rakshasa* Trighata in disguise and not a natural creature. To save Sita, he must quickly kill Trighata.

Figure 4.132 portrays Rama moments before he slays Trighata. He grips her antlers and presses the *rakshasa* to the ground with his foot. Knowing she is about to die, Trighata plays her last trick in the ploy to help Dasagiri abduct Sita – a deceptive lure directed at Sita's guardian. She imitates Rama's voice and cries out aloud the name 'Lakkhana'. Sita hears these fearful cries and concludes that Rama must be in mortal danger. She pleads with Lakkhana to go to Rama's defence and to disobey his solemn injunction to never leave her alone and unprotected. Lakkhana reluctantly succumbs to Sita's appeal, but not before he draws a protective magic circle around her and warns her never to step outside it until he returns with Rama.

Unfortunately, the magic circle cannot protect Sita from her own pious good nature and generosity. When Dasagiri steps out of the shadows in the disguise of an old ascetic and asks for the gift of alms, Sita without hesitation steps beyond the protection of the magic circle and generously offers him fresh fruit. This moment is captured in Fig. 4.133. Dasagiri is dressed in the simple robes of an ascetic and he carries a large alms bowl. He is wearing the headdress of a 'holy man' and his face is deeply lined to underscore his age and wisdom. The silversmith has also included Trighata in this scene wearing the disguise of a deer to symbolize her role in the deception of Sita. In the true chronology of events, Rama had already slain Trighata elsewhere in the forest with the help of Lakkhana.

4.135 Dasagiri attempts to seduce Sita

Sita is now ensnared by Dasagiri. He quickly reverts to his demon form after accepting the meritorious offer of fruit from Sita and bundles her into his magical aerial chariot. The abduction is complete and Sita is flown away to the kingdom of Theinkho. This flight is illustrated in Fig. 4.134. Dasagiri is portrayed with his arms wrapped around Sita's shoulders while she gazes into the distance with indifference, and perhaps defiance. On the ground beneath the chariot an eagle-eyed reader might recognize the back of a monkey who is hanging on to the chariot in a forlorn effort to impede the abduction. This monkey is Sukrit, the only witness to Sita's fate. Another noteworthy feature of this scene is the exuberant display of natural flora common to Burma.

The abduction narrative is now transported to the island of Lanka. Figure 4.135 is a sumptuous portrait of Dasagiri attempting to seduce – perhaps 'assault' is the candid word – the beautiful and voluptuous Sita. Dasagiri leans aggressively towards Sita and reaches out with both arms to embrace her. Sita's face and body language express a total rejection of the demon king. She defiantly rejects his marriage proposal and is uninterested in his material promises and enticements – the status of Empress of Theinkho, enormous wealth and power, and vast lands for her father to rule. Sita is staunchly loyal to Rama and beyond the power of Dasagiri. This induces a murderous response from the demon king. In his fury he proclaims that his female court attendants have one month to persuade Sita to agree to the marriage – otherwise he will kill Sita, cook

4.136 Mandotari pleads with her husband to be patient with Sita

her body for dinner and then cut off the ears and noses of all the attendants!

These dire threats are overheard by the demon Mandotari, the principal wife of Dasagiri. She knows of her husband's evil nature and tries to persuade him to be patient and give Sita more time to agree to the marriage. This conversation is portrayed in Fig. 4.136. Mandotari kneels before her husband, who looks down on her with menace and anger. He also holds a large sword in his hand to symbolize the gravity of his threats. Mandotari reminds Dasagiri that Sita is a human and will need more time to accept her marriage fate. Mandotari also promises to use all her own powers in the next month to break Sita's resistance. In an uplifting contrast to the violence alluded to in this conversation, the silversmith has delightfully framed Dasagiri and Mandotari with exquisite floral and faunal motifs – a kneeling deer, a fruit tree, wild yam plants, exotic grasses and small flowering orchids hanging from the tree on the right side of the image.

Sukrit and Rama Unite Against Dasagiri

The last of the four Ramayana events illustrated in this chapter takes place soon after Sita's abduction in the forest. Rama and Lakkhana have been searching endlessly for Sita and finally take a rest under the broad canopy of an old tree. This scene is illustrated in Fig. 4.137. Rama is sleeping with his head comfortably in the lap of his devoted and selfless brother, Lakkhana. This brotherly devotion is witnessed by Sukrit, who lives, unbeknown to Rama and Lakkhana, in the branches of the tree above them. Sukrit is moved by the close relationship between the two brothers. He mournfully contrasts its compassion with his own broken relationship with Vali, his estranged brother who is the false king of the Vanara monkey race. Years earlier, Vali had stolen Sukrit's beloved wife, exiled him to the forest and usurped the throne. Sukrit's reflections now fill him with emotion and his tears fall onto Rama's face, who is sleeping below.

Now, having woken Rama, Sukrit descends from the tree and introduces himself to the startled brothers. He first allays Rama's fears that he might be a demon in the service of Dasagiri, and then explains his presence in the tree and the malevolent nature of Vali. Sukrit also reveals that he is the only witness to the capture and abduction of Sita by Dasagiri. Rama is profoundly thankful for this intelligence and touched by the injustice suffered by Sukrit at the hands of his brother.

A second illustration of the serendipitous encounter between Rama and Sukrit is portrayed in Fig. 4.138. This scene offers a somewhat different perspective compared to Fig. 4.137. Rama sits majestically on a high tree stump and extends a

4.137 Sukrit watches Rama sleeping from a tree branch

4.138 Rama and Sukrit swear an oath to fight Dasagiri

hand towards Sukrit, who kneels on the ground in a posture that suggests subservience. Rama's status and power are symbolized by his iconic bow and royal costume. Lakkhana holds a sword and points it at Sukrit's back. This precautionary, or perhaps threatening, posture likely reflects Rama's initial suspicion that Sukrit was a *rakshasa* demon intent on killing both Lakkhana and himself. Two figures in the background confirm this threat. They are identified by their demon faces as *rakshasas*, who were known to live in the nearby forests.[10]

The meeting between Rama and Sukrit is a pivotal event in the Ramayana narrative. The oaths exchanged here laid the foundation for the eventual triumph of good over evil. Rama swore to slay Vali and proclaim Sukrit the rightful king of the Vanara race; and Sukrit promised to mobilize his monkey army under the banner of Rama in the great war that followed to defeat the malevolent demon Dasagiri. Strangely, this long and momentous conflict and all the events that follow are not illustrated on any silver artefacts in the Noble Silver Collection, notwithstanding their centrality to the source narrative in both the Valmiki and Burmese versions of the Ramayana. This narrative 'gap' may be a result of the statistically small and unrepresentative number of artefacts in the collection; or, perhaps it simply reflects the contemporary decorative preferences of the Burmese silversmiths and patrons alike.

Figure 4.139 illustrates a narrative event that followed the exchange of oaths by Rama and Vali. Chronologically, it is the last scene from the Ramayana to decorate the silverwork in the collection. The two fighting monkeys are Sukrit and his

evil brother, Vali. They are identified by their monkey faces and long tails. Both are dressed in a royal costume and wear a king's crown or helmet. Sukrit holds two swords aloft and presses Vali to the ground. Rama attempts to shoot Vali during this fight but cannot differentiate him from his ally Sukrit due to the brothers' physical resemblance. Therefore, after the first fight ends inconclusively, Rama smears red betel juice on Sukrit for identification. In the second duel, Rama easily recognizes Vali and slays him with a single arrow. Rama then installs Sukrit as the king of the Vanara race in fulfilment of his sworn oath.

4.139 The monkey Sukrit fights with Vali, his evil brother

10. It should be noted, however, that the facial characteristics of a demon and a monkey are alike and not always easy to differentiate, especially for secondary figures in a complex scene.

Legends and Mythology

Pyu Saw Htee

Burmese legend records that Thamudarit, a nephew of the last king of Sri Ksetra in the Pyu era, founded the first capital of the new Bagan dynasty at Paukkan. At the time, the small kingdom of Paukkan was terrorized by four monsters: the Big Tiger, the Big Boar, the Big Flying Squirrel and the Big Bird. Six narrative scenes on the pierced bowl S57 (Fig. 4.140) illustrate the story of the Big Bird and its nemesis, Pyu Saw Htee.

Pyu Saw Htee was the son of an old Pyu king. His parents were now farmers in the small village of Male. At the age of seven, Pyu Saw Htee was sent away to learn archery and other princely arts from a hermit in a distant village. When the training was complete, Pyu Saw Htee returned home bearing the hermit's remarkable prediction that one day he would become king of Paukkan. Several years later, when Pyu Saw Htee was 16, his father gave permission for him to travel alone to the city of Paukkan. The scene in Fig. 4.141 depicts Pyu Saw Htee departing on his journey. He stands on the right side of the image facing a deity who is presenting him with an old bejewelled bow for protection. Two small deer accompany the deity. The Pyu-era bow was the treasured possession of his father. Pyu Saw Htee's parents stand behind the deity. Their hands are clasped in prayer to wish their son safety on his journey. The details of the scene include a Buddhist stupa, trees, rice fields and a simple farmhouse.

After Pyu Saw Htee arrived in Paukkan, he met an old Pyu couple who welcomed him into their house as an adopted son. Later, Pyu Saw Htee asked the old couple for permission to go hunting with his father's old bow. They reluctantly agreed but first warned him about the four monsters living in the forest that had terrorized the kingdom of Paukkan for over 12 years.

4.140 Offering Bowl S57

Figure 4.142 illustrates Pyu Saw Htee seeking approval to hunt. The old couple sit on a tabular rock in front of their small home and Pyu Saw Htee kneels before them with his head lowered and his hands clasped in respect to his elders and surrogate parents. His bejewelled bow lies on the ground at his side.

Once in the forest, the expertly trained and skilful Pyu Saw Htee quickly hunted down and killed the Big Tiger, the Big Boar and the Big Squirrel. Then he turned to the west in search of the Big Bird. Soon, he encountered a man leading seven terrified young maidens along a forest path. The man sadly explained to Pyu Saw Htee that these women were the next sacrificial meals for the Big Bird. Figure 4.140 dramatically illustrates the Big Bird seizing one of the sacrifices. A giant eagle-like beast is shown clutching a young woman in its colossal talons. The woman's torso and long hair hang down to the ground and her torn dress exposes her breasts. The remaining six maidens look skyward at this scene of horror, knowing they will be sacrificed next to appease the Big Bird's reign of terror.

However, before the Big Bird seized his next meal, the brave and virtuous Pyu Saw Htee intervened and killed it with a single arrow. Figure 4.144 portrays Pyu Saw Htee releasing the deadly arrow from his father's treasured bow. Seconds later, the Big Bird drops to the ground. Now, the kingdom of Paukkan is liberated from the dread power and aggression of the four monsters. It is also worth noting that this scene features a cluster of stupas in the background. Perhaps this is an allusion to the thousands of stupas built during the Bagan period following the mythological victories of Pyu Saw Htee. Many of these stupas survive in Bagan.

Figure 4.145 illustrates an event in the story that is memorialized in Bagan to this day. After killing the Big Bird, Pyu Saw Htee plucked one of its longest wing feathers and instructed the six surviving maidens to carry it back to the king of Paukkan and report truthfully all they had witnessed. They are portrayed in Fig. 4.145 carrying the long feather above their heads. However, the maidens disobeyed their instructions and soon discarded the feather because it was too heavy. Today, there is a location in Bagan known as Hnget Taung Pyit, translated literally as 'Bird Feather Thrown'!

Happily, the young women did not entirely fail their erstwhile life-saver. They did report the death of the Big Bird and

4.141 Pyu Saw Htee receives his father's bow

4.142 Pyu Saw Htee asks permission to go hunting

4.143 The Big Bird seizes a sacrificial maiden

4.144 Pyu Saw Htee shoots an arrow at the Big Bird

4.145 Six maidens carry away a feather from the Big Bird

4.146 King Thamudarit appoints Pyu Saw Htee as his heir

all they had witnessed to the king of Paukkan. The joyful King Thamudarit, in recognition and thanks for the courage and selfless bravery of Pyu Saw Htee, immediately appointed him heir to the throne of Paukkan. He also betrothed his most beautiful daughter to Pyu Saw Htee. Figure 4.146 portrays the king honouring the saviour of the kingdom. The slayer of four monsters kneels before the king on his raised throne and thanks him for his gratitude and benevolence.

Three years later, King Thamudarit passed away and Pyu Saw Htee as the heir apparent was expected to ascend the throne of Paukkan. However, he stepped aside, instead inviting the hermit who had taught him archery as a boy to be the next king. This honourable act rewarded the hermit for his skilful, patient and virtuous training of the young Pyu Saw Htee.

In the conclusion to this mythological tale of early Bagan, the hermit was crowned Yathegyaung Min, translated as the 'Hermit turned layman king'. This unlikely king reigned successfully for 15 years before passing away of old age. Pyu Saw Htee succeeded Yathegyaung and ruled the kingdom of Paukkan with great moral purpose, wisdom and benevolence for 75 years. The righteous Pyu Saw Htee died at the age of 110.

4.148 The spirit tiger carries away Ma Shwe Oo

The Tiger and the Virtuous Weaver

The decorative icon of the Taungpyone legend is a ferocious tiger holding a young woman between its protruding fangs. Burmese silversmiths used this icon as a stand-alone invocation of the legend and its moral story – the importance of honour and courage in the face of malevolence. Figure 4.148 illustrates the icon – Ma Shwe Oo, a virtuous young weaver, held lifeless in the mouth of an evil tiger – on the offering bowl S128 (Fig. 4.147). It is not uncommon to see repetitions of this image in a variety of styles on a single offering bowl.

The legend of the tiger and the virtuous weaver is set about six kilometres north of Mandalay, in the village of Taungpyone. The land was ruled by King Anawrahta (r. 1044–1077 CE), the first documented king of the Bagan empire. The king had two sons, Min Gyi and Min Lay. They were sent to Taungpyone to supervise the building of a pagoda to house a sacred emerald

Buddha. King Anawrahta also commanded each villager in Taungpyone to provide one brick for the construction of the pagoda. This decree led the villagers to believe that each brick would fulfil a personal wish and therefore the pagoda became known as the 'Wish-fulfilling Pagoda'.

The tiger holding the weaver in its mouth is a scene from the very end of the legend. As no silverwork in the collection is decorated with a complete visual storyboard of the legend, a synopsis follows to elucidate the complicated tale. The narrative begins with a long and rather romantic account of King Anawrahta's campaign to defeat the kingdom of Thaton in southern Burma. Thereafter, the focus of the legend is the behaviour of the king's two sons and the events that follow the completion of the Taungpyone pagoda project. In particular, the story focuses on the unwelcome and inappropriate attention of Min Lay towards a weaver girl named Ma Shwe Oo, who was engaged to a local forester. And, importantly, the weaver's father was also the Taungpyone village headman.

Min Lay was handsome, strong, debauched and powerful. He repeatedly tried to seduce Ma Shwe Oo but was always rejected. Finally, Min Lay's aggression became so intolerable that Ma Shwe Oo and her family were forced to flee to a faraway village. Here, Ma Shwe Oo's father waited patiently for an opportunity to inform King Anawrahta of his son's wanton behaviour. This opportunity soon arose. The king announced his inspection of the finished 'Wish-fulfilling Pagoda', and Ma Shwe Oo and her family returned to Taungpyone.

4.147 Offering Bowl S128

4.150 The annual Taungpyone Nat Festival

4.149 Ma Shwe Oo and the spirit tiger –
a *nat* display at Mount Popa

4.151 The brothers Min Gyi and Min Lay and the spirit tiger,
depicted on a marketing poster for the Taungpyone Nat Festival

When the king carefully examined the pagoda, he discovered that two bricks were missing. He was incensed by this omission and called a meeting with the village headman, Ma Shwe Oo's father, to identify and punish the two villagers who had not provided a brick as instructed. At this meeting, Ma Shwe Oo's father bravely informed the king that the two errant bricklayers were in fact his own two sons, Min Gyi and Min Lay. Furthermore, he reported that Min Lay had dishonoured his daughter and many of the village women with his persistent and unrestrained drunkenness and debauchery. These were all well-prepared charges and King Anawrahta quickly realized that his two sons were guilty of serious crimes, punishable by death. They were executed the same day. However, a day later, the spirits of the dead brothers appeared before their father and begged for a place to live. Unwisely and irresponsibly, King Anawrahta decreed they should continue to live as spirits in Taungpyone!

As a result of the king's decision, Min Lay now lived on as an evil *nat* spirit possessed with the awful power to manifest himself as a human. He was also accompanied by a snarling spirit tiger that had served as his manservant in a previous incarnation. And, to no surprise, Min Lay had not forgotten the beautiful Ma Shwe Oo and he soon appeared before her in human form and renewed his malevolent seduction. He also transformed his spirit tiger into a natural beast to threaten and intimidate Ma Shwe Oo. However, neither Min Lay nor the tiger could break her will and determination. Instead, she fearlessly spoke only of her contempt and hatred for the king's son.

Tragically, this was her final undoing. Min Lay was irretrievably angered, and he ordered the tiger to seize the virtuous weaver and carry her away into the forest to meet her death. Figure 4.148 is the iconic image of the spirit tiger with his fangs sunk into Ma Shwe Oo's limp and lifeless body. This is the final act in this wretched legend. The courageous and principled young weaver chose death over surrender to the evil Min Lay.

Today, the mythological forest trail of the tiger runs through fields south of Taungpyone and is marked by shrines and pagodas to commemorate where Ma Shew Oo dropped her flowers, where her girdle fell, and where she eventually died. Her image also appears on a shrine on Mandalay Hill and her story lives on in songs, plays, films and an annual *nat* festival in Taungpyone in August (Figs. 4.150 and 4.151). Ma Shwe Oo and the spirit tiger are also immortalized in a *nat* display at Mount Popa near Bagan (Fig. 4.149).

Zodiac Signs

Figure 4.164 is a small image of a large Shan-style pierced bowl (S11) with the general shape of a lantern. It is embellished with 12 framed zoomorphic figures that represent the Burmese signs of the zodiac. These signs are astronomically equivalent to the Western zodiac, although some of the constellation names and figures are uniquely Burmese and unlike their Western counterparts. The Burmese lunar new year begins in the month of Tagu (April). Figures 4.152–163 illustrate each of the 12 zodiac months on the offering bowl.

4.152 Meiktha (Horned ram) / Aries. Month: Tagu (April)

4.153 Pyeik-tha (Bull) / Taurus. Month: Kahson (May)

4.154 Mei-don (Mythological bird) / Gemini. Month: Nayon (June)

4.155 Karaka (Crab) / Cancer. Month: Wazo (July)

4.156 Thein (Lion) / Leo. Month: Wa-gaung (August)

4.157 Kan (Virgin) / Virgo. Month: Taw-thalin (September)

4.158 Tu (Scales) / Libra. Month: Thadin-gyut (October)

4.159 Byeik-sa (Scorpion) / Scorpio. Month: Tazaung-mon (November)

4.160 Danu (Archer) / Sagittarius. Month: Na-daw (December)

4.161 Makara (Sea monster) / Capricorn. Month: Pya-tho (January)

4.162 Kon (Water pot) / Aquarius. Month: Tabo-dwe (February)

4.163 Mein (Fish) / Pisces. Month: Tabaung (March)

4.164 Offering Bowl S11

Konbaung Royal Family

Octagonal lime boxes are commonly decorated with high-relief repoussé figures of the Konbaung royal family. The figures are inferred to represent King Thibaw (r. 1878–1885) and one or two of his principal wives – Queen Supayalat and her sister Queen Supayagyi.

These three historical figures are portrayed on the lid of the lime box S10 (Figs. 4.165 and 4.166). King Thibaw sits on a low, decorated platform between his two wives. Queen Supayalat holds a nursing child. Each figure wears informal court dress. The family smile warmly and their demeanour radiates an aura of peace and contentment. In contrast, an official sepia photo of the royal group dated 1885 (Fig. 4.167) portrays the family in a more serious and brooding mood. King Thibaw and his two queens look sternly and severely at the camera with tense expressions. Queen Supayalat, the chief queen, sits between King Thibaw and her sister. Note the similarities between the photograph and the figures on the lime box – the court costumes, the headwear, the royal platform and the shoulder-to-shoulder contact between the king and his wives. Perhaps Burmese silversmiths used an available copy of the official royal photograph as a template for the lime box portrait. King Thibaw, the last Konbaung king, is generally a popular totem on Burmese silverwork. Perhaps the totem expressed symbolic political support and nostalgia for the Konbaung dynasty in the years following King Thibaw's exile in 1885 and his death in Ratnagiri, India, in December 1916.

4.165 Lime Box S10

4.166 Queen Supayagyi, King Thibaw, and Queen Supayalat with child

4.167 Queen Supayagyi, Queen Supayalat and King Thibaw – sepia print, 1885

Floral and Faunal

Floral motifs embellish almost all Burmese silverwork as either the primary or secondary decorative element. The style of the floral work derives from the ancient Burmese tradition of *kanote* design. This tradition is believed to date from the Pyu era in the first millennium CE. *Kanote* design work is found in many genres of Burmese art, including silverwork, lacquerware, wood carving, textiles and stonework. One hypothesis suggests that the origin of *kanote* designs can be found in ancient drawings of the flowers, blossom, buds, stems, leaves and seed pods of the lotus plant. This plant, more than any other, is associated with the Buddha and his life story.

Flora and fauna are also important narrative elements in the ancient literature that inspired the work of Burmese silversmiths. Many of the narratives from this literature take place in near-pristine natural environments filled with animal and plant life. Wild, mythical and imaginary animals play important roles in many Buddhist Jataka tales, Burmese legends and the Ramayana. Furthermore, Burma has always been an overwhelmingly rural society, and the animal and plant kingdoms were an integral part of the silversmith's daily life and a ready source of artistic inspiration. Figures 4.168–175 illustrate eight examples of floral and faunal motifs on a variety of silver artefacts.

Shan-style decoration typically gives prominence to motifs from the natural world. Figure 4.168 is a detail from a highly pierced Shan bowl. The classical design theme features a busy display of exotic birds, insects, small mammals and snakes living on the stems and delicate branches of a bamboo clump. Shan silversmiths rarely took inspiration from Buddhist or other ancient literature. Also, human figures are uncommon on Shan silverwork.

Traditional Chinese art also influences the style of Shan decorative art. Figure 4.169 is a detail from a pair of large ceremonial rice storage jars from the Shan States. The decoration features an orchard of old plum trees in full blossom with dove-like birds perched on the twisted branches. The composition and style of this design echo one of the 'Three Friends of Winter' themes from classical Chinese ink brush art. This cross-cultural design is unsurprising, since the Shan

people are ethnically Tai, and their ancestry is traced to the Tai minority populations of Yunnan and Sichuan provinces in modern-day southwest China.

Shan silversmiths delighted in decorating silverwork with miniature yet detailed animal motifs. Figure 4.170 is a magnified image of a small area on the lid of a pierced Shan treasure box. Two whimsical frogs face each other on either side of a single plum blossom set inside a complex floral lattice. The frog is symbolic of rain, fertility and rebirth – all critical aspects of life in a rural, rice-based Buddhist society. There are also two pairs of cockerels in the lid design which are not easily identified. They are located above and below the single plum blossom in the centre of the image. The cockerels in each pair face away from each other and the upper pair is inverted in the photograph. This design also incorporates a yet smaller animal motif. On either side of the cockerels are a line of tiny, and somewhat schematic, ducks. And, to add design complexity, the duck motifs are alternately inverted in each line and partially framed with a scrolling plain silver thread. This is a remarkable example of finely detailed pierced silverwork. It is also a celebration of some of the animals that play an essential, everyday role in Burmese rural life.

Figure 4.171 is a cropped photograph of miniature-scale repoussé work on a hand-sized water cup. The cropping effectively results in a 4x magnification of the workmanship. The image illustrates a chaotic battle between two tusked elephants and three enormous fighting dogs with flared nostrils and gaping jaws. Mahouts, armed soldiers and dog handlers complete the scene. The elephant tusks are minute silver casts soldered to the repoussé decoration. This exceptional work is by the master silversmith Maung Kywet Ni from Moulmein.

The Burmese green peafowl, or peacock, is a classic Burmese motif. It was an official insignia of the Konbaung dynasty kings, appearing on court robes, regalia, coins of the realm, royal thrones and a wide range of art forms, including silverwork. After 1885, the peacock motif became associated with anti-colonial sentiment and rebellion against British rule. The peacock illustrated in Fig. 4.172 decorates the centre of a large, octagonal silver salver. It is portrayed in full display against a burnished background. A regal floral pattern

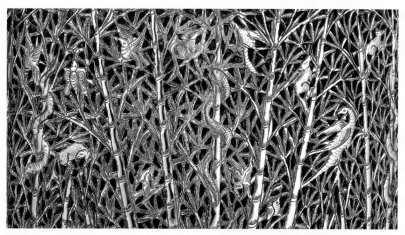

4.168 Shan iconography: Birds, animals and bamboo

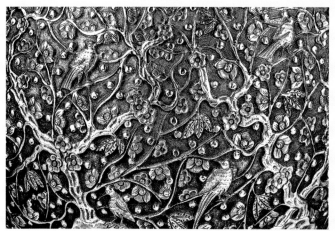

4.169 Shan iconography: Flowering plum trees with birds

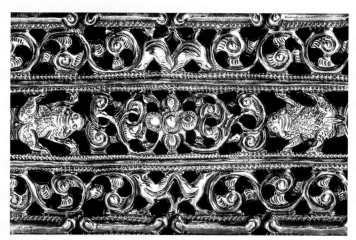

4.170 Shan iconography: Frogs, cockerels and ducks

4.171 Miniature-scale decoration: Fighting elephants, dogs and soldiers

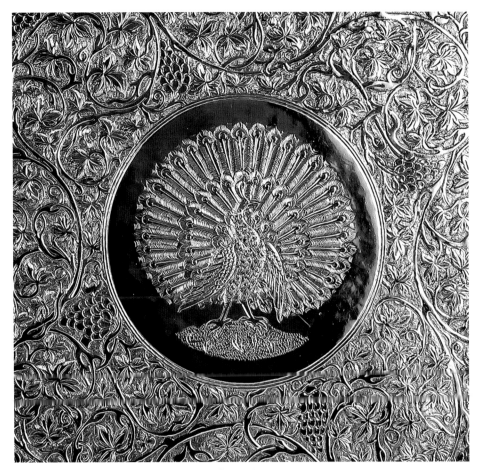

4.172 Konbaung dynasty symbol: A peacock in full display

surrounds the peacock, comprising twisted vines, leaves and grape clusters. Peacocks in display are commonly inscribed on the underside of offering bowls and lime boxes.

Burmese silversmiths also excelled at illustrating the horses and other animals that feature in the Jataka tales, the life of Buddha and the Ramayana. The richly caparisoned and muscular horse portrayed in Fig. 4.173 is the supernatural mount of the *yakka* Punnaka in the Vidhura-Pandita Jataka. This talented horse could fly and walk on water at Punnaka's command. The silversmith has masterfully captured the precise anatomy and dynamism of the leaping horse in high-relief repoussé. The hoofed forelegs are powerfully raised and all its muscles bulge with strength. This superb rendition of a strapping horse required exceptional skills in the art of drawing, sculpting and technical silversmithing.

Figure 4.174 also illustrates Punnaka's supernatural horse. Both the horse and the demon rider are executed in exceptionally high relief and fidelity. They adorn the lid of a 7-centimetre-wide circular box. The photo image is approximately true scale. This is not a relaxed portrayal of a horse. Punnaka is clinging perilously to one side of his disgruntled horse, with one hand pulling hard on the reins and both feet

planted heavily in the stirrups. The horse is depicted with flared nostrils, a gaping jaw, ugly teeth and a speckled body pattern. The controlling bridle is a thick rope thrust into the horse's mouth. Punnaka wears an ornate costume, and in some respects the demon features of his face mimic those of the horse! Unusually, the high-relief representation of the horse and rider overflow the small lid of the box. Also, the horse is almost a three-dimensional sculpture due to the exceptional height of the repoussé work.

The bucolic farming scene in Fig. 4.175 is a decorative detail from an offering bowl attributed to the prize-winning silversmith Maung Yin Maung. In the scene, King Suddhodana, the father of Prince Siddhartha Gautama, is performing the traditional royal ploughing ceremony at the start of the rice growing season. The anatomy and perspective of the two yoked oxen pulling the plough are crafted with consummate artistic skill. The silversmith has also created perspective and subtle depth-of-field by chasing a flight of birds in the background sky. The birds follow the plough in search of food and each bird decreases in size as it recedes into the apparent distance. The attention to narrative detail and artistry are key elements of the special charm and quality of Burmese silverwork.

4.173 Punnaka's supernatural horse

4.174 Punnaka astride his magical horse, sculpted in high relief

4.175 King Suddhodana performing the royal ploughing ceremony

Silver –
A Precious and
Noble Metal

Genesis and History

Silver is made in the stars. All silver in the universe is created in the last few seconds before the life of a giant star ends in a cataclysmic supernova explosion. It is only during these few seconds that the gravitational collapse of the star's core produces the extreme temperature and density conditions required to create heavy silver nuclei from other much lighter elements. The enormous force of the supernova explosion expels the freshly minted silver and other matter into the vast regions of deep interstellar space. This matter eventually accumulates into enormous clouds of gas and star dust. Later, these clouds coalesce under the force of gravity to form new stars and new planets. Figure 5.1 is an image captured in 2007 of a collapsing blue superstar in the constellation of Ursa Major. Ten years later the star exploded to create the giant supernova SN2017ein – the stellar genesis of a vast mass of new silver.

Planet earth was born out of a cloud of gas and star dust about 4.5 billion years before the present. Its mineral composition at birth contained only a trace mass of silver – the average concentration of silver in the earth's crust is estimated to be only 0.08 parts per million (ppm). By comparison, the concentration of the two industrial metals, iron and aluminum, is 41,000 ppm and 82,000 ppm respectively.

However, trace amounts of molecular silver are not uniformly distributed within the earth's crust. Some of the molecules have combined with other elements to form silver mineral species as a result of thermal and tectonic activity over geological time. Silver concentrations produced by these activities are typically in the form of rare macroscopic strands of pure silver metal, more common mineral compounds formed by silver bonding with sulphur, chlorine, antimony, arsenic and other elements, and as silver atoms within the molecular lattice of other more common lead, copper and zinc minerals.

The occurrence of these silver concentrations at or close to the earth's surface is a later consequence of crustal uplift and the relentless process of surficial erosion over billions of years. More recently, prehistoric human exploration and curiosity eventually led to the first discovery of silver in surface rocks and the birth of our love affair with this alluring metal.

History, of course, does not record the moment when a curious *Homo sapiens* first gazed upon native silver and beheld its beauty. The oldest extant silver artefacts date from the Sumerian civilization in Mesopotamia in about 3,000 BCE. Silver is therefore known as one of the seven metals of antiquity, together with gold, copper, iron, mercury, lead and tin. Archaeological evidence from antiquity also indicates that cupellation metallurgy was first used in Sumeria and neighbouring Anatolia during the third millennium BCE. This important early Bronze Age discovery provided ancient civilizations with the ability to separate silver from lead and other metallic ores using a simple charcoal-fired furnace (Fig. 5.14). The only sources of silver prior to the discovery of cupellation metallurgy were rare native silver accumulations and the metal electrum, a natural alloy of gold and silver in variable proportions. Cerro Rico mine, or 'rich hill', in Potosi, Bolivia is the world's largest single source of silver, having produced about 60,000 tons, or nearly 2 billion ounces, of the metal since the 16th century (Fig. 5.2).

Chemical and Physical Properties

Silver is a naturally occurring heavy element with an atomic number of 47 and an atomic mass of 107.87. The internationally recognized symbol for the element silver is Ag, from the Greek word 'Argyros'. The Sanskrit root of 'Argyros' means

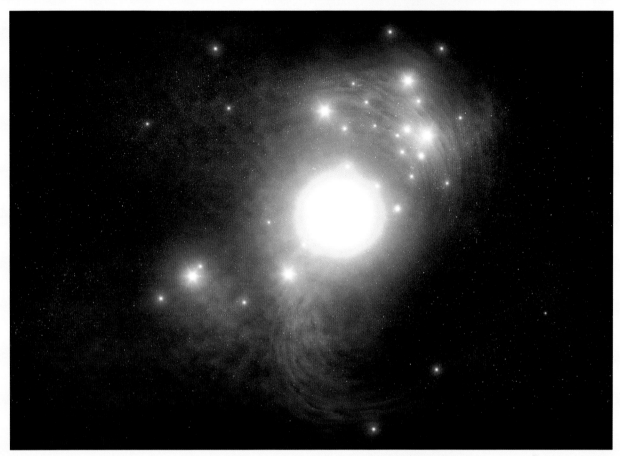

5.1 Blue star in the constellation of Ursa Major

5.2 Cerro Rico mine in Potosi, Bolivia (elevation 4,090 m), the largest silver mine in history

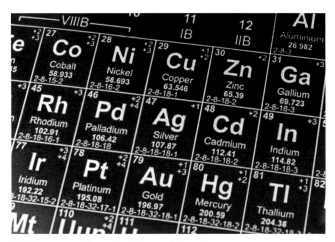

5.3 Silver (Ag) in the periodic table of elements

5.4 Medical dressings coated with silver sulfadiazine

'shining white'. 'Argentum', the Latin word for silver, is also the etymological root of the word 'argent', the French locution for money. Silver (Ag) is one of the Group 11 (1B) elements in the periodic table of elements (Fig. 5.3). It is also more generally classified as a transition, precious and noble metal. The alchemist's symbol for silver is a crescent moon, and many ancient cultures used silver to represent a lustrous, white moon.

Figure 5.5 lists the key physical properties of silver. In its purest form it is soft, white, lustrous, malleable, ductile and the most reflective of all metals (Fig. 5.6). It has high compressive and tensile strength, which gives the metal its characteristic properties of malleability and ductility. These properties make it an ideal metal for cold-working by silversmiths.

Silver is also endowed with the highest electrical conductivity and the highest thermal conductivity of all metals. These properties are utilized in many industrial applications. Silver

is a stable element in air and water and therefore suitable for use in bullion, coins, jewellery and artefacts. Silver dissolves easily in nitric acid to form a photosensitive nitrate that is the precursor chemical for traditional silver photographic film. In low concentrations, silver is also toxic to bacteria, algae and fungi. This anti-bacterial effect is utilized in medical dressings coated with silver sulfadiazine (Fig. 5.4) and silver nano-coated medical instruments. The ancient Greeks first recognized this unusual property of silver and used it to sterilize water and wounds. Also, it was a common belief in the Middle Ages that the wealthy were less likely to die from the plague because their everyday plates, cups and cutlery were made of silver.

On the other hand, the ingestion of colloidal silver over long periods of time for medicinal purposes can produce the unfortunate side effect known as argyria. This condition presents as a purple-blue-grey skin discolouration over much of the body.

Elemental Properties of Silver	
Periodic family	Group 11 (IB)
Atomic number	47
Atomic weight	107.86
Melting point	961.8°C
Density	10.49 g/cm³
Crystal structure	Face-centred cubic
Moh's hardness	2.5
Vickers hardness	26 (annealed) 100 (cold worked)
Stable isotopes	107Ag and 109Ag
Radioactive	No
Crustal abundance	0.1 ppm
Maximum purity	99.95%

5.5 Elemental properties of silver

5.6 A key property of silver – exceptionally high reflectivity

Sources and Utilization

Sources

Native silver is rare in the natural world. Wire silver (Fig. 5.7) and electrum, a combination of native gold and silver, are the two most common occurrences of native silver. The most common silver minerals include argentite/acanthite (Ag_2S) (Fig. 5.8), pyrargyrite (Ag_3SbS_3) (Fig. 5.9), proustite (Ag_3AsS_3) (Fig. 5.10) and chlorargyrite (AgCl). Silver also forms a valuable solid solution phase in lead, copper and gold ores. Argentiferous galena (PbS) (Figs. 5.11 and 5.12) contains up to two per cent silver by mass. The silver produced as a by-product of mining lead, copper and gold ores in 2018 totalled 605 million ounces – equivalent to 73 per cent of the total global mine production (877 million ounces).[1]

1. Source: The Silver Institute – World Silver Survey 2019

5.8 Argentite, Czech Republic

5.9 Pyrargyrite, Mexico

5.7 Native wire silver, Kazakhstan

5.11 Galena, Slovakia

5.10 Proustite, Mexico

5.12 Galena, Bolivia

5.13 Electrolytic silver refining plant

A—FURNACE. B—STICKS OF WOOD. C—LITHARGE. D—PLATE. E—THE FOREMAN
WHEN HUNGRY EATS BUTTER, THAT THE POISON WHICH THE CRUCIBLE EXHALES MAY NOT
HARM HIM, FOR THIS IS A SPECIAL REMEDY AGAINST THAT POISON.

5.14 Silver cupellation furnace
From *De Re Metallica* by G. Agricola (1556)

Silver metal with a 99.9 per cent purity is commonly defined as 'fine' silver and referred to as '999' silver. Refined bullion bars are typically 999 silver. The trace elements in fine silver are normally copper, lead and iron. Fine silver is typically produced from low-purity metallic silver in an electrolytic silver refining plant (Fig. 5.13). Ancient and historical silver metal produced in a cupellation furnace (Fig. 5.14) contained up to about 98 per cent silver by mass. Fine silver is rarely used for silver coins, jewellery or artefacts, because it is relatively soft and easily damaged. To mitigate these adverse properties, pure silver is blended with other metals, commonly copper, to produce silver alloys. The advantageous properties of silver alloys include increased strength, hardness and wear resistance, with a minimal decrease in ductility, malleability or reflectivity.

Figure 5.15 graphically represents the increase in hardness of silver with increased copper content. Note that silver hardness increases more than two-fold as the copper content of the alloy increases from 0 per cent to 10 per cent. The standard silver alloy, commonly known as 'Sterling' silver, contains 92.5 per cent silver and 7.5 per cent copper. This alloy has been used commercially in Europe since the 12th century, and a minimum legal content of 92.5 per cent silver for Sterling silver was established in English law by the 14th-century hallmarking act. No equivalent laws were ever enacted in Burma, although the royal Burmese and British Indian mints strictly controlled the silver purity of their kyat and rupee coins from the mid-19th to mid-20th century. Consequently, Burmese silverwork made exclusively from these recycled coins has a predictable silver content of about 91.5 per cent.

Utilization

Figure 5.16 lists the total global silver demand, or utilization, for the year 2018. Over 212 million ounces of silver were used to craft jewellery (Fig. 5.17) and other silver artefacts. The fabrication of silverware, including cutlery (Fig. 5.18), consumed an

Silver Hardness Increasing with Copper Content

(graph: Annealed Hardness (HV) vs Copper Content (% Weight))

5.15 Silver hardness (HV) increasing with copper content (% weight)

Global Silver Demand 2018	(million ounces)	% Total
Electrical and electronics	248.5	24%
Jewellery	212.5	21%
Coins and bars	181.2	18%
Photovoltaic	80.5	8%
Silverware	61.1	6%
Brazing alloys and solders	58.0	6%
Photography	39.3	4%
Ethylene oxide	5.4	0.4%
Other industrial	146.9	14%
Total physical demand	1,033.5	100%

5.16 Global silver demand, or utilization
Source: The Silver Institute – World Silver Survey 2019

5.17 Silver jewellery

5.18 Silverware

additional 61 million ounces. These two non-industrial groups accounted for 21 per cent and 6 per cent respectively of the world's total consumption of more than one billion ounces of silver. India accounted for 36 per cent of the silver demand for jewellery and 68 per cent of the demand for silverware. The comparative figures for China were 12 per cent and 4 per cent. Photography, once the largest single consumer of silver, now constitutes only 4 per cent of global demand. In contrast, high technology electrical, electronic and photovoltaic applications (Fig. 5.19 and 5.20) now comprise 32 per cent of total silver consumption. Brazing alloys and solders (Fig. 5.21) consumed 6 per cent of demand in 2018. Silver as a financial asset in the form of bullion (Fig. 5.22) and coins consumed 181 million ounces in 2018, or 18 per cent of the total global demand.

In summary, the annual non-industrial silver demand for jewellery, artefacts, silverware, coins and bullion totalled 454 million ounces in 2018, with a nominal value of US$7.94 billion as of October 2019. This data emphatically confirms the enduring demand and financial value of silver after more than 5,000 years of recorded human history.

5.19 Integrated circuits – a high-tech application of silver

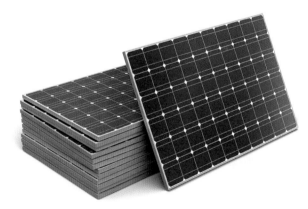

5.20 Photovoltaic cells – a growing demand for silver

5.21 Silver brazing alloys and solder

5.22 999.0 fine silver bullion from Switzerland

Tarnish, Care and Patina

Silver tarnish (Fig. 5.23) is the bane of all silver collectors. It is a consequence of several chemical reactions between silver-copper alloys and corrosive elements in the atmosphere. These reactions can diminish both the aesthetic and monetary value of all silverwork. An understanding of the basic chemistry of tarnishing helps to determine the best means of preventing and reducing the phenomenon.

Tarnish Chemistry

Silver is classified as a 'noble metal'. This signifies it is chemically stable and strongly resistant to oxidation in clean air and water. Therefore, silver tarnish is rarely due to oxidation. It is a misconception that silver readily 'oxidizes'. Silver tarnish is in fact primarily due to the reaction of silver with sulphur (S) and hydrogen sulphide gas (H_2S) to produce silver sulphide (Ag_2S). The reaction formula is as follows:

$$4\,Ag + O_2 + 2\,H_2S \rightarrow 2\,Ag_2S + 2\,H_2O$$

The largest man-made source of atmospheric sulphur is the combustion and processing of oil, gas and coal. These industrial activities contaminate the ambient air with trace levels of both sulfur and sulphur dioxide that are sufficient to tarnish unprotected silver artefacts. Silver sulphide tarnish can also be

5.24 Early-stage silver sulphide tarnish on an offering bowl

caused by food and consumer products in the home. Organic sulphur in eggs and spices are a potent source of hydrogen sulphide. Household cleaners, paint, wool, rubber, acid-paper and packaging materials are all potential sources of sulphur that can easily react with silver to produce silver sulphide tarnish. On the planetary scale, large volcanic eruptions also add enormous volumes of sulphur gas into the atmosphere. This volcanic gas can cause silver tarnishing anywhere in the world.

Silver also reacts to a much lesser extent with chlorine to produce silver chloride (AgCl). This is a transparent chemical that attracts dust and soot to create patchy brown-black tarnish. Bleach and sodium chloride in human perspiration are the most common sources of silver chloride tarnish. The most effective and easiest rule for preventing corrosion due to hand-transmitted perspiration and other oils is simply to wear gloves whenever you handle silver artefacts.

The first stage of silver sulphide corrosion is superficial and appears in different guises, including a light yellowish film, darker yellow-brown circular spots and more extensive dark brown patches (Figs. 5.24 and 5.25). This stage of corrosion is easily removed by light polishing, with negligible loss of silver or decorative detail. Any failure to remove the superficial tarnish will inevitably lead to a second and more pervasive stage as deeper corrosion creates thick layers of dark brown to black silver sulphide (Fig. 5.26). The rate of progress and severity of second-stage corrosion both increase in proportion to the concentration of sulphur in the ambient air, the surrounding temperature and the relative humidity. Therefore, silver will generally corrode at a faster rate in tropical climates compared to temperate climates. Atmospheric ozone, often present at elevated levels close to the ocean, is another corrosion accelerant. And, to further complicate an understanding of silver corrosion, the actual chemical process is unique to each piece

5.23 Tarnished silver betel box

5.25 Middle-stage silver sulphide tarnish on a Burmese one-kyat Peacock coin

5.26 Deep silver sulphide tarnish on an offering bowl

of silver because the alloy metallurgy and work history of each piece is also unique.

In summary, silver corrosion is a multi-faceted phenomenon with no single means of prevention and no one-size-fits-all formula for its removal.

Firestain

This form of tarnish, also known as firescale, is caused by the oxidation of copper in the silver-copper alloy to produce black cupric oxide (CuO) and reddish-purple-grey cuprous oxide (Cu_2O) (Fig. 5.27). This oxidation occurs when the alloy is periodically heat treated, or annealed, in a high-temperature furnace during the fabrication and cold-working process. Annealing is a necessary silversmithing process to restore the metal's workability, softness and ductility. A large artefact may need to be annealed many times, and each time the heated copper is exposed to oxygen it will begin to oxidize.

The silversmith's best means of preventing firestain is to 'pickle' the silverwork in a bath of dilute sulphuric acid after the annealing is complete. This effectively removes surface firestain, although copper oxides in the sub-surface layers of the silver may appear only after the silverwork is finally polished. Full prevention of firescale was difficult in the past because the heat treatment tools were limited to an open-air charcoal furnace and manual bellows.

Silver Care and Patina

The most effective methods, products and tools used to care for silver are determined in part by the personal preferences and experience of the collector. The silver care described herein is specific to the Noble Silver Collection in Singapore and it may not be effective or suitable for silverwork in other collections or locations.

The first line of protection against chemical corrosion is to display the silverwork in a low air-exchange cabinet. This reduces the supply of the sulphur and hydrogen sulphide 'fuel' that feeds the most common corrosion reaction. The best-quality silverwork in the Noble Silver Collection is displayed in showcases made from extruded aluminum and structural laminated glass (Fig. 5.28). These well-sealed units effectively limit the air exchange to approximately 0.25 air changes per day.[2] Other silver is displayed in antique wooden cabinets that allow higher rates of air exchange.

3M anti-tarnish strips (Fig. 5.29) are placed in each piece of silver in the wooden cabinets to help adsorb corrosive chemicals in the ambient air. Activated carbon and zinc oxide in these strips are generally effective for periods of up to about six months. Chemical lacquers and seals are more sophisticated long-term corrosion-protection tools. These are more

5.27 Firestain – copper oxide tarnish

2. These museum-quality cabinets are designed and manufactured by Trika Pte Ltd of Singapore.

5.28 Sealed display case to reduce silver sulphide tarnish

commonly used by national art and design museums. When applying a seal, it is important to verify beforehand that the chemical will not adversely affect the natural surface appearance of the silver. Corrosion is also inhibited by wrapping silverwork in acid-free and sulphur-free paper when it is transported or stored.

There is no 'silver bullet' for the permanent prevention of tarnish. Therefore, it remains the inescapable duty and responsibility of the diligent collector to periodically clean the silver! This is not necessarily such an onerous task as many believe. The cleaning work simultaneously allows the collector to examine their silverwork in fine detail and occasionally results in the discovery of previously unknown decorative detail.

The first appearance of light tarnish is easily removed by a gentle buffing of the affected area with a light polishing cloth or a soft, thick microfibre cloth. The Noble Silver Collection uses a variety of brand name and generic polishing cloths (Figs. 5.30 and 5.31) for light tarnish removal. Hagerty silver polish (Fig. 5.32) is the preferred polish for removing or reducing the heavier and more extensive tarnish sometimes found on new acquisitions that have not been recently displayed or cleaned. This polish and other similar products also contain corrosion inhibitors to reduce the rate of future chemical tarnishing. The polish should be applied sparingly using a thick microfibre polishing cloth and left on the silver for a few minutes before starting the work. The best cleaning results are often obtained by working on one small area at a time to better monitor and regulate the effect of the polish on the silver. Silver polish is a mild abrasive and overly aggressive or uncontrolled

polishing may irreparably damage the surface, particularly the high-relief decorative detail. With time, the polisher will develop the experience to calibrate the required hand pressure on the cleaning cloth to efficiently clean the tarnish and avoid any damage to the important ornamentation. It is also important to work the polishing cloth in all directions to diffuse tarnishing edges and to ensure the cloth doesn't 'miss' the low-relief surface areas. After using the polishing cream, a gentle all-over buffing with a clean microfibre cloth will complete the work and optimize the appearance of the silverwork.

Hagerty silver gloves (Fig. 5.33) are ideal for the light buffing of artefacts with a flat surface or low-relief decoration. Gloves made from cotton, non-powdered latex or nitrile organic compounds should always be worn when handling and cleaning the silver to prevent the transfer of corrosive, chlorine-rich perspiration and to protect the hands.

Silver tarnish also has an aesthetic character. The attractive black sooty 'patina' common on old Burmese silverwork (Fig. 5.34) is a result of differential corrosion and polishing over many years. This occurs because the efficacy of hand polishing is naturally strongest on high-relief surface areas and weakest in the low-relief crevices and hollows. Consequently, the corrosion of the low-relief areas continues until they are

5.29 3M anti-tarnish strips

5.30 Arthur Price silver polishing cloth

5.31 Generic polishing cloths

5.32 Hagerty silver polish

5.33 Hagerty silver polishing gloves

5.34 Black patina – an attractive form of deep silver sulphide tarnish

5.35 Servants 'overpolishing' the household silver, 19th century

5.36 No overpolishing – detail preserved

5.37 Early stage overpolishing – lost details on the face

5.38 Late stage overpolishing – face is smooth without detail

eventually covered in deep layers of black silver sulphide that define the patina. There is often an attractive visual contrast between the deeply tarnished areas in black and the strongly reflective high-relief decoration. The patina also adds value to the general appearance of the silverwork by increasing the perception of decorative depth, sharpening the outline of repoussé work and increasing the range of silver colour tones. Cotton buds and a touch of silver polish can be used to clean small recesses within the decoration. Recessive areas that are more inaccessible can be gently and very carefully cleaned of undesirable patina by using a soft shoe brush or a soft toothbrush.

A final note of caution. Over-polishing of beautifully decorated silverwork will eventually round the edges and obliterate the details of the workmanship. This can materially impair the aesthetic and monetary value of the artefact. The historical custom of delegating silver polishing to the servants (Fig. 5.35) effectively maintained the high lustre of the unadorned family silverware, but often degraded the high-relief repoussé

decoration on more ornamental silverwork. The progressive damage caused by the overpolishing of old Burmese silverwork is illustrated in Figs. 5.36–38. There is no over-polishing on Fig. 5.36 and the facial features of the court minister's head are sharp and well-preserved. The first indications of over-polishing are visible on the female heads in Fig. 5.37. The eyes and ears have lost detail and are unattractive. Extreme over-polishing of the human figure in Fig. 5.38 has left only a trace of the face and a flat, almost featureless torso. Only an echo remains of the silversmith's detailed workmanship.

'Every cloud has a silver lining' is perhaps a fitting proverb that states a general truth about silver care – polishing tarnished silverwork may not be a favoured pastime, but the effort unfailingly reveals the full natural beauty and visual splendour of the silver artefact. The time and effort required to effectively care for a silver collection might seem like a metaphorical cloud, but the superb lustre of a tarnish-free surface or the contrasting tones of an old patina are undoubtedly a glorious 'silver lining'!

Charting the Collection

The EmbArk Gallery Systems database software is used to catalogue the Noble Silver Collection. An object file is created for each artefact with customizable data fields for provenance information, physical properties, artistic features, photo images, inventory control and general descriptive data. A wide range of inventory reports can be generated by searching object files on selected field criteria. The reports are a valuable analytical tool for studying and better understanding the Burmese silverwork in the Noble Silver Collection.

The simple charts below display the frequency distribution of three important data fields:

- Form and Design – Fig. 6.1
- Decorative Narrative – Fig. 6.2
- Year of Completion – Fig. 6.3

These data displays reveal some pertinent information about the collection:

- Traditional offering bowls (75) constitute 49 per cent of all artefacts.
- Jataka tales in total (43) are the most common decorative narrative on the silverwork.
- The Sama Jataka (an allegory of loving kindness) is the most popular Jataka by a wide margin.
- The animal fauna of South and Southeast Asia (22) and stories from the epic Ramayana poem (19) rank the second and third most popular decorative subjects respectively.
- The largest proportion of dated silverwork – representing 32 per cent of the collection – was made in the period 1900–1909.

- Silverwork dated from the 19th century (1850–1899) constitutes 25 per cent of the total.
- The 'Year of Completion' frequency distribution approximately defines a right-skewed bell curve with a steep decline after the period 1920–29.
- The collection includes only one artefact made later than 1929.

A footnote to these frequency distribution charts must record that the data and information described pertains only to the Noble Silver Collection and is not necessarily representative of work from the Burmese Silver Age as a whole.

Figure 6.4 is a scatter plot graphic to illustrate the relationship between the diameter and weight of 210 Burmese offering bowls in a dataset comprising 70 offering bowls from the Noble Silver Collection and 140 bowls from two other private collections. Each data point on the graphic represents a single bowl. The distribution of the data points broadly defines three separate data clusters. This suggests that to a degree the silversmith crafted three preferred, or standardized, sizes of bowl – designated as small, medium and large. The mean diameter, weight and height of these three 'standards' are as follows:

Cluster Name	Weight (g)	Diameter (mm)	Height (mm)
Large	1,272	277	156
Medium	654	192	131
Small	190	106	73

One hypothesis to account for these three 'standard' size bowls is that the silversmiths used a fixed number of recycled coins for each bowl size. The common coins available to

Number of Pieces (Sample Number=153)

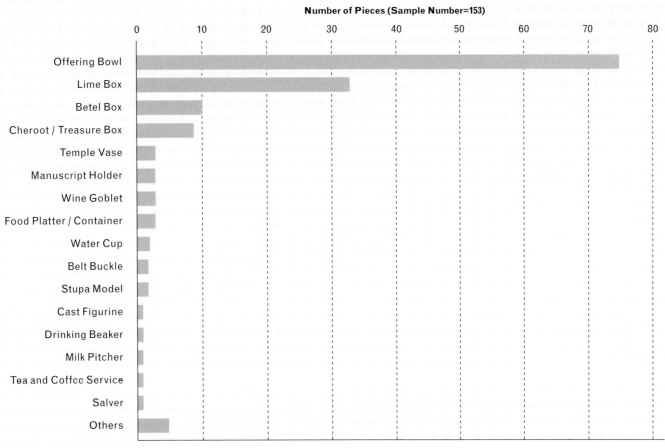

6.1 Form and design

Number of Pieces (Sample Number=153)

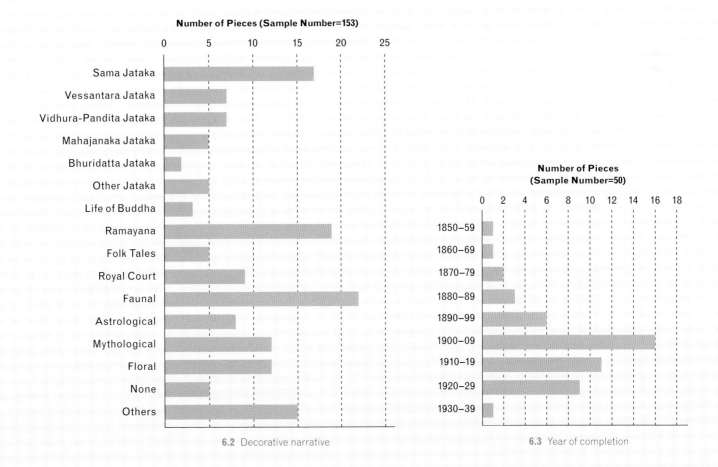

6.2 Decorative narrative

Number of Pieces (Sample Number=50)

6.3 Year of completion

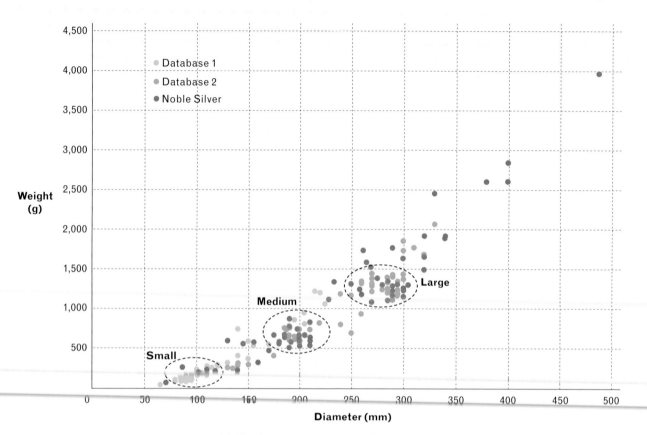

6.4 Weight-diameter relationship of 210 offering bowls

recycle were the one-kyat Burmese Peacock and the British Indian one-rupee silver-copper alloy coins, each weighing about 11.6 grams. Therefore, the mean weight of the 'large standard' bowls is equivalent to about 100 coins. The equivalent number of coins for the 'medium standard' and 'small standard' bowls is about 50 and 15 respectively. An alternative hypothesis is that official silver brokers imposed a degree of regulation on silversmiths during the colonial era, which led to some harmonization of the size and silver content of the offering bowls.

The scatter plot graphic also indicates that most bowls with the same or similar diameter do not vary much in weight. This suggests that the bowl's gauge, or width, and the silver content were also partially standardized. This interpretation of the data is consistent with the hypothesis that many offering bowls were made from a fixed number of coins with a controlled silver content of about 91.5 per cent. If there was a high variance in the weight of bowls with a similar diameter, it would indicate that silversmiths more commonly used uncontrolled silver sources of variable quality. It is also noted that about 10 per cent of the dataset comprises pierced bowls that contain proportionately less silver, and therefore weigh less than a non-pierced bowl of the same diameter. Most of the pierced bowls are found in the 'small' and 'medium' size data point clusters and do not materially impact the overall analysis of the weight-diameter relationships.

There are also data points on the scatter plot outside of the nominal clusters. There are several explanations for these points: the database is not large enough to be representative; individual silversmiths routinely crafted 'non-standard' size bowls; or the hypothesis regarding the use of a 'standard' number of coins is incorrect. The single data point in the top-right corner of the graphic represents the offering bowl S106, which weighs almost four kilograms and measures nearly a half a metre in diameter. This is an uncommon size for the Burmese Silver Age. Modern-era bowls of this size are not uncommon, although the quality of the workmanship and decoration does not compare favourably to the older offering bowls.

Finally, the author does recognize that the 210 silver artefacts in the scatter plot dataset are a statistically small sample of the entire body of work from the mid-19th to early 20th centuries. And, there may be other unknown or random factors that determine the weight-diameter relationships of Burmese silver offering bowls. A larger database is required to better understand the interesting physical and technical characteristics of the silverwork.

Bibliography

Agricola, Georgius, Herbert Clark Hoover, and Lou Henry Hoover. *De Re Metallica*. Translated from the first Latin edition of 1556. New York: Dover Publications, 1950.

Alexander, D. *Buddhism and the Arts*, 2006. www.faithandthearts.com

Anandajoti, Bhikkhu, ed. *Aggatherivatthu: The Stories About the Foremost Elder Nuns*, 2015.

Anderson, James A. 'China's Southwestern Silk Road in World History'. *World History Connected* 6, no. 1 (n.d.).

Appleton, Naomi. *Jataka*. Oxford Research Encyclopedia of Religion, 2016.

Asian Civilisations Museum (Singapore), and Gauri Parimoo Krishnan, eds. *The Divine Within: Art & Living Culture of India & South Asia*. Singapore: Asian Civilisations Museum, 2007.

Aung Thaw. *Historical Sites in Burma*, n.d.

Aung Tun. *History of the Shan State: From Its Origins to 1962*. Chiang Mai: Silkworm Books, 2009.

Aung-Thwin, Michael, and Maitrii Aung-Thwin. *A History of Myanmar Since Ancient Times*. London: Reaktion Books, 2012.

Aung-Thwin, Michael, John N. Miksic, and Geok Yian Goh. *Bagan and the World: Early Myanmar and Its Global Connections*. Baltimore, Maryland: Project Muse, 2018. https://muse.jhu.edu/book/56755/

Aye, Henri-André. *The Shan Conundrum in Burma*. Rev. ed. Bangkok: White Lotus Press, 2010.

Backman, Michael. *Rare Antique Asian and Decorative Arts*. Paul Holberton, 2016.

Baillargeon, David. 'A Burmese Wonderland: Race and Corporate Governmentality in British Burma, 1906-1930', n.d.

Bakewell, P.J. *Silver Mining and Society in Colonial Mexico: Zacatecas 1546–1700*. 1st paperback ed. Cambridge Latin American Studies 15. Cambridge: Cambridge University Press, 2002.

Béguin, Gilles, and Narisa Chakrabongse. *Buddhist Art: An Historical and Cultural Journey*. Bangkok: River Books, 2009.

Bellegem, Maickel van. 'Mylar, Reproductions of a Traditional Burmese Patinated Alloy'. The British Museum, n.d.

Bellegem, Maickel van. 'The Black Bronzes of Burma'. British Museum – Technical Research Bulletin 1, 2007.

Bennett, Anna T.N. 'Gold in Early Southeast Asia'. *Archaeo Science* 33 (2009).

Blackburn, Terence R. 'A Report on the Location of Burmese Artifacts in Museums'. *Kiscadale Asia Research*, 2, 1994.

Blackburn, Terence R. *The British Humiliation of Burma*. Bangkok: Orchid Press, 2000.

Blackburn, Terence R., ed. *The Defeat of Ava: The First Anglo Burmese War of 1824–26*. New Delhi: APH Publ. Corp, 2009.

Booth, Anne. 'The Burma Development Disaster in Comparative Historical Perspective'. *SOAS Bulletin of Burma Research* 1, no. 1 (Spring 2003): 1–23.

Braun, Rolf, and Ilse Braun. *Opium Weights*, 2102.

Bromberg, Paul. *Thai Silver and Nielloware*. Bangkok: River Books, 2019.

Brown, Ian. 'The Economic Crisis and Rebellion in Rural Burma in the Early 1930s'. In *Growth, Distribution and Political Change*, 143–57. Palgrave Macmillan, 1999.

Bryant, Edwin F. *The Quest for the Origins of Vedic Culture: The Indo-Aryan Migration Debate*. Oxford; New York: Oxford University Press, 2001.

Burlingame, Eugene Watson. *Buddhist Legends*. Harvard University Press, 1921.

Burman, Markus. 'This Is The Real Burma', 2014.

Butts, Allison. *Silver: Economics, Metallurgy, and Use*. Huntington, N.Y: R.E. Krieger Pub. Co., 1975.

Cangi, Ellen Corwin. *Faded Splendour, Golden Past: Urban Images of Burma*. Oxford in Asia Paperbacks. Kuala Lumpur; New York: Oxford University Press, 1997.

Carus, Paul. *Buddha: His Life and Teachings*. New York: Peter Pauper Press, n.d.

Chan, David P.L. *Chinese Export Silver: The Chan Collection*. Singapore: Asian Civilisations Museum, 2005.

Chan, Libby Lai-Pik, and Nina Lai-Na Wan, eds. *The Silver Age: Origins and Trade of Chinese Export Silver*. Hong Kong Maritime Museum, 2017.

Charney, Michael W. *A History of Modern Burma*. Cambridge, UK; New York: Cambridge University Press, 2009.

Charney, Michael W., ed. 'The Bibliography of Burma (Myanmar) Research: The Secondary Literature'. *SOAS Bulletin of Burma Research Bibliographic Supplement*, Winter 2004, 1–264.

Chaturachinda, Gwyneth, Sunanda Krishnamurty, and Pauline W. Tabtiang. *Dictionary of South and Southeast Asian Art*. 2nd ed. Chiang Mai: Silkworm Books, 2004.

Cheesman, Nick, Monique Skidmore, Trevor Wilson, and Institute of Southeast Asian Studies, eds. *Ruling Myanmar: From Cyclone Nargis to National Elections*. Singapore: Institute of Southeast Asian Studies, 2010.

Chong, Alan. *Devotion & Desire: Cross-Cultural Art in Asia: New Acquisitions*. Singapore: Asian Civilisations Museum, 2013.

Christie's. *Important American Silver*, 2015.

Constantinescu, B. 'Medieval Silver Coins Analysis by Pixe and Ed-XRF Techniques'. *Romanian Journal of Physics* 54, no. 5–6 (2009).

Conway, Susan. *The Shan: Culture, Art, and Crafts*. Bangkok: River Books, 2006.

Corwin, Nancy Megan. *Chasing and Repoussé: Methods Ancient and Modern*. Brunswick, Maine: Brynmorgen Press, 2009.

Cowell, Edward B., and England Pali Text Society (London). *The Jataka, or, Stories of the Buddha's Former Births*. Oxford: Pali Text Society, 1995.

Craddock, P.T., and Janet Lang, eds. *Mining and Metal Production Through the Ages*. London: British Museum Press, 2003.

Craddock, Paul. 'Production of Silver Across the Ancient World'. *ISIJ International* 54, no. 5 (2014): 1085–92.

Crosby, Kate. *Theravada Buddhism: Continuity, Diversity and Identity*. Wiley Blackwell Guides to Buddhism. Chichester, West Sussex; Malden, MA: Wiley Blackwell, 2014.

Cunningham, Alexander. *The Stupa of Bharut: A Buddhist Monument Ornamented with Numerous Scupltures*. W.H. Allen, 1879.

Danslip, Tanistha, and Michael Freeman. *Things Thai: Crafts and Collectibles*. Singapore; Basingstoke: Periplus, 2011.

Davids, T.W. Rhys. *Buddhist Birth-Stories (Jataka Tales)*. London: George Routledge, n.d.

Dehejia, Vidya, and Exhibition Delight in Design – Indian Silver for the Raj, eds. *Delight in Design: Indian Silver for the Raj* (in conjunction with the Exhibition Delight in Design – Indian Silver for the Raj, held from 18 September to 13 December 2008 at the Miriam & Ira D. Wallach Art Gallery, Columbia University, New York). Ahmedabad: Mapin, 2008.

Deshpande, Olga. 'Three Early Twentieth-Century Silver Burmese Bowls from the Hermitage Collection', n.d.

Dhammika, S. 'Nature and the Environment in Early Buddhism', 2015.

Donovan, D.G., Hayao Fukui, and Toshikatsu Itoh. 'Perspective on the Pyu Landscape'. *Kyoto University Field Reports*, 1998, 119–27.

Driem, George van. 'Tibeto-Burman Phylogeny and Prehistory: Languages, Material Culture and Genes', 233–49, n.d.

Dulayapak Preecharushh. *Naypyidaw: The New Capital of Burma*. Bangkok: White Lotus Press, 2009.

E.M.P-B. *A Year on the Irrawaddy*. Bangkok: White Lotus, 1998.

Edwardson, Morgan. *To Myanmar with Love: A Travel Guide for the Connoisseur*. San Francisco: ThingsAsian, 2009.

Efti, Tay. *Sumeria: The Eastern Source of Western Civilization*. Tay Efti, 2016.

Elliott, Patricia W. *The White Umbrella: A Woman's Struggle for Freedom in Burma*. 2nd ed. Bangkok: Friends Books, 2006.

Enriquez, Capt. C.M. *A Burmese Loneliness: A Tale of Travel in Burma, the Southern Shan States and Keng Tung*. Thacker, Spink & Co., 1918.

Falconer, John. *Burmese Design & Architecture*. Hong Kong: Periplus, 2007.

Fell, R.T. *Early Maps of South-East Asia*. Images of Asia. Singapore; New York: Oxford University Press, 1988.

Ferrars, Max, and Bertha Ferrars. *Burma*. Bangkok: AVA Pub. House, 1996.

Fielding-Hall, H. *Burmese Palace Tales*. Bangkok: White Lotus Press, 1997.

Fielding-Hall, H. *The Soul of a People*. Macmillan and Co. Limited, 1902.

Finegold, Rupert, and William Seitz. *Silversmithing*. Radnor, Pa: Chilton Book Co., 1983.

Fisher, Robert E. *Buddhist Art and Architecture*. World of Art. New York: Thames and Hudson, 1993.

Francis, H.T., and E.J. Thomas. *Jataka Tales*. Mumbai; Delhi: Jaico Pub. House, 2006.

Frank, Andre Gunder. 'Money Went Around the World and Made the World Go Around', n.d.

Fraser-Lu, Sylvia. *Burmese Crafts: Past and Present*. Kuala Lumpur; New York: Oxford University Press, 1994.

Fraser-Lu, Sylvia. *Burmese Lacquerware*. 1st ed. Bangkok: Tamarind Press, 1985.

Fraser-Lu, Sylvia. *Silverware of South-East Asia*. Images of Asia. Singapore; New York: Oxford University Press, 1989.

Fraser-Lu, Sylvia, Donald Martin Stadtner, and Asia Society, eds. *Buddhist Art of Myanmar*. New York; New Haven: Asia Society Museum; in association with Yale University Press, 2015.

Galloway, Charlotte. 'Burmese Buddhist Imagery of the Early Bagan Period (1044–1113)'. PhD thesis, Australian National University, 2006.

Galloway, Charlotte. 'Sri Ksetra Museum Collection Inventory Version 1.0', February 2016.

Galloway, Charlotte. 'The Jewelled World of Burmese Kings'. *Tassa Review* 23, no. 1 (n.d.): 10–11.

Galloway, Charlotte. 'Ways of Seeing a Pyu, Mon and Daravati Artistic Continuum'. *Bulletin of the Indo-Pacific Prehistory Association* 30 (2010).

Gear, Donald, and Joan Gear. *Earth to Heaven: The Royal Animal-Shaped Weights of the Burmese Empires*. Seattle; Chesham: University of Washington Press; Combined Academic, 2003.

George, Watt, Percy Brown, and Narayani Gupta. *Indian Art at Delhi 1903; Being the Official Catalogue of the Delhi Exhibition 1902–1903*. Delhi: Motilal Banarsidass, 1987.

Glanville, Philippa, and Victoria and Albert Museum, eds. *Silver*. London: Victoria and Albert Museum, 1996.

Glover, Ian G. 'The Past, Present and Future of Prehistoric Archaeology in Burma'. *Asian Perspectives* 40, no. 1 (Spring 2001): 119–26.

Goodman, Shona T.S., and Yawnghwe Harn. *From Princes to Persecuted: A Condensed History of the Shan/Tai to 1962*, 2014.

Grabowsky, Volker, and Andrew Turton. *The Gold and Silver Road of Trade and Friendship: The McLeod and Richardson Diplomatic Missions to Tai States in 1837*. Chiang Mai: Silkworm Books, 2003.

Green, Alexandra, ed. *Eclectic Collecting: Art from Burma in the Denison Museum*. Honolulu: University of Hawaii Press, 2008.

Green, Alexandra, and T. Richard Blurton, eds. *Burma: Art and Archaeology*. London: British Museum Press, 2002.

Green, Timothy. 'The Millenium in Silver: 1000–1999'. Rosendale Press, August 1999.

Grimwade, Mark. *Introduction to Precious Metals: Metallurgy for Jewelers & Silversmiths*. Brunswick, ME: Brynmorgen Press, 2009.

Griswold, Alexander, Chewon Kim, and Peter Pott. *The Art of Burma, Korea and Tibet*. Greystone Press, 1968.

Gutman, Pamela. 'The Ancient Coinage of Southeast Asia', 1977.

Gutman, Pamela, and Bob Hudson. 'A First-Century Stele from Sriksetra'. *Bulletin de l'Ecole Francaise d'Extreme-Orient* 99 (2013): 17–46.

Guy, John. 'A Warrior-Ruler Stele From Sri Ksetra, Pyu, Burma'. *Journal of the Siam Society* 85, parts 1 & 2 (n.d.): 85–94.

Guy, John. 'The Art of the Pyu and the Mon'. *The Art of Burma New Studies*, 1999, 13–28.

Guy, John, et al. *Lost Kingdoms: Hindu-Buddhist Sculpture of Early Southeast Asia*. New York: The Metropolitan Museum of Art, 2014.

Hall, D.G.E. 'Burma'. Hutchinson University Library, 1950.

Hart, Mrs. Ernest. *Picturesque Burma Past and Present*. J.M. Dent & Co., 1897.

Harvey, Peter. 'The Symbolism of the Early Stupa'. *The Journal of the International Association of Buddhist Studies* 7, no. 2 (1984).

Hecker, Hellmuth. 'Buddhist Women at the Time of the Buddha'. Buddhist Publication Society, 1982.

Hendrix, Elizabeth. 'A Cypriot Silver Bowl Reconsidered'. *Metropolitan Museum Journal*, no. 34 (1999).

Herbert, Patricia M. 'The Sir Arthur Phayre Collection of Burmese Manuscripts', n.d., 62–70.

Herold, A. Ferdinand. *Buddhism*, 1920.

Higham, C.F.W. 'Archaeology In Myanmar: Past, Present, and Future'. *Asian Perspectives* 40, no. 1 (Spring 2001): 127–38.

Hill, Dorothy Kent. 'Ancient Metal Reliefs', n.d.

Hockerhull Thomas. *Symbols of Power*. London: British Museum, 2015.

Holden, Geoffrey. *The Craft of the Silversmith*. 1954th ed. Stuio Vista, n.d.

Hoover, Herbert. *The Memoirs of Herbert Hoover*. Hollis and Carter, 1952.

Horner, I.B., and Padmanabh S. Jaini, eds. *Apocryphal Birth-Stories (Pannasa Jataka)*. London; Boston: Pali Text Society; Distributed by Routledge & Kegan Paul, 1985.

Htin Aung. *The Stricken Peacock: Anglo-Burmese Relations 1752–1948*. Dordrecht: Springer Netherlands, 1965. https://link.springer.com/openurl?genre=-book&isbn=978-94-015-0420-1

Hudson, Bob. 'A Thousand Years Before Bagan: Radiocarbon Dates and Myanmar's Ancient Pyu Cities', September 2012.

Hudson, Bob. 'The Origins of Bagan: The Archaeological Landscape of Upper Burma to AD 1300'. University of Sydney, PhD, 2004.

Hughes, G. Bernard. *Small Antique Silverware*. London: Fitzhouse, 1990.

Inaba, Masamitsu. 'Tarnishing of Silver: A Short Review'. *V&A Conservation Journal*, no. 18 (January 1996).

Jones, J.J. 'The Mahavastu Volume 2'. Luzac & Company, 1952.

Jordan, Ryan P. *Silver: The People's Metal*. United States: Ryan Jordan, 2012.

Kang, Heejung. 'The Spread of Sarnarth-Style Buddha Images in Southeast Asia and Shandong China by the Sea Route'. *Kemanuslaan* 20, no. 2 (2013).

Kann, Eduard. *The Currencies of China*. New York: Ishi Press, 1926.

Keck, Stephen L. *British Burma in the New Century, 1895-1918*. Britain and the World. Houndmills, Basingstoke, Hampshire: Palgrave Macmillan, 2015.

Kelly, R. Talbot. *Burma: Painted and Described*. London: Adam and Charles Black, 1905.

Kelly, R. Talbot. *Burma: Peeps at Many Lands*. London: Adam and Charles Black, 1908.

Kerlogue, Fiona. *Arts of Southeast Asia*. World of Art. London; New York: Thames & Hudson, 2004.

Khin Maung Nyunt. *A Pot-Pourri of Myanmar Culture*. Yangon: Gon Htoo Books, 2013.

Khin Myo Chit, and Paw Oo Thet. *A Wonderland of Burmese Legends*. Bangkok: Tamarind Press, 1984.

Khin Myo Chit. *Colourful Burma*. U Kyaw Oo Parami Sarpay, 2016.

Kin, Oung. *Who Killed Aung San*, 1993.

Kipling, Rudyard, and Pankaj Mishra. *Kim*. Modern Library pbk. ed. New York: Modern Library, 2004.

Kossalt, Steven M. 'The Art of Southeast Asia: A Resource for Educators'. The Metropolitan Museum of Art, 2001.

Kratoska, Paul H., ed. 'South East Asia, Colonial History: High Imperialism (1890s–1930s)', n.d.

Krech, Volkhard, and Marion Steinicke. 'Dynamics in the History of Religions between Asia and Europe'. Brill, 2012.

Kustel, Guido. *Roasting of Gold and Silver Ores*. Read Books, 2010.

Kyaw, Minn Htin. 'Historical Geography and Urbanization in Ancient Arakan'. *Aseanie* 20 (2007): 55–73.

Lacoste, Anne, and Felice Beato. *Felice Beato: A Photographer on the Eastern Road*. Los Angeles: J. Paul Getty Museum, 2010.

Latimer, Jon. *Burma: The Forgotten War*. London: Murray, 2004.

Law, Bimala Churn. *A Summary of the Mahavastu*. Calcutta and Simla: Thacker, Spink & Co., n.d.

Lay, Myint. 'Certain Rites of Passage in Burmese and Japanese Societies'. *The Journal of East Asian Studies* 8, no. 1 (June 1997): 70–95.

Le May, Reginald. 'The Culture of South-East Asia: The Heritage of India'. George Allen & Unwin, 1954.

Ledgard, Edna. *The Snake Prince and Other Stories: Burmese Folk Tales*. New York: Interlink Books, 2000.

Leider, Jacques P. 'Relics, Statues and Predictions: Interpreting an Apochryphal Sermon of Lord Buddha in Arakan'. *Asian Ethnology* 68, no. 2 (2009).

Leider, Jacques P. 'Specialists for Ritual, Magic and Devotion'. *The Journal of Burma Studies* 10 (June 2005).

Leidy, Denise Patry. *The Art of Buddhism: An Introduction to Its History & Meaning*. 1st ed. Boston: Shambhala; Distributed in the United States by Random House, 2008.

Li, Chenyang, ed. *Myanmar: Prospect for Change*. Singapore: Select, 2010.

Lowry, John. *Burmese Art*. London; Palo Alto: H.M. Stationery Off.; distributed by Pendragon House, 1974.

Lu, Pe Win. 'Some Aspects of Burmese Culture', 1957.

Luce, Gordon. 'Old Burma-Early Pagan'. J.J. Augustin, 1969.

Luce, Gordon. 'The Ancient Pyu'. *Journal of Burma Research Society* 27, no. 3 (1937).

Ma Thanegi. *Gold Leaf and Terra-Cotta: Burmese Crafts Throughout History*. San Francisco: ThingsAsian Press, 2017.

Mackenzie, Compton. *Realms of Silver*. London, 1954.

Mahlo, Dietrich. *The Early Coins of Myanmar/Burma: Messengers from the Past: Pyu, Mon, and Candras of Arakan (First Millennium AD)*. Bangkok: White Lotus Press, 2012.

Mangrai, Sao Khemawadee. *Burma, My Mother: And Why I Had To Leave*. Sydney: Sydney School of Arts and Humanities, 2014.

Marshall, Andrew. *The Trouser People: A Story of Burma in the Shadow of the Empire*. Washington, D.C.; Oxford: Counterpoint; Oxford Publicity Partnership, 2003.

Marshall, Sir John, ed. *Annual Report 1926–1927*. Archaeological Survey of India, n.d.

Martin, Rafe. *The Hungry Tigress*. Yellow Moon Press, 1999.

Martin, Scott V, and D. Albert Soeffing. *Guide to Evaluating Gold & Silver Objects for Appraisers, Collectors, Dealers*. New York: SMP, 1995.

Matthews & Co, Beurdeley. *Burmese Art and Its Influences*, 1981.

Maung, Htin Aung. *A History of Burma*, 1967.

Maung, Htin Aung. *Burmese Folk Tales*. Oxford University Press, 1954.

Maung, Htin Aung. *Folk Elements in Burmese Buddhism*, 1959.

Maung, U Maung. 'Nationalist Movements In Burma, 1920–1940: Changing Patterns Of Leadership: From Sangha To Laity'. The Australian National University, November 1976.

McArthur, Meher. *Reading Buddhist Art: An Illustrated Guide to Buddhist Signs and Symbols*. New York: Thames & Hudson, 2002.

McCrae, Alister, and Alan Prentice. *Irrawaddy Flotilla*. Paisley: James Paton Limited, 1978.

McCreight, Tim. *The Complete Metalsmith*. Brunswick, Maine: Brynmorgen Press, 2004.

McGill, Forrest et al, eds. *Emerald Cities: Arts of Siam and Burma, 1775–1950*. San Francisco: Asian Art Museum, Chong-Moon Lee Center for Asian Art and Culture, 2009.

McLynn, Frank. *The Burma Campaign: Disaster into Triumph, 1942–45*. Yale Library of Military History. New Haven: Yale University Press, 2011.

Meiji Soe. *Culture & Beyond: Myanmar*. 2nd ed. Rangoon: Sarpay Beikman, Printing and Publishing Enterprise, 2014.

Miksic, John. 'The Buddhist-Hindu Divide in Premodern Southeast Asia'. Institute of Southeast Asian Studies Nalanda-Sriwijaya Centre Working Paper 1 (September 2010).

Milne, Leslie. *Shans at Home: Burma's Shan States in the Early 1900s*. Bangkok: White Lotus Press, 2001.

Ministry of Religious Affairs and Culture, ed. *Documentary on Excavation at Beikthano*, n.d.

Ministry of Religious Affairs and Culture, ed. *The Myanmar Royal Regalia & Royal Household Articles*, n.d.

Mirante, Edith T. *Burmese Looking Glass: A Human Rights Adventure and a Jungle Revolution*. 1st ed. New York: Grove Press, 1993.

Mollat, Hartmut. 'A Model Chronology of the Animal Weights of Burma'. Berichte und Kommentare, 2009.

Moore, Elizabeth Howard. 'Ancient Knowledge and the Use of Landscape Walled Settlements in Lower Myanmar'. SOAS, 2004.

Moore, Elizabeth Howard. 'Bronze and Iron Age Sites in Upper Burma: Chindwin, Samon and Pyu'. *SOAS Bulletin of Burma Research* 1, no. 1 (Spring 2003).

Moore, Elizabeth Howard. 'Interpreting Pyu Material Culture: Royal Chronologies and Finger-Marked Bricks'. *Myanmar Historical Research Journal* 13 (June 2004).

Moore, Elizabeth Howard. 'Place and Space in Early Burma: A New Look at Pyu Culture'. *Journal of the Siam Society* 97 (2008).

Moore, Elizabeth Howard. 'The Early Buddhist Archaeology of Myanmar: Tagaung, Thagara, and the Mon-Pyu Dichotomy', 2008.

Moore, Elizabeth Howard. *The Pyu Landscape: Collected Articles*, 2012.

Moore, Elizabeth Howard. 'The Sacred Geography of Dawei: Buddhism in Peninsular Myanmar'. *Contemporary Buddhism* 14, no. 2 (2013).

Moore, Elizabeth Howard, and Pauk Pauk. 'Nyaung-Gan: A Preliminary Note on a Bronze Age Cemetry near Mandalay. Myanmar', 1999.

Moore, Elizabeth Howard, and San Maw San. 'Flights of Fancy', n.d.

Moss, Michael. 'The Nineteenth Century'. Culture and Sport Glasgow, 2015.

Myint-U, Thant. *Lost Maps of Asia*. Faber & Faber, 2011.

Myint-U, Thant. *Where China Meets India*. Faber & Faber, 2012.

Myo, Nyunt, and Myo Win Kyaw. 'Pinle (Maingmaw): Research at an Ancient Pyu City, Myanmar'. *Archaeology Report Series – Nalanda-Srivijaya Centre* 6 (June 2017).

Nair, P. Thankappan. 'The Peacock Cult in Asia', n.d.

Ñāṇamoli. *The Life of the Buddha: According to the Pali Canon*. Seattle: BPS Pariyatti Editions, 2001.

Nash, Manning. 'Burmese Buddhism in Everyday Life'. *American Anthropologist*, 1963, 285–95.

Nelson, Walter Henry. *Buddha: His Life and His Teaching*. 1st Tarcher Lives of the Masters ed. New York: Jeremy P. Tarcher/Penguin, 2008.

Nisbet, John. *Burma Under British Rule and Before*. Vol. 2, n.d.

Northover, Peter. 'Microstructures of Ancient and Historic Silver'. Open Research Online, September 2013.

Nudang, Sopa. 'Styles and Patterns of Silver Work of Ywahtaung Village in Sagaing Division, Myanmar'. *The Social Sciences* 11 (23) (2016): 5710–18.

O'Connor, V.C. Scott. *Mandalay and Other Cities of the Past in Burma*. 1st ed. Hutchinson & Co., 1907.

O'Connor, V.C. Scott. *The Silken East: A Record of Life and Travel in Burma*. Hutchinson & Co., 1904.

O'Reilly, Dougald J.W. *Early Civilizations of Southeast Asia*. Archaeology of Southeast Asia. Lanham: AltaMira Press, 2007.

Olcott, H.S. 'The Life of Budha and Its Lessons'. Theosophical Publishing House, 1912.

Ōno, Toru, ed. *Burmese Ramayana: With an English Translation of the Original Palm Leaf Manuscript in Burmese Language in 1233 Year of Burmese Era, 1871 A.D.* Delhi: B.R. Pub. Corp.; distributed by BRPC (India), 2000.

Orwell, George. *Burmese Days*, 2014.

Osho, and Osho International Foundation. *Buddha: Its History and Teachings and Impact on Humanity*. Switzerland: Osho International Foundation, 2009.

Owens, David C. 'Buddhist Iconography on Burmese Silverware'. *Passages*, November–December 2017: 10–11.

Owens, David C. 'Ceremonial Offering Bowls from the Burmese Silver Age: The Noble Silver Collection'. *Arts of Asia* 48–6, November-December 2018: 110–20.

Pannyawamsa, Sengpan. 'The Tham Vessantara Jataka: A Critical Study of the Vessantara Jataka and Its Influence on Kentung Buddhism, Eastern Shan States, Burma'. University of Kelaniya, 2007.

Pe, Maung Tin, and Gordon Luce. *The Glass Palace Chronicle of the Burmese Kings*, 1923.

Pearn, B.R. 'Three Shan Legends'. *Journal of Burma Research Society* 22, no. 1 (1932).

Pickford, Ian, and Antique Collectors' Club. *Antique Silver*. Woodbridge: Antique Collectors' Club, 2010.

Pisit, Kobbun. 'The Jatakas in Narratives and Buddhist Art in Lao Culture'. *Silpakorn University Journal of Social Sciences, Humanities and Art* 15, no. 3 (2015): 37–60.

Pluvier, Jan M. 'Historical Atlas of South-East Asia'. New York: E.J. Brill, 1995.

Praphot 'Atsawawirunhakan. *The Ascendancy of Theravada Buddhism in Southeast Asia*. 1st ed. Chiang Mai: Silkworm Books, 2010.

Pryce, Thomas Oliver. 'Metallurgy in Southeast Asia'. Springer Science, January 2014.

Reade, Julian. *Mesopotamia*. 2nd ed. London: Published for the Trustees of the British Museum by British Museum Press, 2000.

Rice, D.W., and E.B. Rigb. 'Atmospheric Corrosion of Copper and Silver'. IBM Corporation, n.d.

Rivett-Carnac, J.H. 'On Some Specimens of Indian Metal'. *Journal of Indian Art and Industry* 9, no. 77 (1902).

Robinson, M, and L.A. Shaw. *The Coins and Banknotes of Burma*, 1980.

Rogers, Benedict. *Than Shwe: Unmasking Burma's Tyrant*. Chiang Mai: Silkworm Books, 2010.

Ronachai Krisadaolarn, and Vasilijs Mihailovs. *Siamese Coins: From Funan to the Fifth Reign*. Bangkok: River Books, 2012.

Rooney, Dawn. *Betel Chewing Traditions in South-East Asia*. Images of Asia. Kuala Lumpur; New York: Oxford University Press, 1993.

Roth, H. Ling. *Oriental Silverwork: Malay and Chinese*. Oxford in Asia Hardback Reprints. Kuala Lumpur, New York: Oxford University Press, 1993.

Sai, Htwe Maung. 'History of Shan Churches in Burma', August 2007.

Sangermano, Father. 'The Burmese Empire'. Translated by William Tandy, 1833.

Sao Sanda. *The Moon Princess: Memories of the Shan States*. Bangkok: River Books, 2008.

Sargent, Inge. *Twilight Over Burma: My Life as a Shan Princess*. Honolulu: University of Hawai Press, 1994.

Scott, J. George. *Gazetteer of Upper Burma and the Shan States*. Superintendent of Government Printing Burma, Part 1 Vol 1, 1900.

Selth, Andrew. 'Modern Burma Studies: A Survey of the Field'. *Modern Asia Studies* 44(2), 2008.

Shah, Sudha. *The King in Exile: The Fall of the Royal Family of Burma*. New Delhi: HarperCollins Publishers India, 2012.

Shaw, Sarah, ed. *The Jatakas: Birth Stories of the Bodhisattva*. Penguin Classics. New Delhi; New York: Penguin Books, 2006.

Singer, Noel F. 'Palm Leaf Manuscripts of Myanmar (Burma)'. Asian Art, n.d. http://www.burmese-art.com

Singer, Noel F. 'Vaishali and the Indianization of Arakan'. APH Publ. Corp, 2008.

Singer, Noel F., ed. *Burmah: A Photographic Journey, 1855–1925*. Stirling: Paul Strachan-Kiscadale, 1993.

Singh, Dr. Anand Shanker. 'A Historical and Cultural Study of Buddhist Art in Early South-East Asia'. *International Journal of Humanities and Social Sciences* 2, no. 3 (November 2015): 17–23.

Smith, Grant H., Joseph V. Tingley, and Grant H. Smith. *The History of the Comstock Lode, 1850–1997*. Nevada Bureau of Mines and Geology Special Publication, no. 24. Reno: Nevada Bureau of Mines and Geology, 1998.

Smith, John Sterling Forssen. *The Chiang Tung Wars: War and Politics in Mid-19th Century Siam and Burma*. Bangkok: Institute of Asian Studies, Chulalongkorn University, 2013.

Soe, Aung. 'Myanmar Polity (1819-1885)'. PhD dissertation, Dept. of History, University of Mandalay, May 2011.

Sookksawasdi, S. 'The Pre-Pagan Period: The Urban Age of the Mon and the Pyu'. PowerPoint, n.d.

Spencer, Robert, F. 'Ethical Expression in a Burmese Jataka'. *The Journal of American Folklore* 79, no. 31 (March 1966): 278–301.

Stadtner, Donald Martin. 'The Mon Of Lower Burma'. *Journal of the Siam Society* 96 (2008): 193–215.

Stadtner, Donald Martin, and National Centre for the Performing Arts (India), eds. *The Art of Burma: New Studies*. Mumbai: Marg Publications, on behalf of the National Centre for the Performing Arts, Mumbai, 1999.

Stadtner, Donald Martin, and Phaisan Piammettawat. *Sacred Sites of Burma: Myth and Folklore in an Evolving Spiritual Realm*. Bangkok: River Books, 2011.

Stanton, Thomas H. 'Law and Economic Development: The Cautionary Tale of Colonial Burma'. *Asian Journal of Law and Society*, n.d.

Stargardt, Janice. 'Death Rituals of the Late Iron Age and Early Buddhism in Central Burma and South-East India: Whose Norms and Whose Practices'. Landscape, 1990.

Stargardt, Janice. 'From the Iron Age to Early Cities at Sri Ksetra and Beikthano, Myanmar'. *Journal of Southeast Asian Studies* 47, no. 3 (October 2016): 341–65.

Stargardt, Janice. 'Tracing Thought through Things: The Oldest Pali Text and the Early Buddhist Archaeology of India and Burma'. Royal Netherlands Academy of Arts and Sciences, 2000.

Stark, Miriam. 'The Archaeology of Early Modern South East Asia'. Oxford Handbooks Online, 2014.

Starkey, Sarah. 'Irrawaddy Flotilla Company, 1865–1950'. National Museums Liverpool, October 2008.

Strachan, Paul. 'A Burma River Journey'. Kiscadale Publications, 1997.

Strachan, Paul. *The Pandaw Story: On the Rivers of Burma and Beyond*, 2015.

Strachan, Paul, and Irrawaddy Flotilla Company. *Pandaw: The Irrawaddy Flotilla Company and the Rivers of Myanmar*. Edinburgh: Kiscadale Publications, 2003.

Su, Su Myaing. 'A Study on the Metallic Culture of Pyus'. *Universities Research Journal* 5, no. 9 (2012).

Symes, Michael. *An Account of an Embassy to the Kingdom of Ava, Sent by the Governor General of India in the Year 1795*. W. Bulmer & Co., 1800.

Tan, Terence. *Ancient Jewellery of Myanmar: From Prehistory to Pyu Period*. Mudson Sar Pae Publishing Houose, 2015.

Tansen, Sen. 'Buddhism Across Asia: Networks of Material, Intellectual and Cultural Exchange'. Institute of Southeast Asian Studies, n.d.

Taylor, Robert H. *General Ne Win: A Political Biography*. Singapore: Institute of Southeast Asian Studies, 2015.

Taylor, Roger, Crispin Branfoot, and Linnaeus Tripe, eds. *Captain Linnaeus Tripe, Photographer of India and Burma, 1852–1860*. Washington; New York; Munich; London: National Gallery of Art; The Metropolitan Museum of Art; DelMonico Books/Prestel, 2014.

Temple, Richard Carnac. 'Notes on Currency and Coinage among the Burmese'. *Indian Antiquary* XLVIII (1921).

Temple, Richard Carnac. *The Thirty-Seven Nats*. Gartmore, Scotland: Kiscadale Publications, 1992.

Thailand, and Samnak Ratchalekhathikan. *The Story of Ramakian from the Mural Paintings along the Galleries of the Temple of the Emerald Buddha.* Bangkok: Sangdad, 2004.

Than Htun. *Lacquerware Journeys: The Untold Story of Burmese Lacquer*. Bangkok: River Books, 2013.

Than Tun. *Auspicious Symbols and Ancient Coins of Myanmar*. Kelana Jaya, Selangor, Malaysia; Yangon: Avahouse; distributed by Myanmar Innwa Bookstore, 2007.

Than Tun, and Aye Myint. *Ancient Myanmar Designs*. Bangkok, Thailand: IGroup Press, 2011.

Than, Win. *Myanmar Cultural Property*. Ministry of Culture Myanmar, 2014.

Thant Myint-U. *The Making of Modern Burma*. New York: Cambridge University Press, 2001.

Thein Lwin, Win Kyaing, and Janice Stargardt. 'The Pyu Civilization of Myanmar and the City of Sri Ksetra'. Lost Kingdoms – The Metrploitan Museum of Art, 2014.

Thiri, Nyunt, Dr. 'Sri Ksetra: The Ancient City of Pyu Rising in a Marvellous Dignity for Myanmar-Buddhism'. *Journal of International Buddhist Studies* 6, no. 2 (December 2015).

Thomas, Edward J. *The Life of Buddha: As Legend and History*. Repr. [der Ausg.] London, 1931. The History of Civilization. London: Routledge, 1996.

Thompson, Edward J. *Burmese Silver*. Faber & Faber, 1948.

Tilly, Harry L. 'Modern Burmese Silverwork'. Superintendent of Government Printing Burma, 1904.

Tilly, Harry L. 'The Silverwork of Burma'. Superintendent of Government Printing Burma, 1902.

Tin, Maung Kyi. *150th Anniversary of Mandalay*. Pyinsagan Books, 2008.

Topich, William J., and Keith A. Leitich. *The History of Myanmar*. The Greenwood Histories of the Modern Nations. Santa Barbara, Calif: Greenwood, 2013.

Tylecote, Ronald F. *A History of Metallurgy*. London: Maney, 2002.

Tzang Yawnghwe. *The Shan of Burma: Memoirs of a Shan Exile*. 2nd reprint. Local History and Memoirs 16. Singapore: Institute of Southeast Asian Studies, 2010.

U Aung, Thaw. 'The "Neolithic" Culture of the Padah-Lin Caves'. *Asian Perspectives* XIV (1971): 123–33.

UNESCO. *Wat Phu: The Temple of the Mountain*, n.d.

University of Pennsylvania, Richard L. Zettler, Lee Horne, Donald P. Hansen, and Holly Pittman, eds. *Treasures from the Royal Tombs of Ur*. Philadelphia: University of Pennsylvania, Museum of Archaeology and Anthropology, 1998.

Ward, Francis Kingdon. *In Farthest Burma*. Bangkok: Orchid Press, 2005.

Webster, Donovan. *The Burma Road: The Epic Story of the China-Burma-India Theater in World War II*. New York: Perennial, 2004.

White, Benjamin. 'Silver: Its History and Romance'. Waterlow and Sons Limited, 1920.

White, Herbert Thirkell. *Burma*. Cambridge: Cambridge University Press, 2011.

Wicks, Robert S. *Money, Markets, and Trade in Early Southeast Asia: The Development of Indigenous Monetary Systems to AD 1400*. Studies on Southeast Asia. Ithaca, N.Y: Southeast Asia Program, Cornell University, 1992.

Wicks, Robert S. 'Telling Lives: Narrative Allegory on a Burmese Silver Bowl', n.d.

Wilkinson, Wynyard R.T. *Indian Silver, 1858–1947: Silver from the Indian Sub-Continent and Burma Made by Local Craftsmen in Western Forms*. London: W.R.T. Wilkinson, 1999.

Wilkinson, Wynyard R.T., Mary-Louise Wilkinson, and Barbara Harding. 'Burmese Silver from the Colonial Period'. *Arts of Asia* May–June 2013 (n.d.): 69–81.

Win Kyaing. 'Sri Ksetra and Pyu Ancient Cities'. PowerPoint, n.d.

Win, Naing Tun. 'Prehistory to Proto-History of Myanmar: A Perspective of Historical Geography'. In *Burma/Myanmar in Transition: Connectivity, Changes and Challenges*, 22. Chiang Mai: University Academic Service Centre, Chiang Mai University, 2015.

Wray, Elizabeth, Clare Rosenfield, Dorothy Bailey, and Joe D. Wray. *Ten Lives of the Buddha: Siamese Temple Paintings and Jataka Tales*. 1st ed. New York: Weatherhill, 1972.

Wright, Arnold, Oliver T. Breakspear, and H.A. Cartwright. *Twentieth Century Impressions of Burma: Its History, People, Commerce, Industries, and Resources*, 2015.

Yi, Yi. 'Life at the Burmese Court Under the Konbaung Kings: Part 1'. Burma Historical Research Department, 1982.

Yule, Sir Henry. *A Narrative of the Mission Sent by the Govenor-General of India to the Court of Ava in 1855*. Hard Press, 2012.

Index

Numbers in **bold** indicate photographs.